Alaskan Voyage   1881-1883

Translated by ERNA GUNTHER

Alaskan Voyage 1881-1883

JOHAN ADRIAN JACOBSEN

An Expedition to
the Northwest Coast
of America

from the German Text of Adrian Woldt

The University of Chicago Press
Chicago and London

The University of Chicago Press, Chicago 60637
The University of Chicago Press, Ltd., London

© 1977 by The University of Chicago
All rights reserved. Published 1977
Paperback edition 1983
Printed in the United States of America
88 87 86 85 84 83   2 3 4 5 6

Library of Congress Cataloging in Publication Data
Jacobsen, Johan Adrian, 1853–1947.
  Alaskan voyage, 1881–1883; from the German text
of Adrian Woldt.

  Translation of Reise an der nordwestküste
Amerikas, 1881–1883.
  Bibliography: p.
  Includes index.
  1. Indians of North America—Northwest coast
of North America. 2. Eskimos—Alaska. 3. Alaska
—Description and travel—1867–1896. 4. British
Columbia—Description and travel. 5. Jacobsen,
Johan Adrian, 1853–1947. I. Woldt, A. II. Gunther, Erna,
1896–   III. Title.
E78.N78J3213   979.8′004′97   77–78066
ISBN 0–226–39033–0

Contents

Beaufort Sea
Point Barrow
Point Hope
C. Pr. of Wales
King I.
Port Clarence
St. Lawrence I.
Cape Nome
St. Michael
Unalakleet
Bering Sea
Yukon R.
Andreafsky (St. Mary's)
Anvik
Tanana
Nunivak I.
Sabotnisky
Kozerevsky
Kuskokwim Delta
Kuskokwim R.
Nushagak Bay
Cook Inlet
Chugach Mts.
Unalaska I.
Kodiak I.
Gulf of Alaska
Chilkat R.
Yakutat
Klukwan
Pacific Ocean
Sitka
Fort Tongass
Queen Charlotte Islands

Year by year ethnologists are becoming increasingly aware that European culture is engulfing and destroying the native peoples left in the world. Their customs and habits, legends and memories, weapons and artifacts are rapidly disappearing and there will soon be new and different developments in a large part of the human race. The oral history of these people will be lost and scientific knowledge in philosophy, medicine, and natural history will suffer from it.

Mankind must therefore make every effort to collect, as the most valuable knowledge of the ancient past, all the objects pertaining to the development of culture, for they are documents for the future writing of the "Book of Mankind." But, instead, we are watching while this basic information is allowed to be destroyed. . . . By rights the ethnological museums are the ones that should send collectors out to answer this call and salvage what can still be saved."

With his worldwide knowledge Professor Bastian, the director of the Berlin Museum, is the proper person to send out this call. After each extensive journey he has returned convinced of this need.

As long as mankind has existed there has been no greater and more devastating revolution than the present one. As powerful as were the changes of the Stone Age and the Iron Age, they seem minor compared with this period when the whole world is populated by the carriers of modern culture, which wipes out every stage of the past.

Adrian Woldt

These statements are gathered from the foreword to Jacobsen's book, composed ninety-three years ago by Adrian Woldt, the ghostwriter of the book itself, probably at Professor Bastian's dictation. Bastian, the director of the Royal Museum für Volkerkünde (Ethnological Museum) in Berlin had visited the Northwest Coast of America and was anxious to obtain collections from this area because these native people were not well represented in the major museums of Europe.

When Jacobsen returned with about seven thousand pieces, the staff of the museum in Berlin issued a book that summarized the results of his ethnological expedition. This book, *Amerika's Nordwestküste*, with five color plates, eight photographs, and map, was published by A. Asher and Company in Berlin in 1884 and sold for 50 marks (about $12.50 in American money).

Adrian Woldt's book, titled *Captain Jacobsen's Journey to the Northwest Coast of America, 1881–1883, for the Purpose of Making Ethnological Collections and Obtaining Information, as Well as Describing His Personal Experiences* and published at Leipzig by Max Spohr in 1884, was based on Jacobsen's notes, diaries, and lectures. It is that book that is translated here. As far as I know, it has never been reprinted or previously translated into English. The work has been spread over a number of years; at first I translated short sections for particular anthropologists who needed them, but as the value of the information in the book became better known in our discipline it seemed to me that an English version would be useful.

The text has been condensed to some extent, and I have omitted some sections that reflect impressions so closely rooted in Jacobsen's own time and culture as to be irrelevant today. The final chapter, dealing with Jacobsen' hasty visit to Arizona, has been omitted, since it is likely to be of little interest to those concerned with the area where Jacobsen did most of his work.

On the first usage of a personal, tribal, or geographic name, Jacobsen's original spelling is used, followed in brackets by the modern form. Thereafter the modern usage is employed. The Glossary of Place Names gives further information on this.

The autobiography Jacobsen furnished is included as an appendix to this translation. After his return Jacobsen worked in the museum, unpacking and registering his collection. Since the Berlin Museum was the principal sponsor it had first choice of the objects. When the museum's selection was completed and the smaller institutions had been satisfied, Jacobsen was generously presented with the remainder of the artifacts. He sold a large part to Herr Umlauff, a dealer in Hamburg. Some of this collection was still in the possession of the Umlauff family at the time of World War II, but all, including the records, was lost when the Umlauff house was destroyed. The remaining Jacobsen pieces in museums and private collections in Europe and America are scattered and valuable.

Jacobsen was not the only one collecting ethnological artifacts in Alaska. Until a few months before Jacobsen arrived at Fort Saint Michael, Edward W. Nelson had held a post there as signal officer. Whenever he could get a substitute at the signal station, Nelson was out collecting for the Smithsonian Institution, and on many occasions Jacobsen found that Nelson had already made a clean sweep of the artifacts in the Eskimo villages he visited. Also collecting artifacts and studying the native culture were the brothers Aurel and Arthur Krause, who represented the Geographical Society of Bremen; and the Russians, even after the sale of Alaska, sent collecting expeditions like the Chudnofsky expedition of 1890.

During the first year of his expedition Jacobsen received a letter from Professor Bastian asking him to try to bring back a number of "longheaded" Indians from the north end of Vancouver Island. He was referring to the Koskimo, who deformed their children's heads. Although this trait was found among many tribes in the south and central areas of the Northwest Coast, the Koskimo had a special style of doing it, producing what Boas called a sugar loaf deformation. Jacobsen went out to the nearly inaccessible Koskimo and tried unsuccessfully to persuade a small group of them to come on a visit to Germany. On his earlier trip to Labrador he had brought back a group of Eskimo who both enjoyed their visit and pleased the people in Europe who saw them (see Autobiographical Appendix).

In 1885 Jacobsen went on another jaunt, which brought him to the coast of Siberia facing America. Since his brother Fillip was then living among the Bella Coola, he had also been asked to assemble a group of Indians for a trip to Europe. These people did not have deformed heads, but they had fine costumes and were eager to travel. They stayed for two years, moving from one city to another and collecting a large number of enthusiastic and entertaining newspaper reviews.

When Jacobsen was at home he prepared slide lectures and wrote for semiscientific journals. This activity makes it all the more strange that he did not himself write the books based on his expeditions. His ghostwriter, Adrian Woldt, was a member of the Ethnological Society and published a newsletter called *Wissenschaftliche Correspondenz* (Scientific News), a quarterly that brought important events in science to the attention of the general reading public.

Early in 1973 I was in Hamburg for several months, and through the kindness of Dr. Wolfgang Haberland at the Museum für Uhrgeschichte und Ethnologie, I was given a room to work in that contained a cupboard filled with Jacobsen's field notes, diaries, scrapbooks, maps, slides, and pictures, the material from which Woldt worked.

The photographs I found were a surprise because Jacobsen never mentioned taking pictures. It seemed impossible to think of his even having a camera with him, and many times he was drenched and his canoe was filled with water, making the survival of plates or films unlikely. If the journalist, Mr. Woolfe, took any pictures they could not have been among the ones I found, since he was not with Jacobsen at those places, though there is one photograph of the two men together (the frontispiece of this book). The pictures in the German edition of the book, most of which are reproduced here, are excellent sketches made of the pieces as they were cataloged for the collection in the Berlin Museum.

Alaskan Voyage   1881-1883

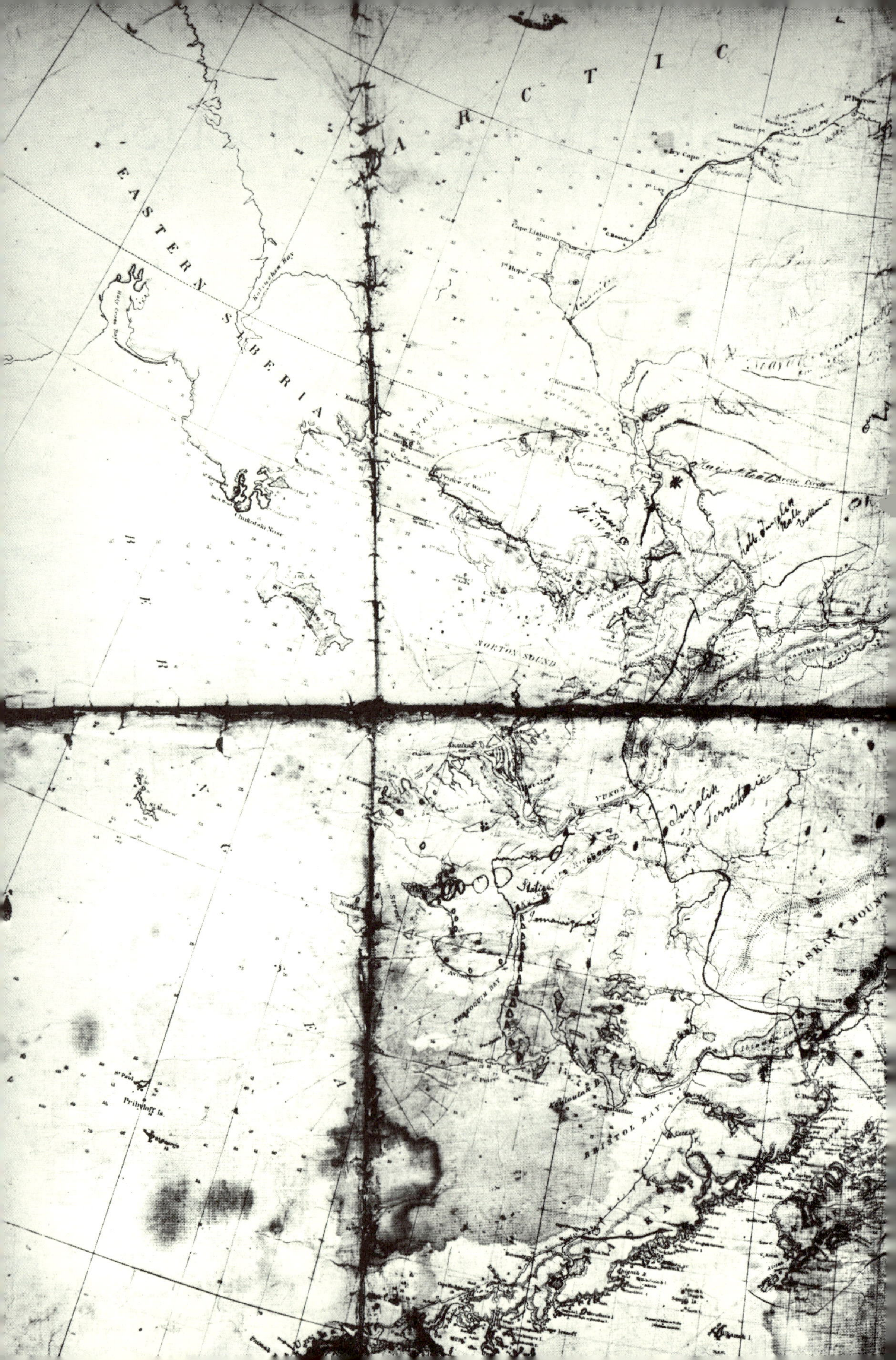

EASTERN SIBERIA
ARCTIC
BERING SEA
Kolutschin Bay
Holy Cross Bay
Chukotski Noss
Cape Lisburne
Pt Hope
East Cape
BEHRING STRAIT
Prince of Wales
Kotzebue Sound
Good Hope
Arctic Circle
NORTON SOUND
NORTON BAY
St Paul
Pribyloff Is.
Nunivak
YUKON
Ingalik Territoire
ALASKA MOUNT
BRISTOL BAY

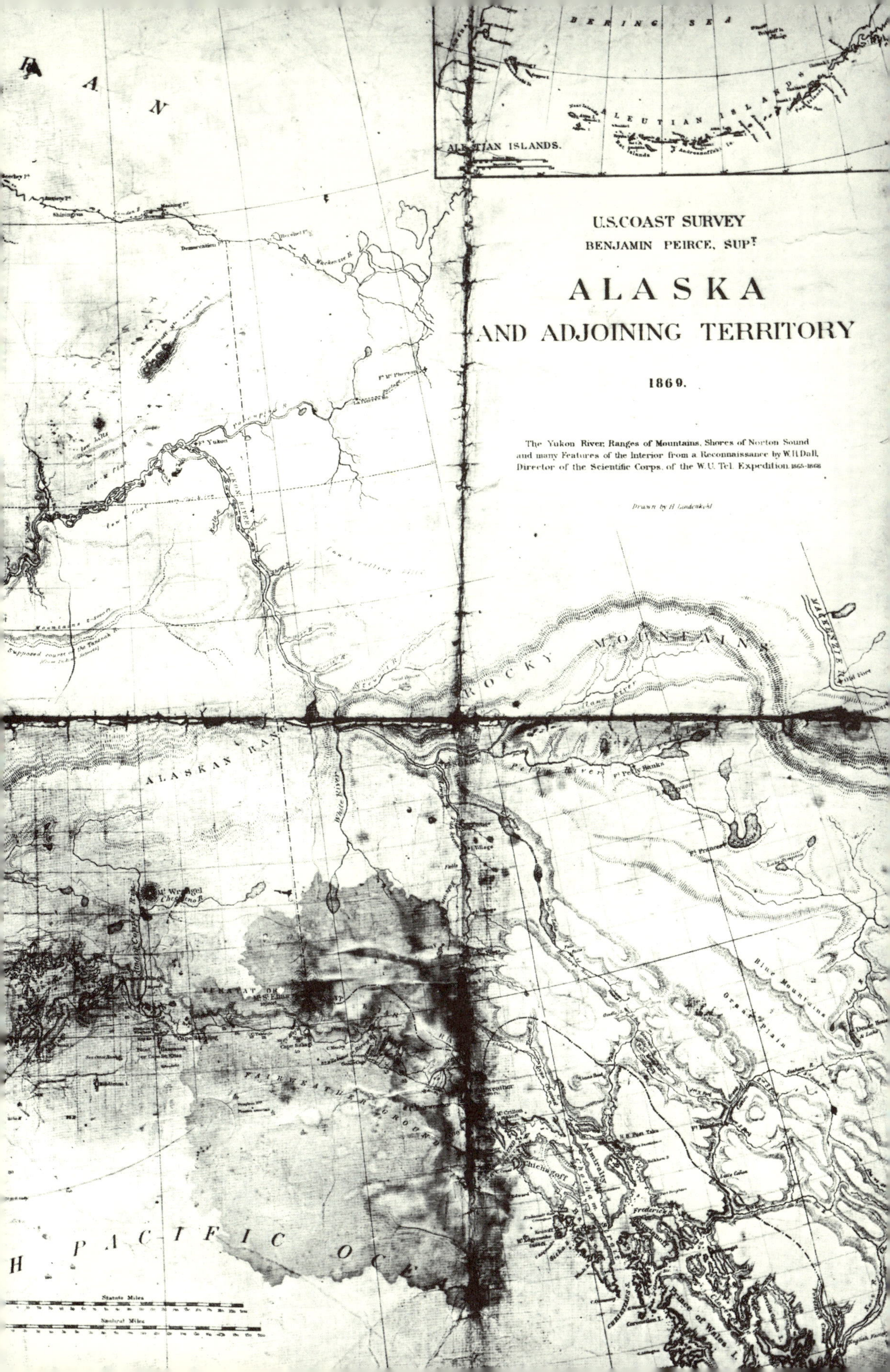

BERING SEA
ALEUTIAN ISLANDS
ALEUTIAN ISLANDS.
U.S. COAST SURVEY
BENJAMIN PEIRCE, SUP.T
ALASKA
AND ADJOINING TERRITORY
1869.
The Yukon River, Ranges of Mountains, Shores of Norton Sound
and many Features of the Interior from a Reconnaissance by W.H.Dall,
Director of the Scientific Corps. of the W.U. Tel. Expedition 1865-1868
Drawn by H. Lindenkohl
ROCKY MOUNTAINS
MACKENZIE
ALASKAN RANGE
Mt Wrangel
FAIRWEATHER GROUND
Blue Mountains
Great Plain
PACIFIC OCEAN
Statute Miles
Nautical Miles

Jacobsen (*on right*) with
his friend H. D. Woolfe,
correspondent for the
New York Herald.

1

On Wednesday, 27 July 1881, I received a request from Director Bastian in Berlin to undertake an expedition of several years' duration to the Northwest Coast of America in order to obtain ethnological specimens for the collections in the Royal Museums in Berlin. The necessary funds had been secured by a number of volunteers who had joined under the title "Ethnological Aid Committee," headed by Mr. J. Richter, a banker in Berlin.

The following Tuesday I went to Hamburg, where I took the steamer *Australia* to New York and from there traveled on the Central Pacific Railroad through Chicago, Omaha, Ogden, and Sacramento to San Francisco, arriving on 26 August. The motley crowds of people in this principal city of California, the future queen of Pacific trade, make a deep and lasting impression on anyone seeing this west coast metropolis of the New World for the first time. According to my instructions, San Francisco was to be the point of departure and return of my various expeditions for the museums, and it was thus necessary to establish some lasting contacts. This was made possible through the courtesy of Mr. Frank of the firm Gutte and Frank, to whom I had letters of introduction, as well as through Mr. Ad Rosenthal, the imperial German consul. During my four days' stay in San Francisco, Mr. Frank was kind enough to help me buy the kinds of wares and articles of exchange I would need with the northern Indians and to get me advice from one of his friends who had lived among these people for many years. At the same time I also arranged with his firm to ship my collections to Europe.

My instructions were that I should go first to the Queen Charlotte Islands, which lie at about 55° north latitude north of San Francisco. Since there was no established route of travel between San Francisco and the Queen Charlotte Islands, I had to take the next regular boat to Victoria on Vancouver Island

and from there use whatever opportunity presented itself to continue the trip.

On 30 August I sailed through the Golden Gate toward Victoria on the stately steamer *Dacota*. One can entertain oneself royally on these well-built steamers, which like all passenger ships in America are floating hotels and provide every comfort. Among the passengers were people of all ages and practically every nationality. One was a rich French Canadian who was returning to his gold mine on the Stikine River in Alaska and brought for his men the best and most select merchandise he could obtain from Stewart's;[1] another was a Scottish world traveler who intended to retire in Victoria with his wife and was collecting notes for his journal. The hilarity of a number of farmers from the northern districts who had been on a pleasure trip to San Francisco with their wives and daughters was a striking contrast to the thoughtfulness of a New York merchant who, after a disastrous business venture, was seeking a new fortune in Alaska. Snatches of national songs could be heard all day from the salon, where the young people sang endlessly and the ladies entertained themselves by discussing the latest styles they were bringing home from San Francisco. Numbers of Chinese, packed together in the lower decks, had just recently arrived from their Asiatic homeland to work for several years on the Canadian Pacific Railroad. Others of their countrymen who had been here longer were on a gold-mining expedition headed for the Mackenzie River.

The weather was fine and the trip incomparably beautiful. We stayed so far off the California coast that only occasionally were its rocky headlands visible. The sea was almost blue, and flocks of gulls hovered gracefully over the ship. Toward the end of the third day, when we were opposite the mouth of the Columbia River, we met a large school of whales. These animals were forty to fifty feet long and were spread out as far as the eye could see. It was fascinating to watch these largest of mammals as they lifted their dark heads above the foaming sea, then raised their tails high in the air and dove straight down into the depths. The entire school traveled in groups of three, four, or six, and there were so many that I cannot think of ever seeing such a mass even in my Norwegian home of Tromsø. As nearly as I could identify them, they belonged to the variety the English call "humpbacks."

On the same day we passed Cape Flattery, the northwestern tip of the United States, and found ourselves in that wonderful island world that extends from here along the entire coast and reaches to Asia, forming that significant bridge over which it seems that a most diverse group of people once migrated. It is this fact, which makes this very region of the world so important in ethnological studies, that brings me here.

The *Dacota* continued her course east into the Strait of Juan de Fuca. The shipping in this strait is very heavy with freighters laden with sawed lumber from many mills and coal from the mines in the vicinity, destined for California, Chile, and even Australia. On 3 September 1881 we landed in Victoria.

The streets of this town swarmed with Indians of all kinds, for Victoria is the Indian center for the coast. Here the Hudson's Bay Company had its original western establishment and sent out its agents with trade goods as far north as Alaska and east to the Rocky Mountains, supplying its numerous branch stations on the coast and in the interior. From here also they sent out the skins, which were taken by way of Cape Horn to London, and received from there items of European manufacture and colonial goods. Consequently Indians came here each year to trade their furs, others came to seek employment, and fishermen came for commissions from canneries.

Since my plans concerning the Indians were dependent to a large degree on the attitude of the influential Hudson's Bay Company, I took my letter of introduction to Mr. Monroe, the second in command, since the general director, Mr. Charles, had left for a trip into British Columbia. My reception was very gracious and promising. The next opportunity for continuing my journey northward was to be on a coastal steamer leaving the next week. I was very impatient, but I calmed myself by becoming acquainted with the capital city of Victoria and its Indians.

During a short trip I made in the company of a countryman of mine, we came across a cemetery where the Chinese are buried. Victoria had a Chinese quarter with several thousand inhabitants. Relatives of the deceased visit the cemetery early in the mornings and leave offerings of food and drink. Wax candles of many colors were burning on many of the graves, and on one grave there was a little obelisk with a kind of oven built in it where many colored papers covered with Chinese script had been burned.

My first visit to the Indians was made in the company of a German from Victoria, who took me to the village of Saanich, about twenty miles from town. We drove in the moonlight on a fairly good road through beautiful primeval forest. Giant trees—fir, pine and cedar—towered two hundred feet and higher into the clear air, showing many shades of green, and occasionally a burning tree lighted up the landscape like a torch. Here and there country houses showed small lights, and the underbrush rustled with deer and elk. The village we reached about midnight belonged to the Cowichan Indians, with whom I at once started trading.

My companion, like all who have lived for some time on the coast of British Columbia, understood Chinook Jargon, an international speech mixture that had gradually developed on the west coast through trade relations. It is said that in the previous century a trader from China, named Meares, brought his ship off the Columbia River near the Chinook to trade for sea otter skins; from this contact a jargon developed based on the Chinook language mixed with numerous phrases in Chinese, Hawaiian, and English.[2] Even using the jargon, my first attempt at trading was not an outstanding success, since most of the young people of the village had gone to the Fraser River to fish for the canneries. During the fishing season the workmen earn an average of fifty to sixty dollars a month. The devaluation of money in this region has reached such a degree that with the high prices of everything a dollar buys no more than a mark does in Germany. The smallest coin in current use in Victoria is a dime, worth about forty-five pfennig, and outside of town, many of the Indians consider a twenty-five-cent piece the smallest change. An Indian working as a guide receives a dollar and a half a day, while a white man performing the same services gets two and a half to three dollars and his keep. We returned from our excursion toward morning, again driving in the moonlight.

The remaining two-day interval until my steamer sailed I used to get acquainted with the various Indians around the city, visiting them and trying to purchase ethnological specimens. Because it was late in the season and most of the Indians had returned to their homes after selling their furs, few were in town. Since I had heard about an old Indian burial ground near the city, I went out to see it. I found it was on a little island, and so I had to leave my horse and wagon on the shore; after a long search I found a boat and crossed over. Since the Indians were accustomed to put the dead away in wooden boxes above the ground, the place was not hard to find. The bodies were wrapped in blankets and were in various stages of decay, and I found clay pipes on a few graves as offerings to the dead. At one place a small wooden house with a pointed roof had been built and inside the tiny structure was just enough room for three grave boxes containing the bodies of a chief and his wife and daughter. The trip back to the mainland was almost a disaster for me and my companion because a storm had come up in the interval and drove us, in spite of our greatest effort at rowing, about an English mile out of our way.

Two days before my arrival in Victoria the steamer *Sea Otter* of the Hudson's Bay Company had sailed for the Queen

Charlotte Islands and there was thus no chance for the next three weeks to get a direct passage; so I chose to join a tour in the little old coast steamer *Grappler*, which had seen better days as an English gunboat and now was spending its last years as a trading vessel for a private company in Victoria. A year after my trip, in the autumn of 1882, it ended its countless adventures in a blazing fire during its voyage and took along to its grave the majority of its passengers—mostly Chinese, but also a few whites. We left Victoria at six o'clock in the evening on 10 September. From spring to autumn the ship maintained its schedule as nearly as its uncertain condition made possible, for it was the only communication between Fort Wrangel in Alaskan territory and all the intervening coastal points which were important for trade. On our trip it looked very chaotic on board since many of the passengers were Indians returning home. There were also a number of Indian girls who, with the blessing of their tribesmen, had spent the season in Victoria, the El Dorado for large earnings, and were returning with heavy pockets to the home treats of fish oil and winter dances. Among the white passengers I have the fondest memory of Mr. Cunningham, a onetime missionary who through changes of fortune had become a prosperous trader and part owner of Port Essington at the mouth of the Skeena River. His wife was an Indian and he had great influence among the Indians along the entire coast. He promised me a test of this last statement and proved his point. The Indians living on the long coast on the east side of Vancouver Island are Flatheads[3] in the south and Kwakiutl in the north. The villages of the people here resemble those of all tribes as far north as Alaska.

Generally a village consists of four to six to twelve houses, each being occupied by four to six families of six to ten persons each. The houses are built of cedar planks and stand near the shore, mostly about thirty to fifty paces from the water's edge. Nearly every house has a wooden platform built four to eight feet over the high-water mark. These platforms serve as gathering places for the men, who squat there facing the sea for part of every day. It is interesting to notice in which direction from these platforms the kitchen middens of the village have been built up. The numerous shells of the shellfish consumed there are thrown from the platform and gradually build a solid heap. Among the Kwakiutl and the tribes north of them one finds beside almost every house a totem pole up to sixty feet high, carved from a single tree trunk with designs relating the history of the owner. I will return to this.

After taking on coal at Departure Bay, where the largest coal mine in British Columbia operates, we landed at noon the following day at Allert [Alert] Bay, near a large Indian village. This is where Mr. Cunningham carried out his promise. During the hour-long stay of the *Grappler* he accompanied me and several other passengers quickly from house to house and called to the Nemkis [Nimpkish] Kwakiutl tribe that they should at once bring out everything they wished to sell. He helped with the selection and finally loaded himself and all of us with the ethnographic artifacts we had bought. We returned hastily to the ship, for its bell had already sounded the second warning of departure.

2

As we left Alert Bay and entered Queen Charlotte Sound we also left Vancouver Island and that ethnological area, which consists of a welter of islands. A fairly broad expanse of open water leads ot the next island group northward, which lies off-shore and forms a new ethnological area. At this point we entered the region of the northern Indians, who have a higher culture, greater development and skill, more intelligence, and a greater love of work than their southern neighbors. This region is inhabited by four tribes—the Bella Bella,[4] the Tsimshian, the Haida, and the Tlingit—who occupy the entire coast northward to the Atna or Copper River in Alaska. These tribes all have a great past, but now they stand on the verge of extinction.

At noon on 13 September we landed at Milbank Sound, the impressive principal village of the Bella Bella. There has been a post of the Hudson's Bay Company here for about half a century and more recently also a mission of the Methodist church. Mr. Cunningham again went ashore with me to look at the village and purchase a few things. The houses of the Bella Bella are of cedar planks like those of other tribes and are likewise occupied by four to six families. Inside the building there is usually one large open space with trampled earth for a floor, and in the middle of the house under an opening in the roof is a communal fireplace. The area around the walls is divided into separate spaces with wooden walls, doors, and flooring; each such section is about seven feet high, six feet wide, and six feet deep. They seem to serve as sleeping quarters for individual families, and goods are stored there in wooden boxes. Money and valuables of the European type do not constitute the wealth of an Indian. He puts his entire fortune into "blankets"—literal woolen blankets. The Hudson's Bay Company reckons the value of two blankets as three dollars, an established price on the entire coast, and these blankets are used like money in the purchase of canoes, totem poles, furs, skins, and so forth. There are chiefs who possess two thousand or even three thousand blankets. Such people have the sleeping rooms stacked to the roof with filled boxes. The Indians do not need long beds, since they usually sleep on their backs with their knees pulled up. They use mats woven of grass[5] as mattresses, and for cover use the same blankets they wear during the day. Generally there are not set times for sleeping or eating in an Indian household, and all night one can hear someone at the fire. Everyone seems to sleep and eat as it suits him.

An object that especially attracted me in this village was a "chief's seat," consisting of four boards, almost square, built into a sort of seat, resembling a coachman's seat in form and gaily painted with mythological figures on all surfaces. Such a seat was placed on the floor in front of the fire, and a chief or a high-ranking visitor occupied it in a squatting position. Since it was not possible to buy the piece I ordered a similar one from the most renowned wood-carver among the Bella Bella, and through the friendly cooperation of the Hudson's Bay Company arranged to have this piece and a well-carved cedar canoe sent through Victoria to San Francisco.

Over the fire in the middle of an Indian house there was generally a framework of wood on which food was smoked— fish, berries, bark, and seaweed. The fish were split from one to three times so they would dry more quickly and thoroughly. The other foods were put into small wooden frames made of sticks, and thus exposed to the smoke and heat. They also were formed into square cakes about one finger thick which were packed in boxes and served as food for the winter. When they were to be used they were usually ground in a large stone mortar, put in an iron pot with fish oil, and placed over the fire.

Among the ethnological articles I brought from the Bella Bella were a richly carved chief's staff and a beautifully carved food box. Since among the Indians the tongue is more often looked upon as an organ of oratory than of taste, the speeches and transactions at feasts were accompanied by gestures made with such a staff. Sometimes the staff is swung through the air, then again the ground is pounded with it, or it may simply be carried as an indication of status. As an introduction to the ceremonials I would see so often later on, my purchases also included numerous artistically carved wooden clappers and rattles that were used like castanets both in dances and by shamans in their cures.

After a stop of barely an hour the steamer went on, and toward evening it brought us to a small Indian village the white people have called Chinaman's Hat [China Hat] because of the shape of the mountains near the shore. Here there was little to buy because most of the men, with or without their families, were far up the inlet fishing for salmon. It has often been described how the Indians spear and hook salmon as they ascend the clear shallow rivers to spawn, but it is less well known that the fish often meet bears, especially in the north, who take up a position in a narrow stream and wait patiently until a salmon leaps out of the water to pass an obstruction. At that moment the bear gives the fish a hefty blow with his paw, throwing it on the bank; the bear then eats it at leisure and, if he is still hungry, takes up his position to catch another.

The fish oil I mentioned above, which is prepared in great quantities and stored in wooden boxes for winter use along the entire Northwest Coast, comes from a small, very fat fish resembling a stint, which has circumpolar distribution. In the spring this fish, a type of salmon that I identify with our northern European smelt (eulachon or candlefish), perhaps the *Mallotus arcticus*, comes from the depths of the Arctic waters, where it serves as food for the cod, and ascends the shallow fjords to the mouths of the creeks where it spawns.[6] Here the well-nourished, strong individuals are carried away by the current. Knowing this, the Indians set up across the stream a bag-shaped net which is quickly filled with fish. A canoe is placed behind the net, and when the net is full the Indians pull it in, untie the ends, and empty the fish into the canoe. Then fires are lighted along the bank and the oil is rendered. The oil is poured into wooden boxes, the tried-out fish are thrown away, and the process starts over.

At the last Bella Bella village I met the chief's wife, who wore the largest labret I saw on the entire Northwest Coast. This lip plug was about three inches wide and 2 inches deep. It is the practice of the Bella Bella, the Tsimshian, and to a certain degree also the Haida to deform the body for artistic ornamentation by piercing the lower lips of young girls. A piece of bone or a small silver plug is inserted in the hole at a communal feast and gifts are distributed to those present. Later the small plug is replaced by a larger one when another feast is held; this is continued, a larger plug being inserted each time. A large plug therefore indicates that many feasts and gifts have been given for a woman and is an index of her social rank in the community. The outer form of one of these plugs resembles a slice of bread about the thickness of a little finger; the lower, flatter side is worn against the lower jaw, while the more concave outer edge appears to be covered with a thin skin. The edge is hollowed out slightly so that the flesh of the lip can be fitted firmly against it to prevent its falling out. It is obvious that the Indian woman, already lacking in classic beauty, is not improved by this plug, which protrudes at a right angle from the face and interferes with speech so that no bilabials can be pronounced, flapping up and down with every movement of the mouth.

However the women wearing these plugs, which are decorated with shells and copper inlay, are very jealous of them. As an example of this attitude, Mr. Cunningham told me the following story: Two Indian women got into an argument that became very heated in spite of the speech-hindering ornaments. Finally, in order to end the argument, the one who had the larger labret pointed proudly to it and said, "What are you anyway? Have you a labret as large as mine or have you given as many gifts as I have? Go home and when you can come back with a labret as large as mine, I will accept you as an equal." At that the other bowed her head in shame and left without a word.

After a short stop at China Hat to take on wood as fuel, the *Grappler* continued its journey. For a whole day we went through narrow channels between islands and saw beautiful landscape like that we had seen the day before in Saint George Canal [Gulf of Georgia]. It is with cedar that the Indians build their houses as well as their totem poles, canoes, and beautifully carved dance masks, their boxes, rattles, and paddles, and with cedar that they make their fires. They weave their artistic mats, blankets, baskets, and other containers of cedar bark, infants are wrapped in shredded cedar bark when laid in the cradle, and cedar bark is used for head, neck, and arm rings. Some tribes twist cordage of cedar bark, from the finest strings to the strongest ropes used for whaling, and finally the coffin is also made of the wood.

Toward evening on 14 September we landed at Port Essington, where I left the *Grappler*, since I was only forty miles away from the Queen Charlotte Islands. My next problem was to find transportation across this short distance. Mr. Cunningham, who lives at Port Essington, gave further indication of his kindness by not only trying to arrange this passage for me but also inviting me to stay at his house until I could leave, and I increased my collections considerably during my visit. Otherwise I would not have had much chance at Port Essington, because the majority of Tsimshian there had become Christians and were no longer using their original and interesting ethnological pieces. Here Mr. Cunningham helped from his store, where he had pieces that dated from the "good old days" and sold me, among other things, some handsomely carved women's dance masks, a few stone axes, utensils, and silver bracelets and earrings, as well as model totem poles, some of wood, others of stone[7] about three to four feet tall. I also obtained from him a beautiful dance blanket such as was worn by chiefs at great ceremonials. This blanket was made of mountain goat wool woven with mythological figures of animals and people.[8] I also secured from the natives another collection of household goods and fishing gear, a suit of armor made of stiff leather, and some ornaments.

The Indian wife of my host made my visit very pleasant, especially since she spoke good English. She is very religious, and on the day after our arrival she arranged a prayer and thanksgiving service in the small church built by the Indians of the community, because we had brought her son with us for his vacation from his school in Victoria. I took part in this along with the whole community. Since there was no preacher at hand Mrs. Cunningham led the service herself, kneeling and praying loudly in the Tsimshian language, after which the congregation sang hymns. She repeated this church service the following day.

Port Essington is about eight to ten miles up the Skeena River. During my visit this river became the scene of a tragedy that revealed the Indian beliefs of the community in spite of their superficial Christianity. A little boy about four or five years old fell into the river and drowned. When he was missed his parents ran to the riverbank, crying and wailing in true Indian fashion over the recovered body. Far into the night the resounding cries of the unfortunate parents could be heard as they wept for their child and recited his praises. The practice of wailing for a child is widespread among the Indians.

After much effort, it was possible to persuade three Indians who were on their way to the Queen Charlotte Islands to stop at the heathen village of Ketkatle [Kitkatla], and when I had packed my collection and sent it and letters for Europe to Victoria I joined them. Kitkatla is the first real Indian village I visited. It is rather remote from the usual line of travel and therefore not influenced by modern culture. It is a handsome town with a totem pole about fifty feet high beside every house.

The four tribal deities that belong to the Tsimshian, Haida, and so forth, are the bear, eagle, wolf, and raven. Everyone belongs to one of these groups and documents this by having a figure of one of these animals at the top of his totem pole. Through this the whole tribe is divided into four large families for whom there are ancient myths that can no longer be explained. For example, a man of the Raven family cannot marry a girl who is also a Raven but must find a mate among the Eagles, Wolves, or Bears. Even among those Indians who have

Fig. 1. Cedar-bark shredder; resembles the Polynesian type of bark shredder.

become Christians the custom is still followed. A story is told of an Indian who was preparing to become a Christian but still held strongly to this belief. He went to the missionary with this statement: "A man of the Raven family fell in love with a girl of the same group. Being fully aware of the custom that two members of the same group should not marry, they kept their relationship secret. Since they could not understand the prohibition the man went to the missionary and asked him if he had an explanation. The latter said that he also could see no crime in breaking this regulation if two young people in love wanted to marry. The young people agreed to this and became Christians in order to marry. When this was found out by the Indians the whole village talked of nothing else than this unheard-of frivolity. That they wanted to become Christians was accepted, but that they wanted to marry could not be understood. The young man suffered so much humiliation from his peers that at a great feast, when all the chiefs and warriors were assembled, his patience was exhausted and he rose and made a speech that ended with the following words: 'Can any of you show me that an eagle ever married a bear or a wolf or a raven? In the whole world an eagle marries an eagle and a bear, a bear. My fiancée is a Raven and I am a Raven, and that is why I want her as my wife. Those of you who disagree with me should go into the woods and look at the animals. If you find that I am not right, come and tell me so. Then I will abstain from this marriage.' In the gathering no one could refute his argument and the marriage took place, but the young couple soon found nothing but hatred and contempt toward them and no one paid them any attention. At feasts they were not invited and while the speeches were made and the great wooden drum was beaten for the dances, the man sat with his wife in the house, socially ostracized, a living example of the truth of their ancient belief: Love is joined with hardship."

In Kitkatla I experienced an example of how the Indians support one another. The people I had engaged to take me to the Queen Charlotte Islands and for whom I had deposited the fee with Mr. Cunningham suddenly demanded more, saying they had no sail for the boat. I naturally protested this breach of contract and threatened to go to the neighboring village of Metlakatla to start out. They laughed and asked if I intended to swim with my baggage. In the end the inhabitants were so unified in their demands that I could get no one, and I had to pay the extra few dollars to reestablish the former relationship. I made several interesting purchases in Kitkatla, but they were expensive because the Indians operate together in trade also. In addition, Dr. Powell, the Indian agent from Victoria who was eagerly collecting for the governments of Canada and Washington, had paid high prices and had promised to come back.

At noon on Wednesday, 21 September, we started, passing a number of islands before we came to the open sea. Since it was too late in the day to cross the sound we stopped at an island and spent the time hunting and fishing. In the course of the afternoon I had a small adventure in which, unfortunately, I lost my gun. A large sea lion about eleven feet long came up on a rock and fell asleep. I approached him from the water and fired a shot into his eye. With a loud roar he rose and tried to come down to the sea, but I was occupying the only place where he could do this. Mad with shock and pain, the large beast started directly toward me, turning the hunter into the hunted. I turned my gun around and hit him over the head with the stock, which broke. At this point an Indian who had seen this happen fortunately came in his canoe and killed the sea lion with an ax blow on the head. The hair of the sea lion was yellow. The Indians took the flippers and the tongue as food for the journey. We went on to Bonilla Island in Queen Charlotte Sound and spent the night there.

The storm we had feared broke the next morning, and the weather made the passage impossible for two days. There was nothing else for us to do but stay and use the time for hunting and fishing to increase our food supply. There are many flatfish here, especially halibut, which weigh up to several zentrum [100 pounds]. Unfortunately we did not catch any of these very large fish, but we did have a bite on our line from one. The waves were so high that as we tried to bring a lively halibut aboard the canoe was half filled with water and at last the hook broke and our catch got away. However, in catching other fish we were more successful. I went hunting and shot nine ducks, and in the evening the Indians dug for shellfish, especially the one Americans call "clams"—probably *Venus mercenaria* Linn. It tastes very good, almost like our oyster, and I would have eaten many more if I had had a lemon. Another favorite food of the coastal Indians, for which I could not develop a taste, is the devilfish, a kind of squid, whose tentacles they like to eat. This species is very large and strong and often dangerous to the fisherman. A missionary told me of an experience he had with a devilfish. He was traveling along the shore with a few Bella Bella Indians when a strong headwind came up and they decided to land. While they were landing one of the Indians saw a devilfish in the shallow water, so he threw aside his blanket and thrust in his arm to pull him out. No sooner had he touched the devilfish than he began to scream for help because the creature started pulling him over-

Fig. 2. Model of totem pole with house crests. Tsimshian, New Gold Harbor.

board. Luckily a third Indian stood on the shore and drove the point of his paddle through the animal several times and freed his companion. The devilfish was pulled ashore and proved to be a very large one, though by no means the largest of its kind. The Indians cooked the tentacles in an earth oven with hot stones covered with earth. In half an hour the meat was cooked, and after the skin had been pulled off it was eaten.

On my many little walking trips while we were delayed on Vancouver Sound[9] I found that every bay had a beach piled two or three meters deep with driftwood and great trees that were tangled with small sticks so that it became impassable. At one point on the beach I found five human skulls—the remains of a quarrel between two Haida groups that had taken place some time before. One group of Haida were returning from Victoria, where they had sold the skins they had collected, and the others came from elsewhere. They were going to the Queen Charlotte Islands and were detained by a storm, as we were. They stayed there and began to drink whiskey, which both parties had in quantity, and this developed into a murderous fight. The Indians who told this story said that the Haida are the heaviest drinkers of all the Northwest Coast tribes; so it is not surprising that they also die at an early age.

Finally the weather cleared, and we left on Sunday, 25 September, at five o'clock in the morning. The sound was so calm that we had to resort to our paddles for about half the journey. When the Indians go on trips they always take a short, trowel-shaped paddle along with which they stroke in perfect rhythm, sitting close to the sides of the boat. We worked hard, I handling the tiller, and later some wind came up and brought us to the Queen Charlotte Islands toward evening. Through an error on the part of my people we arrived south of Skidegate Inlet instead of at Copper Bay, where I wanted to go, so we spent the whole night aboard, since we did not dare to land. The next morning in beautiful weather we went north again, traveling along the beach for about three English miles until we finally came into Skidegate Harbor at noon and landed at an oil establishment behind the town. The Tsimshian Indians unloaded my baggage onto the beach and departed immediately, leaving me standing at the site of my next adventure.

The Haida of the Queen
Charlotte Islands

Just as the eyes of the ethnologists are directed toward this region as a promised land, so I approached these islands with great expectations. Among the problems of ethnographic research on the Northwest Coast of North America are many that perhaps might be solved through studies of the Queen Charlotte Islands and their inhabitants, the Haida Indians, who are most secretive and uncommunicative.

After my baggage had been brought to the house of Mr. Sterling, the director of the oil refinery, and he had welcomed me, I immediately ate my noonday meal. Opposite the establishment is a small island where a number of Indians from the town of New Gold Harbor [Kaisun] on the west coast had settled with all their possessions, even part of an immense house post. I decided that these people should be the object of my first visit. Here I at once realized what was ahead for me in this group of islands. The objects I wanted to purchase were very expensive, and the people offered them at such exorbitant prices that only an antiques collector would be able to buy them. Actually, Skidegate Inlet is on the itinerary of every steamer, and the tourists generally buy "curiosities" and order others for large sums. To this circumstance the scientific collector must unfortunately accommodate himself, realizing that in the future prices will probably be higher. In this village I learned the characteristics of the principal ethnographic specialty of the Haida, the beautifully carved totem pole that no tribe on the mainland can produce. The immense cedar trees, which often grow as tall as two hundred feet, are the finest material at their disposal. I will return to this.

The totem poles on the Queen Charlotte Islands are often seventy to eighty feet high and completely covered with carving. Such a column is wide enough so that the open mouth of an animal carved on the pole is used as the entryway to the house. Next to this opening there is generally also a large door

in the front wall. I found that the poles of the Haida are painted in brighter colors than those on the mainland. Another difference between these groups is that the Haida poles, though older, are more beautiful and more artistically developed. It is also obvious that this artistic skill is diminishing, not surprisingly, because the Haida for several reasons are gradually dying out. One cannot see any ship or settlement without meeting Haida Indians, especially girls and women, who also overrun Victoria to earn money. These funds are used to help their husbands with the expenses involved in having a totem pole carved and giving a great feast at its erection in order to achieve the prestige necessary to become a chieftain.

For more than one hundred years these people of the Queen Charlotte Islands with their native strength have withstood the devastating impact of the white man, which began in 1786 with the profitable fur trade, especially the sea otter, when they became acquainted with modern customs, good and bad, and lasted up to the gold rush of the fifties, which cast its pall even on these islands and brought present-day corruption to the natives. The Haida altogether give the impression that they are no longer of unmixed blood; one finds many individuals with lighter skin color, even children with blond hair, where European-American ancestry is unmistakable, though they do not admit it. The Haida men even take their wives to Victoria for the summer for such purposes as mentioned before, and after they each go their own way for making money, they meet again for the journey home. The sad consequences show in the destructive diseases of the women, and they would be much worse if the remarkable sulfur springs in the southern parts of the islands did not give them some relief.

In (New) Gold Harbor—as I should probably call the town —I did not find many wooden masks, and the few there were were not particularly good. As I heard and later verified, the Haida buy many of their masks and rattles from the Tsimshian. These rattles used in the dances have a standard pattern—a bird form with pebbles in its hollow body and a man resting on its back. A frog bites the extended tongue of the man, whose feet rest on another bird. On the ventral side of the body a face is carved in low relief and painted, and the tail of the animal forms the handle of the rattle. The Haida have developed an exceptional artistic skill in silver work, making earrings, rings, and bracelets. The ethnological motifs they use in this work, like everything they create, come from their mythology, but the figures of the whale and eagle have been used so long that they have become stylized into pure ornament. Even in the newer techniques, where arabesques are used in the designs, the practiced eye of the ethnologist can discern historical motifs. One could call the Haida, and also the Bella Bella, Tsimshian, and Tlingit, who have the same mythological concepts, nations of artists, for there is nothing they use that is not skillfully decorated with meaningful designs. Examples are the carved wooden dishes of the Haida and the spoons made of mountain goat horn. They also distinguish themselves in carving stone pillars. The houses of the Haida are larger than those of the other tribes and are kept cleaner. The chiefs' houses I later saw at Skidegate, Masset, and Klu [Klue] were fifty to seventy feet long and thirty to forty feet wide and had a special arrangement inside so they could be converted into amphitheaters during the big winter feasts and dances. For this purpose every house had a square inner space that contained the fireplace but also served as a stage, a dance area, an orator's podium, and the seat of honor for the chiefs. This area was lower than in other houses and was surrounded on all four sides by a terrace consisting of three large logs on which the guests sat during the feasts and where several hundred people could watch the performances. In the chiefs' houses the posts supporting the roof were beautifully carved with the forms of whales, bears, and humans.

Among the Haida, when a family member dies he is put in a little house behind the dwelling and his masks, rattles, and weapons are placed there with him. But it seems that these

Fig. 4. Raven dance rattle. Queen Charlotte Islands.

Fig. 5. Dance rattle: eagle's head and whale. Queen Charlotte Islands.

Fig. 6. Copper plaque, symbol of wealth, used in potlatches. Northwest Coast.

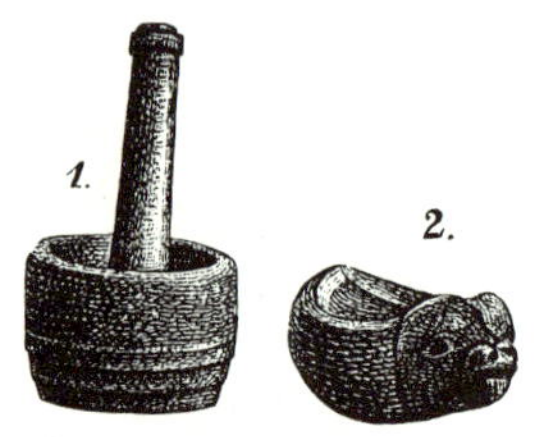

Fig. 7. Mortar and pestle for grinding food and tobacco, and small mortar in animal form. Haida, Queen Charlotte Islands.

articles are taken back by the family after several years, since I never saw them on old graves, though there were many with more recent ones. When a chief dies he is buried in his house and his wife and children are placed beside him. Many of his possessions are laid around his body, as I saw at Klue and Kamschua [Cumshewa]. When a chief dies a pole is attached to his totem pole to indicate that he is no longer living.

In the house of the Haida I saw many examples of the unusual copper plates that for many years have played an important part in the economy of the Northwest Coast Indians. These plates, resembling a shield in shape and etched with very primitive designs, weigh about ten kilograms and were made on the Copper and Stikine Rivers in Alaska and sold for a high price. I saw one for which 1,700 blankets (woolen blankets) were paid. Soon the traders, especially the Hudson's Bay Company, began to imitate them and gave them to the Indians instead of money. In this way they became widely distributed, especially among the Haida and Tsimshian.

When I finished my purchasing at Gold Harbor, I returned to the oil establishment, which belongs to three former prospectors—Mr. Sterling, Mr. MacGregor, and a mechanic whose name I have forgotten. These men are aggressive and industrious and have established trade relations in a wide area. They catch dogfish in great quantity in the inlets of the Queen Charlotte Islands and press the oil. South of Skidegate they have a fishing station deep on Kamschua [Cumshewa] Inlet. Communication between this station and the main plant is by means of a small boat belonging to the company. This craft arrived at the same time as I did and brought five thousand freshly caught dogfish. I had spent a pleasant evening with these gentlemen, and the following morning I inspected the plant. The main building stands on piling so that it is flooded at high tide. In this way it is possible to bring the boat close to the building, and the fish are loaded on wooden frames that are hoisted up and set on tracks to be sent to sorting stations. The liver of the dogfish is taken first and is made into a fine, yellowish liver oil for medicinal purposes; the remainder becomes less valuable, thicker oil. The oil is extracted by steam. In this way the company handles two to three thousand fish daily from June to November. Few Indians work in this plant, and the white men employed are mostly former gold miners. The oil is sent to Victoria in great quantities.

Since Mr. Sterling kindly invited me to join him on his next trip on the little steamer to Cumshewa I engaged a Haida who spoke some English to go with me, taking his canoe. We soon started out and by evening reached a fishing station near the village of Cumshewa. Since all the fishing gear had to be un-

loaded, I took the time to go with my Indian to Klue, which is the southernmost and most populous archipelago and includes at its east end the small island of Tanoo [Tanu]. A favorable wind brought us there toward evening. I discovered a very unhappy situation for my purposes, for the entire population had gone about fifteen miles away for salmon fishing to supply

Fig. 8. Canoe model with two canvas sails that may have been adopted from Europeans.

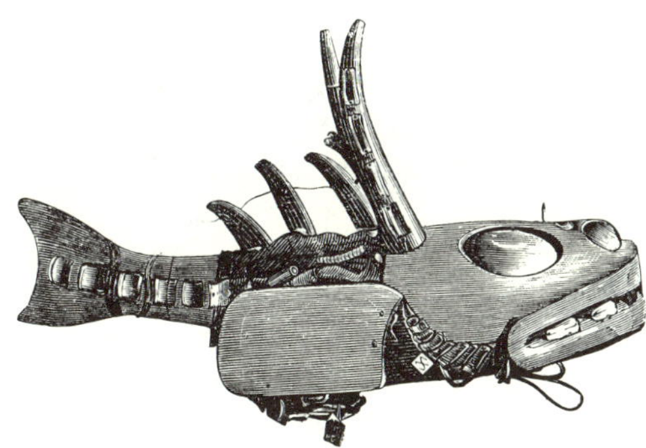

their winter needs. It would have been useless to follow them, because they would not come back with me to their village, where I found many ethnological pieces as I went through the houses. The few men and women who remained in Klue could not sell me very much. The village has some very fine totem poles, and on a chief's grave lay several masks, blankets, and the orator's staff he held when making speeches. The next morning we went north again and stopped at the village of Skedans before coming to Cumshewa, where we got the same old story. There were only four families present, but in spite

Fig. 9. Dance mask in the form of a killer whale with three dorsal fins. Probably Haida.

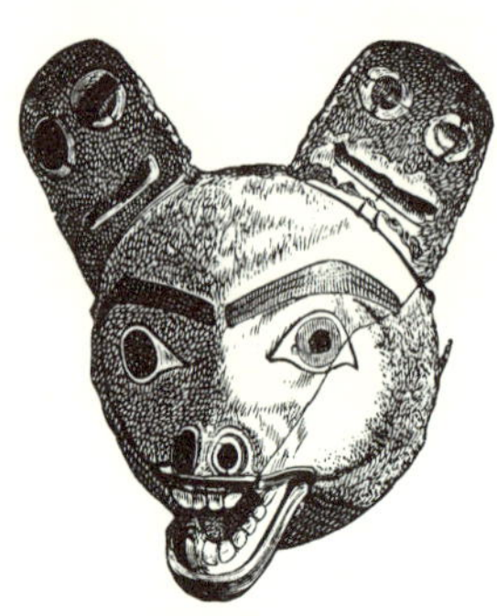

Fig. 10. Wolf mask, with
erect ears and teeth in
mouth. Haida, Masset.

Fig. 11. Soul catcher of
hollow, carved bone, used
by medicine man to carry
soul back to patient.

of that I did get several good pieces. An excellent carver lives in Cumshewa, from whom I secured a beautifully carved pole about five feet tall, even though the price was high because the strangers, especially Americans, spoil the price range here too. In Cumshewa I took the opportunity to examine the Indian grave houses at closer range. Most were locked, but it was possible to look in. Almost all the houses were full of coffins in which there were bodies. These boxes were only two to three feet high and wide, so that it was impossible to lay a human body in them. But on the entire Northwest Coast it is customary to set the body in a sitting position with the knees pulled up high and then it is wrapped in mats and forced into the box. Cumshewa was formerly an important village, but it has lost many of its inhabitants through contagious diseases and through the current desire to leave the villages.

Toward noon on 1 October the steamer came back from the inner fjords and took us aboard, so we arrived at Skidegate that same evening. The next day was Sunday, and I spent the day visiting the village of Skidegate, where in return for a small gratuity I used the chief's house to set up a sort of "swap shop" for exchanging European goods for Indian "curiosities." The trading went very well, even though I had to pay high prices. In the evening I returned to the oil establishment.

I had now been away from San Francisco for one month, and I still had had no mail from home. This, however, might come very soon, for the Hudson's Bay Company steamer *Otter* was expected from the south at any moment. This ship had a double meaning for me, for I also intended to continue my trip to Masset, the northernmost Haida town. But before this could take place the objects I had purchased had to be carefully packed, numbered, and described to be sent off to the museum. All this was accomplished, and I found myself in New Gold Harbor again, when suddenly about noon the whole population broke into great excitement because the *Otter* came into sight. They had scarcely thrown out the anchor when I was the first one aboard, since I was understandably anxious to get my mail from them. The captain handed me a large packet, mostly from Berlin, including authorization forms and letters of introduction.

Many inhabitants of New Gold Harbor came aboard to take the trip to Victoria. Since the ship was not sailing until the next morning, I could take my things aboard in a leisurely fashion. However, I had some very bad luck. I had brought all my goods out on a small boat, including a heavy chest. Through the carelessness of the Indian to whom the boat belonged, when he tried to pass the chest, the boat tipped over near the shore and we fell into the water with the baggage. We both

Fig. 12. Haida village at Masset, Queen Charlotte Islands.

reached land quickly by swimming and I immediately started to pull my goods out of the water; then I grabbed the Indian and ducked him several times. After this he jumped up in fright and ran for the bushes, never to appear again. I lost much of the food I had purchased for the journey, and many objects were thoroughly soaked. I spent the whole night on shipboard drying and repacking the ethnological objects.

The ship finally sailed at about five o'clock in the afternoon. On board were eight young Haida girls who were going to try their luck in Victoria and about twenty young men who expected to find work in the Fraser River valley or Puget Sound. At Masset, where we landed the following day, I became acquainted with Mr. MacKenzie, the head of the local Hudson's Bay trading post, a pleasant and intelligent man who was familiar with the customs and habits of all the local Indians as a result of years of residence in Alaska and British Columbia. How much gratitude I owe him for the information he gave me in a single day's visit the following pages will show. In Masset I also made the acquaintance of two gold miners, one of them a nihilist, Count S——, who had both been prospecting and so had been in many unfamiliar places on the west coast of the islands. While we were landing Chief Weah, an old, well-preserved man who did not seem to have the usual characteristics of an Indian, came aboard to greet us.

Mr. MacKenzie eagerly helped me with my purchases. Even though many earlier visitors, especially the officers of a British warship that called there every summer, had bought almost everything, we went from house to house and found a few items. At the same time Mr. MacKenzie, at my urging, inquired if it was possible for me to purchase a large totem pole. We actually found several people who were willing to consider such a transaction. The poles under consideration were in a deserted Indian village about one English mile away. In the company of Count S—— and an Indian I went there and found several about fifty feet high, much decayed with age but still suitable for my purpose. As we were going back to Masset to make arrangements for the purchase we took another path and came upon a well-preserved pole which I had admired on the way down but which was not for sale. However, in the meantime the owner, a lesser chief by the name of Stilta, who also went by the name of Captain Jim, had changed his mind and declared he was ready to sell the pole. We soon came to an agreement when I offered him fifty dollars, which he accepted, and it was arranged that with Mr. MacKenzie's help the pole would be put on the next steamer that called. This took place and without any injury the pole arrived at the Berlin Museum, where it is the largest exhibit from America. Captain Jim is a very intelligent young man who in the summer of 1881 was the guide of the gold miners mentioned above, and during their

Fig. 13. House with totem pole, bearing a flag, and memorial pole. Haida.

roaming in the interior of the island he found that caribou were there. He shot several of them and I later saw their skins and antlers in Victoria. The fact that Captain Jim had been converted to Christianity and had adopted many ways of the white man accounts for his readiness to sell the pole. Captain Jim was also the first Haida Indian in several generations who had visited the west coast, since communication had long been broken between the natives of the east and west because of a legend of giants who lived in the west and would kill all strangers who came there.

It is perhaps time to relate a few facts which I found out about a totem pole: the Haida, like many other coast Indians, believe that once a great flood covered the earth and few people survived. One of the survivors was an old Haida, according to the story, who was busy one day collecting sea urchins on the east coast of the Queen Charlotte Islands between Skidegate and Masset. It was a clear day and the Indian, "Father Noah," went blithely along the coast in his canoe looking down into the transparent water and now and then picking up sea urchins. Suddenly he saw in the depths of the water a village where a beautifully carved totem pole stood in front of every house, some being so tall that they almost showed above the level of the water. Highly pleased, "Noah" paddled home and made a similar pole, and since then the Haida have had their totem poles.

At present, when a Haida decides to erect a totem pole, the whole village kin participate, which causes no difficulty because almost every Indian is an artist in the techniques of carving. The most skilled and experienced men oversee the whole work, which sometimes takes several years to complete. The master carver selects from among the giants of the forest the one that seems right for the project on hand. Not all of the cedar tree is used, only the lower end of one about ninety to one hundred feet high, and of this about ten feet at the butt end is not carved, since that part will be in the ground when the pole is erected. Then along the entire length of the tree parallel lines are drawn about four to eight feet apart, which should take up about a third or a quarter of the tree's circum-the surface of the cylindrical form is divided into sections, each of which will contain one of the principal figures. The master ference. The lines are cut about one foot deep so as to create a cylindrical form. The remainder of the tree is discarded. Then carver assigns each of these parts to one of the artists who has been invited to participate in the carving by the man who initiated the project. Each artist is told what part in the overall design is his, and then the master carver starts on the main figure himself.

Fig. 14. Model of totem pole with crest symbols. Haida.

Fig. 15. Hat woven of
spruce root with painted
crest designs.

Now the work can begin, and many busy hands take hold, accompanied by the uninterrupted sound of pounding with simple tools: the Indian hand ax and a pair of chisels are all these artists use, and gradually there appears a bizarre composition of human and animal figures. When the pole is finally finished the neighboring and friendly kin are invited to a big feast. The pole is laid on rollers and tied with heavy tow ropes. Then a hole is dug where the pole is to stand, about four to six elles deep, and with the help of all present-—men, women, and children—the pole is pulled into position, the upper end supported with poles and props, and slowly raised erect. As soon as this is achieved the feast begins. All those who worked on the pole are given woolen blankets, and the invited friendly tribes also receive presents. The erection of a pole may thus cost the owner from 600 to 1,600 blankets, the savings of many years of work. For this outlay the owner of the pole may take on the title of chief.

At my request Mr. MacKenzie at Masset one year later sent me a description of the totem pole I had purchased.

Such a pole as yours, is called Kee-ang in Haida, namely, a carved totem pole. This is the general term for poles, but each has in addition an individual and distinctive name. The name for the one purchased for Berlin is "Qwee-tilk-keh-tzoo," meaning a lookout for approaching people or a marker for those who are approaching. Which meaning is more correct I cannot say, because I am not sufficiently familiar with Haida. The pole was erected six years ago at the place where you saw it when a Haida chief named Stilta decided to build a new house. This occasion, as usual, involved the distribution of much property on his part. Hundreds of blankets and other valuable things were given to all who were at the feast. Stilta belonged to the Eagle phratry and according to their customs all those who received presents belonged to the other phratry. The Eagles received nothing. Soon after the erection of the pole and before the house was built, Stilta became ill and died. His brother, from whom you purchased the pole, succeeded him in the position of chief and took his name. At once he erected another pole as a memorial to his dead brother and for the occasion of his assumption of the title. On this occasion a great feast was also given and food was distributed to the guests and blankets to the carvers of the pole. It must be mentioned here that a burial pole differs from a totem pole. At the base of the pole is a whale which has a supernatural relationship with the medicine man. The Haida name for a whale is "Qw-oon." Above the whale is a Haida medicine man or woman (Haida: Sah-gah). These emblems were carved by Edensaw, head chief of the northern part of the island, who is still in Masset. The medicine woman above the whale announces when a whale is stranded on the north coast. This was possible for her because her helpers are helpers of the whale. She also had the power to bring whales into smooth waters.

In this description Mr. MacKenzie mentioned only the lower group of figures on the pole; however, including the eagle at the top there are seven or eight more sculptured figures, with an Indian medicine man and a whale repeated. It must remain for future scientific investigation to finish the description of the entire pole.

After I had completed my purchases at Masset I went on board. The tide was so strong that I have seen nothing like it except in my home in Norway. It was difficult to get away, but in the early morning of 7 October we left Masset and the

Queen Charlotte Islands and headed in a northerly direction toward the mainland of British Columbia. I was very anxious to see Port Simpson, the largest village of the Tsimshian, and never in my life was I more disappointed than when I first saw this place. Instead of stately high totem poles that beckoned the approaching people, I saw nothing but modern European-

Fig. 16. Front of chief's house at Masset; planked walk, house door to right of pole. Guests are assembled for a feast.

type houses with little front gardens, and in the middle of the town carefully laid out streets and a Gothic-type church. This was the result of ten years' missionary work of the Methodists. So Port Simpson was the first Indian village in which I bought nothing because there was nothing to obtain. The local missionary, Mr. Crosby, greeted me very kindly when he came aboard to go to Victoria with his family. However Count S——— and I had the opportunity of seeing a small collection of Tsimshian ethnological pieces. Port Simpson has about nine hundred inhabitants, of whom usually about one-third are at home while the remainder are out hunting and fishing or seeking employment in the southern states. After a stay of a few hours the steamer *Otter* started her journey southward, which was very fortunate for me, because I wanted to get to the northern part of Vancouver Island. Before getting there, however, we made two landings—one at a cannery on the Skeena River called Inverness, and the other at Bella Bella. At midnight we landed at Fort Rupert on Vancouver Island.

4

**The Northern End
of Vancouver Island,
Visiting Kwakiutl
Villages**

My next area of work was the long stretch of Vancouver Island which in its northern half runs parallel to the mainland with its islands and fjords—an excellent region for ethnological research. If anyone had foretold me all the incidents I would experience on this trip and the length of time I would spend here I would never have believed it. Fort Rupert appeared to me to be an excellent place because it had a central station of the Hudson's Bay Company from which I could make excursions in various directions. The local manager, Mr. Hundt[10] [Hunt], quickly became my trustworthy friend, and from him and his family I received constant support. He rented me his sloop at a reasonable price and gave me as a guide his son George, who was about twenty-six years old and a half-breed. He was well acquainted with the local Indian customs and was trusted by the Indians, since he spoke their language fluently. The Fort Rupert Indians are "Quakult" [Kwakiutl, or Kwag.ul].[11] On the evening of our arrival, when I expressed a desire to see some Indian dancing, Miss Hunt, the sister of my newly engaged guide, got together a group of Indian girls who performed in their costumes.

On 10 October 1881 I made my first excursion to as many Kwakiutl-speaking villages as I could. This included all the villages on the northeast and north coasts of Vancouver Island between Comox and Quatsino Sound, as well as between this part of the coast and the islands off the mainland of British Columbia and the fjords in this region. This represents one of those regions where the geographical subdivisions agree with the ethnological boundaries. The principal occupation of the inhabitants, fishing and hunting sea mammals, binds the area together. The inhabitants of this region and also of the almost unknown west coast of Vancouver Island are some of the wildest and most robust specimens of mankind known today. Practices of the ancient past, like murder, cannibalism, and other horrors, have been kept under control by British gunboats. The Kwakiutl Indians have among themselves a series of ranks, of which the most important is that of "Hametze," the cannibal [Hāma′tsa of Boas].[12] The ones that belong to this group indicate their positions with pride and are the recipients of great respect from their tribesmen. Now the "good old days" are over when they could kill slaves and prisoners of war and eat them without hindrance, but they have found another way, one might say more horrible, to gain their ends. Nowadays before their great feast they eat the bodies of the dead; and not those of recent origin, but some that have been dead for one or two years.

One must not regard cannibalism as practiced here—or any other place in the world—as a means of satisfying hunger or some need of the human body which only human flesh could satisfy, for the Kwakiutl Indians have available to them all that the sea can furnish—tasty seals, fish, shellfish, and squid as well as aquatic birds of all kinds, which together give them more nourishment than any other people in the world. To eat human flesh is considered an extraordinary privilege which only distinguished people can indulge in after a series of difficult and castigating preparations. A common person could never aspire to this, for one must be the descendant of a chief or other person of high rank to be initiated. The period of preparation lasts four years during which the novice may be recognized by the cedar bark shoulder ring he wears over his left shoulder and under the right arm. During the last four months of this period the novices leave their families for lonely vigils in the forest, during which they fast and prepare themselves bodily for the last great ceremony. The villagers then already consider them beings of a higher level, and on seeing them they shudder and get out of their way, as they also do when they hear the sounds of their pipes in the morning indicating their presence near the village. At last the time arrives when they become "Hāma′tsa" in its true meaning. For this purpose it is not necessary that they have tasted human flesh, but they must have tasted human blood. This act is performed in the following way: a future Hāma′tsa suddenly leaps out of the woods into the middle of the village, throws himself upon a person there, and bites him in the arm or leg and sucks the blood. That is all.

Naturally the person who is attacked in this way is fully prepared and has an understanding with the Hāma′tsa, who pays him in blankets, often as many as forty, for his willingness to be bitten. I saw several persons who had been bitten in this way, and when showing me their scars they assured me that the bite was not painful, for the Hāma′tsa tears a little

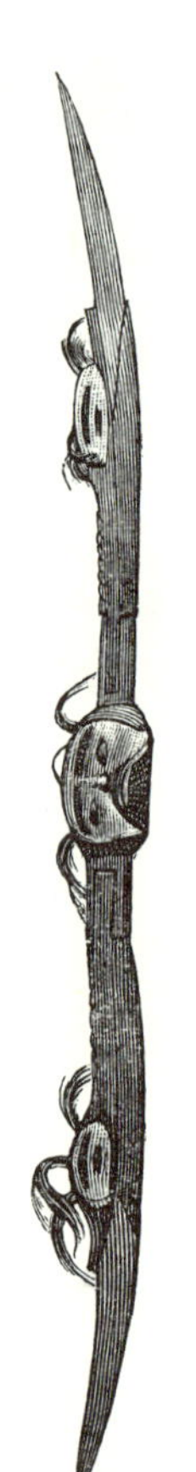

Fig. 17. Self-torture instrument used in preparing for ceremonial dance.

Fig. 18. Two very fine masks: Raven and sea monster used in Hāma'tsa dances. Kwakiutl.

skin with his teeth and knows how to get some blood quickly so that in a few seconds he will have a mouthful. As one can see, there is very little left of this initiation ceremony.

The Hāma'tsa enjoy extra privileges in every respect. Their dance masks, their rattles, their cedar bark head and neck rings are well constructed and ornamented. When a Hāma'tsa takes part in a large general dance it takes four chiefs to invite him, one after the other, before he consents to come. By fasting and isolation in the darkest part of the house he prepares himself for the occasion, because one of the rules of the cult is that a Hāma'tsa should appear pale and haggard. When he goes to the ceremony he dresses in all his finery. He leaves the house accompanied by the four chiefs, walking at the slowest pace possible and taking several hours to reach the festive house, which may be only a few hundred steps away. This snaillike progress makes a great impression on the other Indians; young people who meet him stand still and respectfully lower their heads while he passes. During the feast the Hāma'tsa consider themselves worthy of attention and expect to be regarded as supernatural beings.

With the drinking of some human blood the Hāma'tsa has still not reached the highest rank because he has not yet eaten human flesh. The ceremony when this takes place is carried on with the Hāma'tsa alone in greatest secrecy, and each Hāma'tsa who takes part in it is permitted to add a carved wooden human skull to his mask. I saw a Hāma'tsa who had no fewer than eight such skulls on his mask. When the corpse of which they take a few bites is old enough it is supposed not to be harmful, but in using a recent cadaver some have died of blood poisoning.

Little more than twenty years ago conditions were very different. Fort Rupert, which was founded by Blankenship, who is now Indian agent, was engaged by the Hudson's Bay Company and during the first generation of its founding had a hard struggle against the surrounding Indians, who were then numerous and warlike. It was a custom of the natives, of whom approximately a thousand lived in Fort Rupert, to go on the warpath to capture slaves and take heads. One can still find many human scalps in the region. The power of the Indians was so great that the whites had to be constantly alert, and once the town was besieged. The Hudson's Bay Company always made an effort to be on friendly terms with the natives and soon made peace with them. But the fights among the Indians themselves did not cease, and in these the Hāma'tsa played an important role. In 1859 or 1860 Mr. Hunt watched with his own eyes while the Fort Rupert Indians bound a captured slave to a post and cut his abdomen open, whereupon the Hāma'tsa filled their hands with the flowing blood and drank it. Later the slave probably was completely devoured. At that time the town of Victoria at the southern end of Vancouver Island had sufficient prestige that the governor sent a gunboat to Fort Rupert to punish the Indians, who felt their strength was enough to offer resistance, and as a result the village was destroyed and all their canoes were burned. The Indians themselves fled into the woods, as they customarily did at such times. When the gunboat had left they came back gradually, but their strength had been broken and many went across to the mainland into some of the fjords in British Columbia while others, about 250 to 300, rebuilt the devastated town. Since then they have become lazy and sullen, impertinent and impolite toward strangers, an attitude parallel to the former bloody arrogance of the Hāma'tsa.

Our first excursion in the sloop was to the Indian village of Nooette [Newette] on Hope Island, a little island north of Vancouver Island. Here the old Indian ways continued unchanged, and consequently the people were not inclined to sell me their dance masks and rattles. Only the persuasiveness of George Hunt, our interpreter, who was well regarded in the whole region, finally convinced the chief that in return for a goodly amount he should sell some outstanding ethnological pieces. After a visit of several hours we got under way again, heading for Knight Inlet, which cuts deep into the mainland of British

Columbia. On the way we had to stop at Fort Rupert, and we arrived the next day at Alert Bay, where, as I related at the end of the first chapter, I had stopped on the trip northward and with the help of Mr. Cunningham had made some purchases. Everything was very expensive. Near the settlement was a native burial ground, to which I made my way through thick underbrush. The little burial boxes and the grave houses, which stood on pilings above the ground, were all firmly nailed down. This was not the only reason I could not get any human remains to take home for scientific study; practically the entire population went along with me even into the thickest underbrush.

Soon we continued our journey, but since we could not reach Knight Inlet we spent the night at Beaver Cove on Vancouver Island, riding at anchor. The next morning we made the crossing of a narrow channel to the fjord that has been mentioned, and toward afternoon we reached the Indian village of Mamelellika [Mamaleleqala]. This place is inhabited by a ferocious people who shortly afterward tried to plunder a trading ship and were fought by a well-armed crew, who sent them home with bloody heads. In this way most of the attempts of whites to land have been resisted. An attempt was made to establish a trading post there, but it was soon plundered and the owner driven away. As punishment a gunboat bombarded and burned the village, but it was rebuilt. A Catholic missionary sought to convert the people, but he also had to give up. The only stranger who has dared live in the neighborhood is a native of the Sandwich Islands [Hawaii] who deserted his ship and was a castaway there.

My interpreter described the inhabitants of Mamaleleqala as the greatest thieves, as I later found was true. We anchored at the village and went ashore to make our purchases. Contrary to our expectations the first meeting was good, and I obtained a few articles which were not very valuable for originality, since the Indians, as George Hunt explained, can buy such things from Fort Rupert and Newette. I asked the chief of Mamaleleqala if he would give a dance, since I was very much interested in seeing what these wild people would do, but he gave me to understand that in the middle of October the yearly dancing season had not begun. If he were to allow dancing before that time the neighboring tribes would be very angry and might start a war. The next highest man in rank in Mamaleleqala was of a different opinion and said that he was not afraid of war. He was prepared to have his young men perform a dance if I would give them some tobacco.

This arrangement was settled and the next house was cleared, as nearly as possible, and a large fire was built in the middle. I allowed some of the masks I had bought in Newette to be brought in, and the dance began. They performed not winter dances, which required many performers, but summer dances in which single dancers were used. At the back of the house the large wooden drum was set up and the song leader —every village has one—placed himself beside it with his painted staff. Then he beat on the drum, an ordinary wooden box without a lid, and the singing began. All the young people who sat around the house joined in and beat time on a wooden plank. It seemed as though each one was bent on making as much noise as possible. The partitions which usually served to divide the sleeping quarters now separated the dressing rooms for the dancers. After taking some time to dress, the dancer opened the door and stepped forth with all eyes trained on him. On his shoulders he had a "north blanket" [Chilkat]—a very expensive one made of mountain goat wool with many figures of eyes and faces skillfully woven. On his head he wore a wooden mask, which came from the Tsimshian and was inlaid with shells. The most expensive and highly desirable ornamentation on this type of mask was an arrangement of sea lion's whiskers across the top.[13] Quickly the dancer adjusted his steps to the beat of the music—if one can call this noisy shouting music—until he came into the open area in the center, then he danced around the fire, holding in his right hand a wooden rattle which he shook to agitate the small pebbles that filled its hollow body, producing a castanetlike sound. On the top of the mask one could see some eagle down, and whenever the dancer shook his head it would fly out like snowflakes. It was a wild dance he carried out around the bright fire while the large house was filled up to its darkest corners with redskinned people with their faces painted red and black, moving to the rhythm of the music with their eyes shining with pleasure. The ear-rending howling and noise suited the improvised act so completely that I will never forget this scene. Several dances were given, and among them the masks I loaned them were used, but it was impossible for me to persuade them to do any of the winter dances. The season for these begins in January and is associated with feasts and the giving of presents that are supposed to bring new retainers into the host's retinue by their generosity; so all the Indians watch carefully that nobody starts too soon. The chief's statement about this was not contradicted. The evening and part of the night was spent in dancing, and after we distributed the promised tobacco they lighted us back to our sloop with torches of pitch and parted from us for the night.

The next morning the deck of our ship was turned into a shop. The natives came from everywhere and brought items to

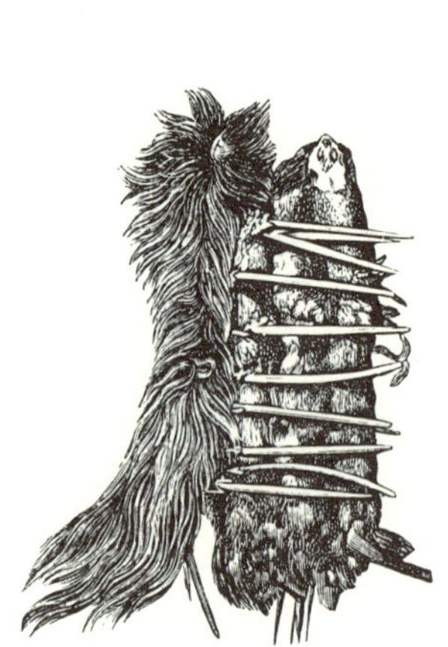

Fig. 19. Medicine man's cap, cedar bark and fur; worn during curing.

sell. But these good intentions did not last long before the Indians began by first taking little things and then stealing valuable articles, and finally they became so bold that they took everything away from me right before my eyes. Unfortunately, among the things they took were two beautifully carved wooden death's-heads which decorate the Hāma'tsa mask. It did not take me long to realize that these wild people were planning with their superior strength to take both our ship and ourselves. Naturally I was very angry, and since we were well armed I demanded, revolver in hand, that they return the stolen pieces. The women and children of the Indians began to scream and fled in their canoes. With screams and yelling the men jumped into their canoes and paddled toward the nearest shore, threatening that they would return in greater numbers. By then my interpreter George Hunt became frightened and raised the anchor and set sail. The Indians raged, but they were helpless and let us pass unhindered.

The next morning we landed among the Queka Indians. This name meant "the beheaders," a designation they fully deserved, because they formerly had the custom of attacking all the northern Indians who passed the narrow passage at Beaver Bay on their way to Victoria, taking their lives and their goods. These Indians, who are the greatest pirates in British Columbia, live in the village of Klawitsches [Klawitches; on Cracroft Island]. When we arrived a great feast was in progress, and we shared it. A woman was in the process of taking over both her father's and her mother's property. It is the custom among most of the coast Indians that at the death of the parents the sons inherit in the order of their birth. If there are no sons, then the daughters take over, but in case there are no children one of the close relatives is chosen by the whole tribe as the legitimate heir. The recipient is then expected to give a feast and to give away a large part of his inherited property. After that moment no one may mention the name of the dead because it would be a sad reminder for the heir. We saw an instance in this village of the hypocrisy of this concern. The Indians leave their sick and dying relatives alone. During the feast I saw in Klawitches an old man lying off to one side moaning, which no one heard, and dying of hunger and thirst. This happens there to all the sick whom the medicine man has given up. These ignorant people, who consider themselves great magicians, are more dangerous to the health of the Indians than all the diseases. One must see their rough way of manipulating the body of the ailing or kneeling on the abdomen of women and girls to bring about an abortion!

The feast at Klawitches was solely for the men, and the few women who were there waited on the guests. The men sat in

Fig. 20. Bone harpoon with many barbs, used for sea lions and fur seals.

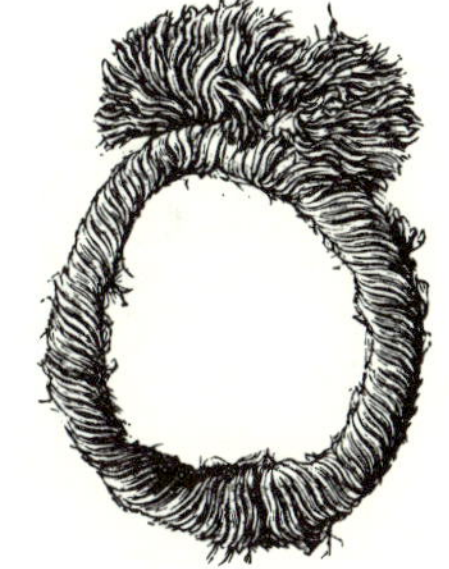

Fig. 21. Cedar-bark head ring used in dancing.

a large circle around the fire and made many long speeches. The famous art of oratory that is often attributed to the Indians was well demonstrated here. Proud and confident with his woolen blanket draped over his shoulders and fastened with a metallic pin so that his right arm is free, in a voice now loud, then modulated, with well-chosen words and lively gesticulation, the Indian stands before such a gathering and speaks to his tribesmen. To emphasize a particularly important point he uses his right arm, but not by lifting a finger skyward as though imploring the help of heaven; the Indian seizes a small piece of wood and throws it forcefully on the ground.

When the speeches were finished, the food was prepared by boiling two fat seals in the large wooden container that was also used as a drum; this is a peculiar custom in that the drum is a square-cornered box or whole carved animal body that can also serve as a cooking pot. The drum was filled with water, and glowing hot stones were thrown into it until the water boiled. Then the seals were put into it, and it was not long before they were boiled. In front of each guest was a small mat on which the food was laid. Each portion was so large that a whole family could be satisfied with it. This actually was the point of these helpings, for after the meal was over the remainder of the food was carefully picked up and carried home in the hands. As napkins long strands of cedar bark were laid in front of the guests, and on these they wiped their hands and mouths. Then a pail of clear water was carried around from which everyone drank. Generally the main dish of the Indians was dried fish, especially salmon, which was dipped in oil; large quantities of cod and halibut were also eaten.

It was still early in the day when I was through with the inheritance feast, and after making a few purchases I went hunting under the guidance of a few Indians who had been recommended to me by the chief. We paddled up a narrow river against the current. On the way several ducks were taken, and at the delta of the river we surprised a family of raccoons who were so frightened that they could not escape. I captured one of them alive, and an Indian carried it to the canoe and tied it, but the others unfortunately fell to the cruel desire of the hunter. In the fresh snow we also found tracks of black bear and deer, but it was too late to follow them.

Our questioning about the Indians of Knight Inlet brought poor results. We discovered that at this time of year they move far inland to hunt and fish so that there was no possibility of buying anything from them. We therefore had to decide to go back to Fort Rupert, where we arrived after a seven-day absence. We spent a full day arranging the purchases and getting extensive information about them from George Hunt. In Fort Rupert I made only a few purchases at this time.

On 18 October 1881 I decided to undertake a strenuous walking trip through the primeval forest across the northern peninsula of Vancouver Island in order to visit the villages of Koskimo and Quatsino on the west coast. I again engaged a half-breed Indian as interpreter and guide and started out with him the next morning. There was a sort of trail through the forest which the Indians could recognize, but for me, although I had experience in many parts of the world, this trail was un-recognizable. Certainly it was the poorest that my feet ever trod. It went over great fallen trees, real giants of the primeval forest, that were so large in circumference a grown man could not see over them; the Indians had cut steps into them on each side in order to pass. At other times one had to work his way along the length of great trees, on slippery bark, and in other places one had to crawl under fallen trees. These giant trees also served as bridges over little creeks and ravines and some-times were the only means of crossing from one hill to another. This was even more difficult for me with shoes than for the Indians, who went barefoot and could get a toehold when nec-essary. As usual I strode forward in a great hurry to reach my destination, but the farther we penetrated into this dense for-est the thicker the undergrowth became, and it seemed we would suffocate in this sea of green. The branches and the thorn-covered twigs hit me in the face, and the soaked floor of the forest often was so swampy that I sank in up to my waist. When we reached the divide in the watershed of the peninsula, it consisted of a swamp. The trees stood farther apart and were smaller, and in order to cross the swamp it was necessary to walk on fallen trees like a tightrope walker, for which I used my rifle as a balancing pole. In the middle of the swamp one of the thin trees suddenly broke and, as we had feared, I fell into the slimy mess over my head. It was no easy task to get out because the swamp was too thick to swim in but also im-possible to stand on. Also, in falling I lost my rifle. Since my Indians were about an English mile behind me, I could not ex-pect immediate help from them. I worked myself forward un-til I reached the next stump, onto which I pulled myself with great effort. Once I had gotten my feet on terra firma again I fished my gun out with a forked stick and continued walking on these thin trees until I reached the end of the swamp, where I waited until the Indians came along. It was fortunate for me that on this trip I had no paper money with me, for it would undoubtedly have been ruined through this incident. Toward evening we arrived at the far end of a deep inlet, which was to be our destination.

Since there was a heavy frost and I was soaked through and stiff with cold, it was lucky that we found an Indian family fishing for salmon at the mouth of a small creek. They were very friendly and took us into their temporary shelter, made of boards set in a tentlike form, where there was a fire to dry my clothes. They offered us an evening meal and the use of the tent for the night. I was painfully cold that whole night, since I had only one woolen blanket and all my clothing, even my shirt, was drying at the fire. The next morning I hired a small canoe and went to Koskimo. On the way we came upon an old Indian cemetery. Since my guide was a half-breed and had lived for some time among whites, I proposed that we visit the cemetery so that I might find a skull I could take with me for scientific study. My companion consented, not for the scientific purpose but because I offered him extra money for his silence and his help. The skull had special importance for me because it was artificially deformed. The Indians of Newette, Koskimo, and Quatsino pressed the heads of their small children, especially the girls, so hard with a peculiar type of binding that the head took on the form of a sugarloaf. The pressure was sometimes so great that the poor infant bled at the nose. We succeeded in getting two of these, one male and one female. I stowed these away in a sack and later in Koskimo I had great difficulty keeping the nosy and aggressive Indians, who examined every piece of my luggage, away from this bag.

We arrived in the aforesaid village about noon and were well received by the people. I stayed with the chief, Negetze, whose name is derived from the great boulder that overhangs the village. Negetze is a kind of Indian white man, over whose door is the following inscription: "Negetze Chief vont to be Frend of Wheit-Mand, thek in his house, he leik to see you."

So I moved into the house of the friend of the whites who loved us so much, and I must say that Negetze, and even more his son and son's wife, who also is of high rank, since she is the head chieftainess of Koskimo and Quatsino, treated me very well. After I had bought the ethnological objects that were available we spent the evening around the fire in the chief's house, listening to war stories, which my interpreter translated. It appeared from these stories that the Koskimo were a friendly people and were not the aggressors in conflicts. However, I saw by a letter Negetze showed me that in 1864 two sailors had been murdered by them, though I could not find out whether Negetze himself had been involved. It had recently become the custom for the Indians to ask for a written statement from every white man they worked for. Then when a traveler came to their village they came running with these papers, which they guarded carefully. In these letters

some of them were characterized as rascals, thieves, idiots, stupid fools, and so forth, so that it was hard not to laugh while reading them. However, these papers occasionally contained some important historical information. In this instance the writer, an Indian agent at the time, stated that Negetze had for some time played the role of middleman in questionable dealings and that he had paid a certain number of woolen blankets as punishment for the murder.

The daughter-in-law of Negetze, the chieftainess and the most powerful person in the whole northwestern part of Vancouver Island, took me under her protection. The worthy lady, who retained only her sugar-loaf deformed head as a sign of her former youthful beauty, showed her concern for me by making up an especially good bed. This she did by simply giving me her own sleeping quarters, which were supplied with many extra blankets. I must confess that the contrast between the cold bath of the day before and this could scarcely be greater. The younger Negetze, this lady's husband, suggested that I go to Quatsino, which was several miles away to the west and lies in another inlet, since it was possible that they might have for sale some blankets made of cedar bark.

Fig. 22. Chief Negetze of Koskimo and his daughter-in-law, chieftainess of Quatsino. Kwakiutl, west coast of Vancouver Island.

Naturally I followed his advice and hired a larger canoe, and my protectress and her husband, the younger Negetze, as well as my interpreter and I, all got aboard and merrily sailed away. This inlet, which leads into the Pacific Ocean, is not more than two to three nautical miles wide at any place and is enclosed by fairly high cliffs, out of which grows an extremely luxuriant vegetation. As we approached the mouth of the inlet we found, as one might expect, a strong current. I paddled until my arm ached in order to get my company, who seemed inclined to be seasick, to calmer waters. Soon we came to the entrance of a little inlet where the summer camp of the inhabitants of Quatsino was located. To my surprise there was nobody at the camp, for the Indians had moved five or six miles farther up the inlet to their winter village. For better or worse I had to take up my paddling again and came there late at night, having covered a respectable thirty-five English miles. The wife of the younger Negetze was in her principal residence here, and to show her hospitality she immediately went to work and cooked a most palatable meal of fish and potatoes.

The situation was most peculiar. Even though it was late at night the inhabitants had heard of my coming and brought many objects they wanted to sell to the house of their chieftainess. The paradiselike condition of the people here was already apparent at Quatsino. These good people, especially the older women and men, in spite of the raw, stormy weather, considered wearing clothing a complete luxury to be indulged in at feasts and dances; they squatted without embarrassment around the fire, although the young people, especially the women, showed a little more concern.

The custom I have already discussed of deforming the heads of infants still in the cradle by binding their heads with considerable pressure so that blood often issues from their eyes and noses produces, particularly in the women, such a high, pointed head that it is justifiably regarded as resembling a sugar-loaf cap. The people also regarded me as a sort of curious animal, but since I was under the protection of their chieftainess, their attitude was friendly.

The trading proceeded very smoothly. I bought a number of rare and original items, among others the prized blankets of cedar bark, as well as one invaluable blanket of mountain goat wool. The whole population of Quatsino was about fifty persons living in seven houses. It made a very good impression on me that here I was free from the usual begging that one finds in all Indian villages on the Northwest Coast.

After a few hours' sleep we rose the next morning and started back to Koskimo. The earlier passage had shown to me the dangers a small canoe could encounter on this coast of the

Pacific Ocean even in calm weather, but today I learned the worst conditions the stormy weather could bring. After we had paddled against the wind out of the inlet of Quatsino, a sea of terrifically high breakers came upon us. The Indians worked with all their strength to bring us around the cliff and into the more sheltered waters of Koskimo Inlet. It is a peculiarity of these Indians to kneel while they paddle and therefore look forward, so that my people looked into the oncoming waves and were so frightened that they wanted to turn back. I, however, sitting in the stern and steering, forced the canoe on the right course and so we luckily came around the projecting highlands. In the evening we were again in Koskimo. Here I engaged the younger Negetze to go with me and my interpreter to Fort Rupert to help us carry through the forest all the things I had bought in the two villages.

We left that evening and went to the mouth of the river where I had spent the first night after my original departure from Fort Rupert. The cabin, which was even then too small for the Indians fishing there and us, now had to serve as a night's shelter for two more persons, the young Negetze and his wife, who accompanied us thus far. We laid pressed together like spoons but soon fell asleep, exhausted from the day's strenuous activity, until the howling of the wolves woke us and kept us awake almost the whole night. This region is plentifully supplied with fish and wild game; on the day of our arrival the owners of the cabin had gotten two black bears and harpooned several hundred silver salmon.

The next morning we started on the return voyage. I had about a hundred pounds of baggage, my rifle, and the food kettle to carry, and my companions each carried one hundred and fifty pounds. One can imagine how difficult the path through the primeval forest was under these circumstances. On the way, near the swamplike little lake, we met three Indians from Fort Rupert who said that they had been sent by the Indian agent, Blankenship, already mentioned, to make a report on the conditions of the Indians living at Koskimo. After overcoming all these difficulties and after many falls on the slippery terrain, we came toward evening to Fort Rupert, where old Blankenship, who was the most knowledgeable person on the Indian customs and habits, gave me valuable information. I spent the next few days providing the articles I had purchased with the proper labels and packing them for their long journey to Berlin. I also bought some objects from the Indians, at high prices, since the Indians thought of these prices only in gold. At this time the highest chief at Fort Rupert returned from a trip and brought the last building articles for a new house that was expected to be completed in the next few weeks. A great feast was planned, to which tribes from as far away as the Queen Charlotte Islands in one direction and Victoria in the other had been invited for a housewarming. By this means the head chief hoped to strengthen his position and his wealth by giving away 1,600 blankets to selected guests. Although I was disappointed that I could not stay for this occasion, still I was very happy when on 31 October the steamer *Princess Louise* arrived and my many pieces of luggage were unloaded in Victoria a day later.

5

During my visit in Victoria a small exhibition opened that had, among other things, objects from the Haida and the Tsimshian. The exhibitor was Dr. Powell, who had bought and collected the pieces. There were many handsome pieces, especially several well-carved and well-painted house posts that supported the roof beams, also some carved wooden heads of a man and of a woman with a labret, and some ethnographic pieces from Alaska. My visit lasted ten days, during which time I sent off to the Royal Museum in Berlin my constantly increasing collection. Then it was necessary for me to find a way of reaching the west coast of Vancouver Island, which is seldom visited by today's travelers. Because this was during the winter season it was not easy to accomplish, for there were many reports of disasters at sea because of the severe storms. There were, however, two commercial firms that maintained small trading posts on the west coast with which they had to communicate, and in this way I found passage. On 11 November 1881 I started out on the schooner *Thorenton* with Captain Billie of the Warren Company, after I had taken on board twenty dollars worth of provisions. The voyage went around the south end of Vancouver Island, but as soon as we passed into the Strait of Juan de Fuca we met a severe storm that drove us into Beecher [Becher] Bay to anchor. Since I never missed a chance to make purchases, I went ashore. The population here consisted of people known as Flatheads.[14] These people have come strongly under the influence of the neighboring principal city of Victoria and have not kept many of their cultural traits.

The next day we set forth through the Strait of Juan de Fuca, and during the day we passed Cape Flattery across from the southwest coast of Vancouver Island and toward eight o'clock in the evening reached Cape Beale at the entrance of Barclay Sound. In the meantime it had become very stormy again. In addition night began to fall, and it became so dark that we could see absolutely nothing. We also found ourselves among the numerous islands that dot the entrance to Barclay Sound. We cruised about among these islands without seeing the mainland. The storm took on such force that it suddenly tore the mainsail. The total crew of the ship consisted of the captain, who was steering, a sailor, and a mechanic, while a half-breed Indian and I were the only passengers. When the sail tore we drifted toward an island that was surrounded by hidden rocks, on which the sea broke with great force. It looked as though we might be killed in the next moment, for the storm roared with such strength that we could not even hear each other shout. The line to the foremast sail broke, and the sailor tried hard to thread a new one to the block. During this time I took down the two rear sails to mend the splintered clew. At the last moment, when we were heading for the rocks without sail or steering, the sailor finished his work and the sail was set again and the captain with good luck managed to make his way between two high breakers. This was our deliverance, for we reached the lee side of the island where we were protected from the wind and could drop anchor. For the whole next day and the second night the storm raged with great force. I had never believed it possible that the elements could have such fury. Our schooner, which has a twenty-fathom line, was dragged some distance without resistance. The storm allowed itself some pranks; everything that was not firmly tied down was simply torn up by the wind, and to our astonishment it lifted up an Indian washbasin as though it were a feather and blew it away.

The island where we sought protection was inhabited in summer by the Indians from the village of Eckult, whose winter village was at the east end of Barclay Sound. Since there was a trading post of the Warren Company at Eckult, it was our destination, which we reached after a four-hour trip. While the captain attended to his business I engaged two Indians and a canoe and went with them to the Indian village of Oheiaht [Ohiat] to the south. Here there was a Catholic mission with the Belgian priest Father Justus in charge. I must gratefully acknowledge here the unusual support I received from him and all others of his faith whom I met on my travels.

After a friendly personal welcome, Father Justus went with me to the Indian village and helped me select the rarest objects, giving me the correct information about their usage. I obtained many pieces and went on the same day back to Eckult, because I wanted to take the opportunity of going with the schooner to Alberni Canal. But since the weather proved unfavorable the next morning, I stayed in Eckult another day and became acquainted with the head of the station, Mr. Loggen , and the Indian agent, Mr. Gilbert, who happened to be there. Both expressed great enthusiasm about going on this excursion, which would take us far into the middle of Vancouver Island. It was interesting that here at the most distant end of the canal was the only white settlement, consisting of four farmers. The distance from this place to the east coast of Vancouver Island was about a two-day strenuous trip through the dense forest. In former times there was a large sawmill here that employed about two hundred men, including the loggers who felled the trees and other workmen. After this mill burned down the establishment was not rebuilt, and it has fallen into ruin. Mr. Sproat, the head of the mill, lived here for four years and gathered full information about the local Indians that is published in his well-known work *Scenes and Studies of Savage Life*. Sproat included all the Indian tribes on the west coast of Vancouver Island between Cape Flattery and Cape Cook, whom he called the Aht [Nootka] tribes. The reason for this name seems to be based on the use of "aht" as the customary final syllable in many of their village names. The inhabitants of the west coast compose an isolated ethnological unit.

On the night of 17 November we went up Alberni Canal under steam, since the wind had calmed a little. At its broadest places the canal is scarcely a thousand paces wide, and in some places it is only the width of the current, so that it is so swift one cannot make any headway with sails alone. The current is further increased where a number of rapid streams flow into it. After we had gone about twenty English miles into the canal an interesting sight met our eyes, when we met twenty laden canoes tied together in twos with boards supported by logs on which the Indians carried all their extra household goods. This was about half of the Seeschaht [Tsisaaht] population, who were moving their place of residence about sixteen English miles farther downstream to be nearer the dogfish run. The liver of this fish was prepared and used for fish oil here as it is in the Queen Charlotte Islands and along the entire coast. Because the fishing grounds of these Indians in the deep inlets of the west coast produced more dogfish oil than the Nootka Indians could consume, they carried on a trade with their neighbors and with dealers. I was not very pleased at meeting the Tsisaaht because it deprived me of the opportunity of visiting their village and buying from them.

We approached our goal slowly on account of the strong tide, so that the evening was almost spent by the time we reached the site of the destroyed sawmill, where we were forced to anchor because of the shallowness of the water. The next morning when the tide was high we could at last cover the few miles that had separated us from our destination, the

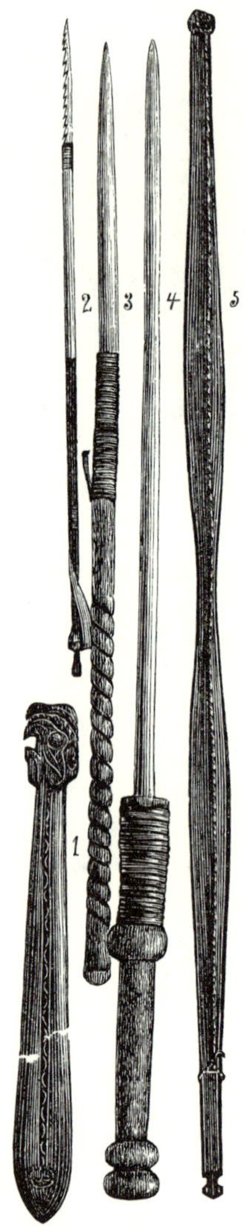

Fig. 23. Weapons from the
west coast of Vancouver
Island: (1) old war club of
whale bone, Nootka;
(2) arrow with barbed
bone point; (3, 4) bone-
tipped lances with wooden
handles, used in canoe
fighting; (5) bow for
hunting and war.

settlement of the farmers. This was in four clusters at the mouth of the Somass River, and close by are the villages of the Tsisaaht and Opettisaht [Hopachisat]. Immediately after we landed I visited these two villages, but because of the reasons stated above, I did not have good results. Nevertheless, I did secure a number of blankets made of cedar bark and one very valuable old sword-shaped war club of whale bone. The weapon is not in use today; it closely resembles the war club of the Maori in New Zealand. I found only three examples on the whole west coast and secured them all.[15]

A comic, but nearly tragic event happened to me on the second day when I went hunting with Mr. Loggen. The delta swarms with geese and ducks, which we pursued vigorously. In the excitement of the hunt I was separated from my companions and wandered farther alone. We started the trip at low tide and I had no idea how far the tide came in. The path, and in fact the whole area, was covered knee-high with water, to which I had paid no attention because I was wearing high rubber boots. The water rose higher and higher and soon it reached my chest and I could no longer see the unevenness of the ground. I stumbled along and almost had to swim, which was not comfortable in water that was almost at freezing temperature. With great effort I held my rifle above my head and made my way through overrun thicket to the bank of the river, where I was opposite one of the Indian villages and climbed a tree to make signals for them to come and get me. While I was sitting in the tree I shot two ducks, which I later recovered.

In the village, which was not reached by high tide, two feet of snow had fallen during the night. I saw here an example of the hardening process of the Indians, for young and old were running around in the snow barefoot. One man who had been carrying wood and gotten dirty went naked into the water chest deep, washed himself in a leisurely way, stepped out, and hung his blanket around himself, which, soaked with moisture, began to steam. Truly, if there are any people on earth who can endure cold, these are the ones. While I was drying my clothes I was asked by an Indian to come to another house to see some ethnographic pieces. I thought that here was an opportunity for me to show my hardiness, for if the Indians could go around all day barefoot in the snow, I could imitate them for this short distance. I therefore went through the village without shoes or stockings, and I must admit that I was painfully cold, but I stuck it out. In the afternoon Mr. Loggen came with an Indian to look for me because he was afraid that I had had an accident. I went with him on board, put on dry clothing, and went out duck hunting again. There were many ducks, and all the Indians joined in the hunt.

During the night more snow fell. This did not hinder the Indians, young and old, who lived in the house along the shore, from going naked to the goose marsh early in the morning and bathing. Then they slung blankets around themselves and returned to the village.

The riverbed had a curious appearance. It was full of dead and decaying fish—dog salmon. It would be very worthwhile if some scientist would explain this phenomenon: it is said that the fish, which go up Alberni Canal to spawn, do not eat while they are in fresh water and try to go back to the salt water after the spawning but die on the way from starvation. According to my observation these thousands were not all old fish; there were many small and young ones too.

The captain and I were invited to spend the evening with one of the farmers who lives about an English mile inland in the deep forest. In order to take a shortcut we went in another direction, and since it was already dark we lost our way. The thicket we tried to cross without a path became so dense and dark that we could not see, and our progress slowed to a crawl on hands and knees. The fallen trees that were lying at all angles forced us to do the most difficult climbing, and often we slipped on the slimy trunks and fell into pools of water. Often we ran into a tree, then a branch would hit us in the face—altogether a confusing situation. But that did not stop us in the least; in fact, we got some humor out of our troubles and often laughed out loud. To add something gruesome to the situation, Mr. Loggen told about a farmer who went hunting in these woods about a year before, and even though he knew the area got lost and has not yet been found. The groping around in the black darkness separated us, and all at once the captain screamed that he had fallen over an animal, probably a wolf. But it was really not that bad, because on closer examination it proved to be a fallen tree trunk. At last by accident we found a path that had been used by cows. We tried to follow this and lost it several times, but always regained it. Finally a light could be seen in the distance and we aimed for it, finding our anxiously waiting host, who gave us a fine meal as a reward for our mishap. When we returned that night our host accompanied us for some distance, and since we watched our directions very carefully we reached home safely.

Our return to Barclay Sound took a whole day, going against headwinds. We spent the night at Eckult and set out again the next morning. That day we came to the trading post of Jucklulaht [Ucluelet] on the west coast at the entrance of Barclay Sound, where the firm of Spring and Frank from Victoria had a store. The schooner anchored there for the night and then started the next day along the coast to Clayoquot Sound, where we had to stay near a small island because of heavy fog. We were directly opposite the winter village of the Klayoquaht [Clayoquot] Indians, where there was also a trading post of the firm of Warren, which was managed by a half-countryman of mine, a Dane named Fredrik Thorenbeck. This was also the end of the trip of the schooner, and I had to find some canoes and Indians to continue my journey. Because of the fog we could not go ashore, but we had a visit from a number of Indians, among whom was the son of Setta Canim, the most powerful chief and most renowned warrior of the west coast of Vancouver Island. I was told that Setta Canim had killed a number of people, including a white trader. He was the greatest gallows bait on the island. This of course raised his status and his reputation so that everyone who came to Clayoquot was anxious to establish contact with him. I fell for this also, so I engaged young Setta Canim and three other Indians to take me to Kayokaht [Kyuquot] in a large canoe and also to bring me back. Meanwhile I brought my baggage from the ship to the home of Mr. Thorenbeck, where I was to stay. The next day I waited in vain for the arrival of the Indians I had engaged, but they delayed until after the departure of the steamer in order to have full control of their own movements. After the ship left I took a canoe and paddled over to the Indians, whereupon they told me they intended to go on the planned trip the next day. When no one appeared on that day, I received a message stating that the trip could be carried out only if I paid twice the price that had been agreed upon. My Danish host, who understood the character of these Indians, knew that after that message it was useless to try to hold them to their agreement, since they thought that I was at their mercy. My next thought was to give up any relations with the people I had first engaged and not go to their village, but to engage a crew from a neighboring town. Mr. Thorenbeck was very kind and offered the use of his canoe, taking his wife and daughter and sister-in-law for the trip to the Indian village of Tschilso-maht, four miles to the north. But the Indians were as smart as we were. The Clayoquot had already sent a canoe to Tschilso-maht with an order not to offer a canoe or services. So the pleasure ride bore no results. Naturally we were not satisfied with this situation and continued our trip to the next village [Ahousat]. This time we did not set out alone; an Indian canoe pushed off from Tschilsomaht with grinning men abroad who swiftly paddled to Ahousat and spoiled our plans there.

At Ahousat I met the steamer again, and the captain, together with the trader, Mr. Niels, a Dane, increased our white contingent against the redskins. The influence of these men looked promising for a short time, but when the steamer left

Mr. Niels sailed to Victoria and Mr. Thorenbeck and his family returned home, leaving me to cope with the Indians. None of them recalled any arrangements that had been made, and only after long discussion was I allowed to engage two men to take me to Hesquiaht [Hesquiat], an Indian village where there was a Catholic mission whose influence could help me with the Indians. Before leaving Ahousat I made a few purchases, not old or valuable, since the village had just recently been rebuilt. In 1864 the treacherous inhabitants had lured a fishing schooner into their bay to attack and murder the crew, whereupon a British warship was sent out the same year to burn the village down.

We departed for Hesquiat the next morning. At noon we stopped for a meal where there were two Indian houses. Here I exchanged my canoe for a larger one because my purchases for the museum needed more space. The waves were high as usual, but favorable winds brought us to Hesquiat in the evening, where I was greeted in the most friendly manner by the Belgian priest, Father Brabant, who invited me to stay with him. There was a trading post of Spring and Frank in the village, with a man from Hamburg as the agent.

The trip to Hesquiat was very important for my purposes because I found many rare pieces to buy, among them two sword-shaped bone clubs similar to the one I had purchased in Alberni Canal. I also acquired numerous pieces of hunting and fishing gear, as well as household utensils.

Father Brabant lived here in what appeared to be comfortable circumstances. The country around the village is fertile, so that twenty cows can be put to pasture. The animals come under shelter only when there are young calves because of the roving wolves. These predators even break into the houses at night and kill chickens. This village also was active in attacks on the whites. It is related that twelve to fourteen years ago the Indians plundered the ship *Havarie*, which had been driven ashore. The captain's wife was mercilessly attacked, and in their fear of punishment for this they killed everyone. Some of the headless bodies were later found in the brush near the beach. I obtained this story from the Clayoquot, who also pointed out two individuals of the Hesquiat who are supposed to have been leaders in this episode. Father Brabant tells a milder version of the event, in that he believes many on the ship were killed in the wreck, not by the Indians. The whole affair is still not cleared up and probably never will be. As a result of the incident a gunboat was sent to Hesquiat, and five Indians were arrested and taken to Victoria, where, when threatened with death, they gave as the leader of the attack a slave living at Hesquiat; after he was arrested he in turn named the chief of the village. Both were executed. The Hesquiat now assert that the real leaders are still alive and that the chief and his slave, though innocent, allowed themselves to be executed to save the village from destruction.

I believe Father Brabant, with his mild character and love of mankind, was trying to absolve the village from this crime; otherwise he would be the first to condemn their disgraceful uncontrolled urge to commit murder. Three years ago the current chief attacked him and shot him in the shoulder and arm. This act was not directed against the priest personally, but the chief had a disagreement with his fellow townsmen and thought that if the priest died a gunboat would come and destroy the whole village. But the priest did not die, for he was well cared for by the people of the village, and when a gunboat appeared he was taken to Victoria for recovery, which was so complete that he returned with only some stiffness in two fingers. The chief who had attacked him fled from the village and hid in the woods, where he probably starved; his body was found later. The Father returned to the village and renewed his efforts at conversion. The village escaped punishment.

The heart-warming friendliness of Father Brabant and his great influence also helped my plans. All the influence of the traders and the requests and promises were disregarded, but the good Father was successful in hiring a crew for me to go to Kyuquot, for which, however, I did have to promise a rather higher price. But here I must defend their demands, since we were not traveling at the time the Indians were accustomed to and through the speed I required I made myself and everyone very uncomfortable because of my burning desire as a collector.

On the forenoon of 30 November we departed with a north wind and a high sea. We had no sooner turned north at Cape Estevan than a terrific wind hit us. We had to end the first day of our voyage right there and land where there were a few deserted houses that were used in summer by seal hunters. In order to add to our commissary I went hunting and shot some sea fowl. In the evening I made a bed of thin boughs and fell asleep at eight o'clock.

The month of December began with cold weather and a high sea. The Indians began to protest, saying that it was too cold to travel and the wind was against us. It required an hour of argument until they agreed at least to make an attempt. So we remained courageous during the trip and arrived toward evening at the headland of Nootka Island called Bajo. There lived several families from Nootka Sound, which we passed during the day. I visited the houses and made a few purchases. We passed the night with these people. The next day we continued in a northwesterly direction, and at noon we passed Esperanza Inlet without stopping but continued with a good wind and arrived at evening at Cape Raget; as darkness fell we reached the object of our journey, the Indian village of Kyuquot.

It is the custom of all coastal residents to greet an incoming boat with loud cheers and to run to the beach. We were greeted in this way. I found quarters with the local representative of Spring and Frank, a Mr. Brawn, who was married to a white woman.

Kyuquot Sound was, like Barclay Sound, Clayoquot Sound, and Nootka Sound, a fjord area with long narrow waterways with beautiful shores rich with fish and wildlife as well as settlements for an isolated population. Such groups acted communally in all important activities such as war and peace, hunting and fishing, feasts and ceremonies, as well as production and storage of food. The inhabitants of Kyuquot Sound were not on the coast during the winter but lived farther inland along these sheltered inlets.

The next morning I hired a canoe and visited the Indian villages of Chawispa and Markaht, where I made some purchases. In the first village a large feast was in progress with a dance in a circle around a large fire in which thirty men and women took part. Their faces were painted black and they had feathers stuck in their hair. My appearance caused great confusion to the feast, since when the word spread that I was a collector the people ran home to get their goods made for sale. The greed for money was so great that the feast was abandoned during my presence. In the second village the same scene was repeated. Here, in the chief's house, the action was principally in the dancing of children, who also had their faces painted black and feathers stuck in their hair. It was very droll to see children from three to eight years old wearing these decorations dance in vigorous movements while the older ones beat a wooden drum. It appeared that this was a children's festival. We spent the night at Markaht and in the morning went on to Deep Inlet [Amai Inlet], visiting the villages of Queka and Oales, and returned to Kyuquot that evening. On a small island here are a church and school under the care of Father Nicolai, as well as the trading post of Spring and Frank I have mentioned. The next day was spent in making a short but profitable trip to the mainland, where there were four settlements. Even though there were only four dwellings at each place, it took until nine o'clock that evening before we returned.

It was now time to consider my return to Victoria. I had visited all the settlements and bought everything that served my purpose. My collection had become so large that I had to spend a day listing and packing it. Then with Father Nicolai's help I made a proposition to four Indians that they take me and my baggage to Victoria.

The return journey started early the next morning with a high sea and a strong wind. The crew became afraid of the high waves, and when we were close to Esperanza Inlet we encountered a severe hailstorm. They entreated me to find a harbor. Since they were right in their request we headed toward the rocky shore, where we found the mouth of a small creek that would serve for a canoe harbor. While we were waiting for the end of the hailstorm I harpooned three salmon.

I urged my crew to start out again, since the wind had lessened though the waves were still high. The crew wanted to return home, but I argued that this would be more difficult than to go ahead, since we were in Esperanza Inlet. After almost superhuman effort we arrived that evening at Nutschatlitz [Nuchatlitz] at the south entrance of Esperanza Inlet. Here we found a trading post of Spring and Frank with Mr. Schmidt, a Canadian, in charge. During the night, when I heard the pouring rain, I prepared my arguments to persuade my Indian crew to continue the journey. When the discussion started in the morning the people at Nuchatlitz took the part of the Indians. It was impossible to argue with the fact that the Indians were only one day's trip from home and I was eight days of good weather away from Victoria.

In order to protect my collection from the weather I took it out of the canoe and locked it in Mr. Schmidt's house. The Indians were now pressing me for pay for the trip to this point, to which I replied that they had not carried out their contract. But what is a contract to them? It is only made to break. I reminded them that I had paid in advance for the rental of the canoe all the way to Victoria. So passed a day and again a stormy night, during which they fled with the canoe. I heard later that they arrived home safely.

So here I sat in the middle of the winter, abandoned by everyone at the stormiest spot of the "Pacific" Ocean [in German, *Stillen Oceans*]. The unrelenting storm prevented me from continuing my journey, but I found that I could use the time well by buying everything I could find at Nuchatlitz.

I must admit that nowhere on the west coast did I meet such importunate and insolent inhabitants as at this place. A natural and understandable excitement is aroused when a white trader comes into an Indian village, but the good people of this village carried this to the point of trying to break their way into Mr. Schmidt's house, where I was staying. The whole next day I spent trying to get a crew and found the shamelessness of these people beyond all bounds. They became a little more reasonable when I told them that if I did not hurry I would not be able to get a steamer that was due at Hesquiat.

Even on Vancouver Island the rain is followed by sunshine, and after five days of downpour the weather improved. I found four crew members for a trip to Hesquiat, since I could not get anyone to take me the whole way to Victoria. We started the trip in the morning and did not go along the outer coast but followed the inside passages through the fjords from Esperanza Inlet and Nootka Sound around Nootka Island. The first village we saw was Ehattesaht [Ehatisaht] on Esperanza Arm. I was anxious to go ashore here, but I was afraid my Indians would try to break their contract again. In the evening we came to Moaht [Moachat] at the upper end of Nootka Sound. I was very tired because I had paddled strenuously all day to spare one of the crewman.

Our arrival caused the usual excitement, with the inhabitants rushing to the beach when someone called "Mammertla!" meaning a white man. I came ashore and went to the house of the chief to eat my supper, which I cooked myself, while an active trade was carried on. The goods were not very important since there were no objects of stone or bone, which led me to believe that a collector must have preceded me there.

As long as we were in Nootka Sound my relationship with my crew was good, but in the morning, when we had just left Moachat and passed Friendly Cove and were approaching Cape Estevan, the most dangerous place on the whole coast, another storm broke, this time with snow, so that sailing was impossible and we could not even see the prow of the canoe. Again we had to fight for our lives with all our strength. The storm was trying to push us into the open sea and we could not return to Friendly Cove. Since we also could not reach the dangerous cape, we had no choice but to drift, hoping to see a landing place; but when we came anywhere within half an English mile from shore we were surrounded by breakers that confused the Indians so that they accused me of having gotten them into this situation. And they were right, since they had not the slightest interest in the Berlin Museum, which was the cause of this dangerous trip.

As long as a person can still make accusations he is not without hope, and when the Indians saw that I was paddling with all my strength they followed my example and worked hard too. Our entire effort was bent on not drifting out to sea. Toward evening, when it was almost dark, we saw a little break in the shoreline where the waves were not so rough and there were no rocks visible. With great effort we reached this spot and landed by waiting for a high wave to carry the canoe onto the shore. Before the wave receded all of us jumped out and pulled the canoe beyond the tide. We succeeded in doing this and found on the shore a deserted house that was used in summer by Muschlaht [Muchalat] Nootka who tended potato fields close by.

We took possession and, after minor repairs, started a fire. Only water was lacking, so the Indians, who were barefoot, went out in the snow to find some, but without success. I went out in another direction and found a spring. We had no cooking pot, so we filled a wooden bucket with water and threw hot stones into it to boil some rice. After the trouble and effort of the day it tasted good. After we dried out our things we slept very well all night.

The next morning the weather had improved, so I decided to make an attempt that day to reach the destination I had set out for fourteen days before, when I had left Hesquiat with a crew I hired to take me to Kyuquot. This place near Cape Estevan was in a better position to get into the open sea. We carried all the goods back to the canoe and with great effort got through the breakers into the open sea, which was still stormy; but since we had only two English miles to reach a designated emergency harbor we landed well before evening. We were very glad to find another "shipwrecked" party there, consisting of two men, two women, and two children who had been there for three days waiting out the storm. These people had been in Moachat several days before us and were on the way to their home at Hesquiat.

This was also our destination, and so we made our fellow travelers and ourselves as comfortable as possible in the deserted house and prepared ourselves for several days of waiting. The next day all the men went hunting, and we shot ducks and gulls in order to supplement the larder, while the women prepared the meals. This continued for two more days, when we were only five English miles from Hesquiat. The Indians were having a more pleasant time than I, for they could converse in their mother tongue, while I was committed to silence and could communicate only by signs and gestures. My isolation touched one of the Indians who, like so many of his tribesmen, probably had worked along the coast of British Columbia and picked up a little English; he approached me in a ceremonial manner when I was sitting on a log staring at the sea and said in funereal tones in pure pidgin English, "What is the matter with you?" His pronunciation of these words was so unintelligible that I was afraid because of his solemn behavior that he was calling down some curse on me. It was later explained to me by Father Brabant that this is one of the most common questions asked in the camps as a greeting. The storm lasted four days, and on the fifth we ventured out into the sea and paddled strenuously the five English miles to Hesquiat, where I stayed for the next week with Father Brabant.

I tried for six days to find a crew, but everyone was afraid of the storms and therefore asked exorbitant prices. I thought that by going up the fjords where ten to twelve families lived I might have better luck. I took just one Indian with me and came back with no crew, but with two silver salmon I bought.

Good luck eventually strikes everyone, and now it was my turn. As we returned to Hesquiat, paddling with all our strength, I could not believe my eyes when I saw a vessel in the distance. I shouted for joy to see the steamer from Victoria. But as though fate was determined to play me false, just as I recognized the ship a storm blew up that tore our sail and half filled the canoe with water. My Indian companion, who had not shared in my jubilation, was more concerned about the storm and appealed to his gods for help. Everytime a high wave rolled toward the boat and threatened to engulf him in his seat in the stern he shook his head and spit into the water and in a loud tone uttered "Brr!" Since I did not have much faith in this procedure, I quickly bailed out the water and tried to repair the torn sail. For a short time things went well and I thought the danger was over when a sudden wind caught the sail again and tore it to shreds. The wind brought a driving rain, and even though we both sat high we were in danger of drowning. We tried to steer away from the wind but lost control of the canoe. I must confess that this experience did not increase my respect for the local gods as we drifted like a piece of wreckage in a canoe half full of water until about three miles below Hesquiat we were tossed ashore by a thunderous wave, fortunately on a sandy beach, and lay there filled with salt water. It was my first necessity to find my rifle and the two silver salmon. I moved the rescued objects, and as I squeezed them against my breast to dry them, the Indian gave me a sad look when he remembered that he was not a heathen but belonged to Father Brabant's congregation and had foresworn all his previous gods. We walked toward Hesquiat, where everyone was surprised to see us, for they were certain we had drowned when they no longer saw our sail. My companion had the good grace to make a speech to his people in which he called my behavior "Indian courage" of the highest order. More important to me was a conversation with Father Brabant concerning the chances whether the schooner that had sailed past Hesquiat would return. The next morning I went with three men to the beached canoe and bailed it out, and we put forth all our strength to bring it through the breakers and follow the schooner. The ship *Favorite*, belonging to the firm of Spring

and Frank, with Captain Frank at the wheel, was the one I had
waited for in Victoria six weeks before to make the trip to Vancouver Island. Captain Frank lives during the winter in Ucluelet in Barclay Sound, where he has a house and a half-Indian
wife. It was two days after I left Victoria that the ship arrived
and made an agreement with the company to open a station on
Nootka Island and from there to forward goods brought from
Victoria to the other stations at Esperanza Inlet and Kyuquot.
If I had known this I would have saved myself much trouble
and money. I did not hesitate for a minute to make reservations
for myself on the schooner even if I did repeat the northern
part of the trip. So I arrived at Victoria, the capital, happy to
see this city again.

6

Even though the wind was still blowing hard I sent the three
Indians back to Hesquiat in their canoe and with my woolen
blanket went aboard the schooner *Favorite*. The very stormy
weather also affected the schooner, for they lost an anchor on
a twenty-fathom chain in Hesquiat Inlet. The next day, since
the weather was good as we approached Father Brabant's residence close to the trading post, we had the good fortune to
find the anchor and chain. Since the superintendent of Hesquiat—the man from Hamburg named Charlie, whom I have
already mentioned—had been appointed to the new business
on Nootka Island, he and his movable possessions were put on
board and his replacement was brought ashore. I also had to
load my baggage, which had been stored at Father Brabant's.
Before this was done I made a last effort to engage a few men
to go with me, but they set such high prices on their services
that I could not afford it. The reason for this was that in the
winter they do not travel because of the weather, and they had
to prepare themselves ceremonially for the fur seal hunting in
the spring.

It is perhaps appropriate at this time to include a few remarks about the fur seal hunt on the west coast of Vancouver
Island. This hunting of fur seals and sea otters has long been
an activity of the west coast people and it has built up cultural
similarities. Dependent almost exclusively on the sea and its
vagaries, the inhabitants of the west coast, and those even
farther north on the mainland, have developed a detailed procedure that resembles a sacred ritual. This was already recognized by Captain Cook in the past century, and the great
trader Meares used it as a trading device. Today the hunt for
fur-bearing sea mammals by the Indians of the west coast is
carried on commercially in a manner similar to that in many
other parts of the world: the natives are allowed to hunt and
fish in their traditional ways, but a number of traders in their

larger craft supervise the operation and buy the catch on the spot. Both the firms already mentioned—Spring and Frank, and Warren of Victoria—are such entrepreneurs, with stores in nearly every village where the natives can obtain modern goods, food, blankets, tools for their economy, and even actual money in return for their fish and furs. With their schooners, which have steam engines, these firms are in continuous contact with the inhabitants of the west coast and substantially support them through their sea hunting.

The season begins in February and lasts until midsummer. During this time almost the entire population moves from the winter villages deep in the inlets to summer quarters on small islands on the coast. The construction of the summer villages is much simpler than that of their winter houses because there are no feasts or ceremonials to disturb their single objective.

For months before the beginning of the season the fur seal hunters prepare themselves physically. Every morning they rub their bodies with sand and stones while uttering certain prayers for a successful hunt. At the same time, and especially at the beginning of the hunt, the medicine men play an important role. How important this can be is illustrated by the fact that the people at Hesquiat, who were outstanding whalers, gave this up just because they believed that the "medicine" they had inherited from their forefathers had lost its strength and was exhausted. The people were not in a position to get a new medicine because this is in possession of the Thunderbird (Hotloxom) and the Thunder (Tootosch) and nobody has at present been able to secure it from this source.

The fur seal hunting is now carried on in this manner: during February and March the steamers sail from Victoria and Cape Flattery to the several Indian villages, where each takes on from thirty to fifty Indians with fifteen to twenty-five canoes. The crew of the schooner consists only of three or four men to take these men and canoes aboard. In good weather they go out into the open sea, often even as far as two hundred English miles. The fur seals, which travel in great herds, have the habit of sleeping as they swim in still water, which should be an unusual sight, as they lie on their backs and cover their faces and eyes with their foreflippers. When the watch in the crow's nest gives the sign that a herd is in sight, the steamer approaches quietly. Just as quietly the canoes are let down into the sea, each manned by two or three Indians. The weapon is a fork-shaped pole ten to twelve feet long, with harpoons on each arm made of bone and iron or a shaped mussel shell. On each harpoon there is a long cord of twisted cedar bark that is tied to the canoe. The Indians paddle softly on approaching the herd, and when the canoes are about twenty feet away the men in the front seats rise and throw the carefully aimed harpoons into the abdomens of the animals, where the barbs on the harpoons fasten them. This releases the pole. The struck animals flee in fright, dragging the canoes with them. As the seals swim with all their strength, the paddlers move their canoes close enough to the ever-weakening animals so that they can be hit on the head with a heavy club. Often an enraged animal will raise himself at the canoe and bite a piece out of the wood with his sharp teeth. When the seals are dead they are pulled into the canoe. Later on board the schooner they are skinned and the pelts are salted for transportation to England. The Indians sometimes eat the meat. They receive five to twelve dollars each for the pelts. Because the canoes approach a sleeping herd from all sides they become scattered over a large area of sea and the schooners often have to act quickly to find them before a fog or storm endangers them.

On the west coast of Vancouver Island during the months of November, December, and January the sea otter is hunted without the support of the schooners. At this time of the year the animals come to the rocky coast and small islands looking for food, and the Indians kill them with harpoons. The sea otter pelts are very expensive and bring the Indian from thirty to one hundred dollars apiece. In contrast to earlier times, not many are now taken at Vancouver Island.

On Sunday 25 December we were on the schooner in the inner harbor of Hesquiat near the mouth of the river. The celebration of Christmas in my present situation was not pleasant, since I had originally planned to be back in Victoria with my fellow-countrymen. Instead, it was a long and tedious journey with long periods of waiting. After the holiday was over Captain Frank brought ashore the goods for Hesquiat and my baggage in order to receive a large quantity of fish oil processed by the natives. The Indian who first brought me to Kyuquot came aboard with his wife and father to visit relatives in Muchalat.

The next morning we started in a strong southeast wind and sailed rapidly northward on the west coast. We soon came to Friendly Cove, where the new store was to be started. As we approached the moorage the wind stopped and Captain Frank ordered a canoe with four Indians to tow us in. Scarcely had they started than a sudden squall came up and with its first impact tossed one of the men out of the canoe and drove the schooner on top of it. The schooner was quickly released and the man was saved. We arrived at Friendly Cove at noon. A canoe was immediately sent to the two chiefs at Moachat with whom I had spent a night on my recent visit, and at once an argument started about the purchase price the firm should pay for the land they needed for their establishment. The deal was closed; the chief was well pleased that Moachat was to have a store, and he pocketed what I believe was sixty dollars. It is interesting that this is the place where the first white man, Captain Cook, moored one hundred years ago, and not until now has it been settled. As a matter of fact, after the discovery of Vancouver Island the Spaniards built a fort and a trading post in this vicinity, but after a few years these were abandoned and the people left. A few Spanish words have been retained in the speech of the Indians at this place, and the place the Spaniards occupied still shows signs of their agriculture in the growth of wild carrots and kohlrabi. Shortly before we arrived an Indian died here who could count to ten in Spanish. Also, many of the people, including the two chiefs, have Spanish features. The place where we were is the summer village of the Moachat. These people now want to participate in fur seal hunting like other Nootka.

Since it took some time to organize the new establishment, I had the opportunity of taking a few trips into the deep inlets of Nootka Sound. I attached myself to the Indian and his wife and father who were leaving the ship to go twenty English miles to the village of Muchalat. The wind was blowing when we started, and we made a flying trip until a giant wave broke into the canoe and we sat up to the chest in ice-cold water. The old man, who sat in the stern, lost his courage and began to weep bitterly. I bailed the water out with my hat as quickly as possible and called to the old Indian to keep the boat before the wind, because in this way the waves coming from behind could do us little damage. But the poor old man had lost all control and steered so that the wind and the waves caught us on the side. The canoe now turned sideways and began to sink. Up to this point I had held onto the sail line, but I now had to let go. Thereupon the young Indian, with great strength of arm, picked up the mast and sail and heaved them overboard. This righted the canoe so I could bail out the water. Throughout all this the Indian wife sat patiently without a sound, though the water came up to her neck. We soon came into a narrow passage where there was no danger. It rained all day, and out of sympathy I gave the poor woman my raincoat, which I afterwards sorely regretted, for the trip seemed endless and the rain came down as though it was a second Deluge. Yet I really cannot say that the rain was difficult for me, for I was already wringing wet.

At last in the evening, long after darkness, we reached Muchalat, where our wet little company came to the Indian relatives' house. According to the custom of the country, we stripped and dried our clothing by the fire. Naturally I had no choice but to do likewise, and since my blanket was soaking wet I had nothing with which to cover myself; so the woman on the trip, in return for my raincoat, lent me a blanket. Little as this was, it was something, and hindered the young ones at Muchalat, who were fingering and pinching my white skin with exceeding thoroughness.

The next morning I made my usual turn round the village looking for ethnographic objects to purchase for the Berlin Museum; but here as at Moachat there was very little, for this village, like its neighbors Clayoquot and Moachat, has been conquered and plundered repeatedly, even though the inhabitants of Muchalat were held in a kind of captivity since they were not allowed to leave the inlet where they lived and had to buy trade articles from the Moachat at higher prices. Those who tried to escape were captured and sold at Cape Flattery as slaves.

During the first night I spent at Muchalat the whole village was in an uproar because of a situation that developed in the house where I was staying. A medicine woman had been called to attend a sick child. This old witch gave the poor little patient gruesome treatment. All evening she chanted hideous medicine songs while she blew like a wildcat at the child and drew blood from near his heart cavity on the premise that the blood would take away the sickness. Since her cure did not seem to have any effect and the little one lay there almost lifeless, the father paid her the proper fee but did not allow her to continue her work. At this she flew into a rage, and, stating that her colleague who would continue the cure had been sent to Moachat, she made loud complaint, screaming from her sleeping place and being answered by the patient's father. This brought the rest of the occupants into the quarrel, which lasted until two o'clock in the morning, when one of the Indians, to bring this to an end, sprang up and beat her thoroughly. Now her husband came into action, insisting that he should be allowed to beat the wife of the man who had just beaten his wife. Both women screamed, which brought more people from their sleeping places, and with shouting and blows the household fought around the fireplace. It took on such proportions that I became afraid and took my revolver and dagger in hand. As the bedlam reached its height a young Indian jumped up and poured a basin of water over the fire, throwing the house into total darkness. This ended the fighting and everyone went to bed.

The next morning the famous shaman came from Moachat. He took hold of the child and kneaded and pinched him for about an hour and sucked blood from his body while making horrible grimaces. Meanwhile the mother, who obviously had great faith in the shaman's art, held the child on her lap and wailed in a dull voice, often repeating the words *Kjukwah* and *Claddai*. It was interpreted to me as an appeal to the evil spirit of the illness to leave the child. All this time, in order to make the performance more hellish, a large drum with a head of bearskin was beaten. When the shaman finished his ministrations the father of the child gave him three blankets. Then the mother took the little one and repeated the cure.

It is perhaps useful at this point to make a few remarks about the medicine men or shamans on Vancouver Island and the Northwest Coast in general. These people believe they have supernatural powers, and the Indians agree with this and have faith in their ability to cure illness. There are two kinds of medicine men, as Sproat reports: those in the second category include medicine women, as was related above, who cure only minor ailments, and the men of the first class help with serious sickness that demands more power. These men often undertake to restore a soul that has left the body, to exchange souls, interpret dreams, prophesy, and drive out evil spirits from the body. Shamans are seldom of high rank, but they have considerable power and often great influence, which becomes greater as they gain wealth through their profession. I did not observe on Vancouver Island that shamans had their own language as those among many native peoples do, in which they can carry on a conversation among themselves not understood by others. Training to be a medicine man is necessary because each cure depends on some details of movements and manipulation as well as on chants. Every doctor develops his own methods within a tradition, but sometimes to be more impressive he creates new ones. The more extravagantly a shaman can sing, moan, and gesticulate, and the greater his sleight of hand tricks, which as we shall presently see are very crude, the blinder is the faith in his powers. But there are shamans who by fasting and mortification will bring themselves into a supersensitive state with the greatest faith in their methods. The medicine men are considered not only doctors for physical ailments but also "soul" doctors. The cares and uncertainties an Indian has when he faces a decision that depends on luck or chance he carries to his shaman, asking him to say the right prayers for him. This is the way it is at the beginning of the fishing season, for the whale hunt and the fur seal hunting, and also before a war or other large undertaking. The belief in one deity that can bring good luck and the fear of the influence of evil powers are both reasons why in addition to his shaman the Indian also has many superstitions. I have often heard them in the forest praying aloud to a good or an evil spirit.

The next morning I left Muchalat after this weirdest New Year's Eve of my life and spent the first day of 1882 getting back to the *Favorite* with my friend Captain Frank.

The first days of the new year were spent organizing the new trading post, while I listed and packed my collection. By 6 January we were ready to leave Nootka Sound and continue northward to our next port of call, Esperanza Inlet, where I had been a month before. We landed at the firm's post at Nuchatlitz, and I rented a canoe and two Indians, who happened to be the same who went with me in December from here to Hesquiat, and we went deep into Esperanza Inlet to Ehatisaht.

When we arrived, in darkness, we found the people from Moachat visiting to take part in a big feast and dancing, which I had the privilege of attending. The dances of the west coast are different from those of the north and east coasts; also, the dances differ in winter and summer. On my first visit to the north coast of Vancouver Island and the mainland only two to four dancers were on the floor together. The west coast Indians are also supposed to have a greater variety of dances than the north coast people—it is said they have fifty-three different dances. In Ehatisaht there was a dance leader who arranged the performance. There were round dances as well as set spectacles.

Fig. 24. Woman's dance mask. West coast of Vancouver Island.

The leader and master of ceremonies assigned each dancer to his place, and for an individual dance he would give the performer his beat with his rattle. All the dancers were in full regalia, with the men's faces painted black and red, the women's in red alone. There were very few masks used on the evening I attended, but among the last dances a worthwhile drama was shown, with the great eagle or firebird (Hotloxom) and the thunder (Tootosch) represented. The head, the tail and both wings of these birds consisted of wood while the body in which the dancer was hidden was covered with cloth, and in the half-darkness the whole presented an eerie appearance. Such presentations always suggest their supernatural beliefs. Another noteworthy dance performed at the same time showed how little preparation was really necessary to create illusions for these audiences. Three naked Indians represented wolves, and for this the first held a well-carved wolf's head in his hand while the other two covered themselves with a canoe sail and stood bent over. This represented the body of the wolf. The third man, half-naked, was at the end of the sail and held in his hand an iron handsaw, a so-called fox tail, which he held

behind him and moved like a tail. This three-part figure moved
in unison, looking like a six-legged being. This giant wolf
opened and shut his mouth and ran toward the audience, which
fled from him in terror all through the house.

After this scene another dance began which reminded me of
the terror of the cannibal Hāma'tsa on the north coast of Vancouver Island. A naked Indian representing a slave or a pris-
oner of war was led around the fire, his captor carrying a large
dagger with which he made motions as though he wanted to
cut open his victim's abdomen. The slave was very frightened
and tried to escape, but he was caught, and in pantomine his
captor carried out his threat and supposedly slit him open and
then caught his blood and drank it. During this pantomine all
present screamed and danced. After the dances I bought some
of the masks and accessories, unfortunately at considerable expense, since these pieces were considered very valuable. To my
great sorrow I could not acquire the costume of the firebird.

The people of the west coast have more feasts than those on
the north and east coasts. There are celebrations during the
year on such occasions as the building of a new house, but the
real ceremonial period is from November to January. Ordinary
feasts are called Klooh-quahn-nah. According to Mr. George
Hunt in Fort Rupert, this means "sudden wealth." As the invited guests enter the house their names are loudly announced,
and each is assigned a seat. When he enters each guest is given
a bundle of shredded cedar bark with which to clean his feet.
The chiefs and the most distinguished guests arrive last. After
the guests have been placed all around the fire, the meal is
cooked in a large wooden box filled with water that has been
heated with hot stones. When the water boils, the food, principally meat, is put into the box and cooks very quickly. This
is the method I have already described for the Kwakiutl Indians. Before the meal begins a small cedar-bark mat is laid
before every guest. The host walks around during the meal to
see that every guest is well served, while the hostess and her
helpers pass the food around. During eating there is little conversation, for that is not considered in good taste. Each guest
receives his portion on the mat. The meal usually consists of
dried fish and oil served in finely carved bowls. Freshly cooked
fish is eaten with a wooden spoon, and the other food is held
with the fingers. The teeth of these Indians are worn down
almost to the gums because of the large amount of sand in the
dried fish that is their principal food. A favorite food for feasts
is whale blubber. The portion of food for each guest is so large
that only half can be eaten, so they take the remainder home.
After the meal every guest is given a strand of shredded cedar
bark to wipe his mouth and hands. The meal is followed by

speeches and conferences. Women are seldom invited to these gatherings, but they have their own feasts, to which friendly neighbors are invited. There are also feasts for those not so highly placed, and it seems that this is the kind I saw on the mainland on an earlier visit.

The next morning I returned to Nuchatlitz from Ehatisaht. It was impossible to begin our journey to Kyuquot because of poor weather. On the same day a big feast and dance took place in Nuchatlitz, in which we participated. The honored guests were the Indians from Clayoquot, who arrived with the Moachat whom I had met the previous evening in Ehatisaht and who were especially invited. The captain was also invited to the feast, which seemed to proceed like the others I had attended. On the left side of the entrance the entire length of the house was occupied by festively dressed Clayoquot, while opposite them were equally well dressed Moachat and the people of Nuchatlitz, who did not take part in the dancing. This audience consisted of about eighty to one hundred persons, including women and children. Since the feast began in the afternoon there was no fire in the middle of the house, but the whole inner space was clean. While the gathering in the house was being seated, the dancers were being organized by the leader of the ceremonial in an open space by the door. The dancers included both men and women; almost all the men were painted black, with long feathers in their hair but without masks, while the women had their faces painted red, wore black blankets over their shoulders, had their hair hanging loose down their backs, and were also without masks.

Across the back of the inner space in the house the singers and dancers were assembled and started their music in a lively tempo. The dance leader allowed four to six persons to enter the house at a time. They moved in dancing and turning figures, gesturing with their hands, until they formed a closed circle, and in this pattern they performed a short dance. When one circle finished the dancers stepped aside for a new group until all the dancers had gathered in the house. Then speeches were made and gifts of blankets, guns, canoes, and sails were distributed and more dancing took place. Then I saw a most surprising and unexpected action when at a signal all the dancers threw themselves on the floor in a great mass from which arms and legs protruded, sometimes to be quickly pulled in again. I noticed by chance that the chief's daughter allowed herself the luxury of spreading a small blanket on the ground where she would fall. When the order came they rose again just as quickly and continued dancing. I noticed that on such occasions as this as well as in everyday life the Indians have the habit of chewing spruce gum. This seems to be a universal practice in North America, for I found it also among the Eskimo of Labrador. The Indians trade the gum and often pay high prices for it.

We could not stay until the end of the feast, which lasted until midnight, because it was necessary to prepare for our departure. Toward evening we went aboard, and we left at about five o'clock in the morning. A good wind took us to Kyuquot, where we arrived in the afternoon. The people there were surprised to see me, for they had imagined that I was either in Victoria or at the bottom of the sea. Captain Frank began at once to unload while a storm was gathering from the southwest.

The next day we had an example of how dangerous this area can be for a white man. The missionary, Father Nicolai, who had visited the neighboring village of Tschuklesaht [Chickliset] came back and related that the local Indians, who were regarded as the most aggressive on the west coast, had threatened him with axes and knives. When the howling, enraged mass moved toward him he stepped forward and told them in a quiet voice in their own language that they could kill him, but if they did a gunboat would soon appear whose captain would most certainly hang at least half the population of Chickliset. This helped; for the Indians knew that whenever such a crime was committed, like this proposed murder of Father Nicolai, the guilty had been punished together with the innocent. So they desisted but told him that he must leave at once and not try to convert them, since they were well satisfied with their own religion.

The Indians of this region not only are opposed to strangers but are unusually brutal among themselves, as stories of wars between the villages relate. I will repeat a story that was told me from several sources, in which the warrior chief Setta Canim played a major part.[16]

For a long time this overbearing and cruel man had been wishing to increase the reputation of his own home village by going on the warpath, so he invited the villages between his Clayoquot and the Kyuquot to a joint venture. For months the sly, villainous chief took every occasion to make speeches against the Kyuquot. However, his own tribe thought the Kyuquot were very numerous as well as brave and that they would be hard to conquer. They finally concluded that they must undertake this war, but only if they could get the support of the Muchalat and Moachat who lived between them. So they sent a canoe with their best orator to these villages to win their consent. This was obtained with amazing speed, and the three united villages decided to annihilate the Kyuquot together.

After this agreement there was great excitement at Clayo-

Fig. 25. Two Indians from the west coast of Vancouver Island. The man on the right is Setta Canim, chief of the Clayoquot.

quot as everyone prepared to fight. War canoes were put into condition and war paddles finished off with sharp points. When everything was in perfect condition the assignments were made to each canoe and the leaders selected. One morning twenty-two large canoes were ready, each with ten to fifteen Clayoquot warriors on board. In usual Indian fashion their faces were painted black, and they left their homes singing loudly while the women cheered them from the beach. They all sang for the success of their expedition and the conquest of the enemy.

With great jubilation the expedition started northward under the leadership of Setta Canim, and by evening they arrived at Hesquiat, where they disembarked. Setta Canim took this opportunity to impress the Hesquiat with his might and win their support. During the night the Clayoquot slept in their canoes, and the next day they continued to Friendly Cove, where the Moachat were awaiting them.

It was said that the campaign proceeded with the loud singing of war songs accompanied by the deep tone of the war drum, as they cruised close to shore while Setta Canim himself, seated high in his canoe, wearing only a red blanket and with his hair in military fashion in a large knot on the top of his head, made a fiery speech. In his right hand, with which he gestured, he held an ancient dagger. He understood like nobody else how to convince his audience that this war was necessary.

After a half hour of speaking they approached the shore, where the Moachat answered with a short speech and a greeting to the chief and warriors. They all went ashore and took part in a large feast prepared by the Moachat and carried out with formality. After the feast there were more speeches and conferences. Every chief gave his thoughts of how the enemy should be attacked, and finally they all assembled around a flat sandy place where in rough lines a sketch was made of the main Kyuquot village. The fabricator of this received his information from a friendly Kyuquot Indian, even to the point of showing each house by a small pile of sand. Especially exact was the location of Chief Nancis's house and that of the leader of the warriors, Moschenik, so that every warrior knew where to find the most dangerous opponents. As the conference continued, everyone present gave his opinion of how many inhabitants were in each Kyuquot house.

Then Setta Canim revealed his plan of operation: fifteen canoes of the Clayoquot should be in the center and fourteen canoes of the Muchalat and Moachat were to be the right wing, and the remainder of the Clayoquot canoes should join with the Hesquiat on the left. The whole force was to attack Kyuquot at night when all were asleep and massacre them. It was determined that the houses should be burned down, and for this purpose they would bring some resinous wood.

After these plans were agreed upon the Moachat and Muchalat made their final preparations. Still on the same day a quarrel erupted between the two chiefs of the Clayoquot as to who should attack Chief Moschenik of the Kyuquot. This would have become an open battle had not an old warrior of the tribe stepped between them. In the evening there was again a feast, at which it was announced that they would continue their journey the next morning at first light. Before sunrise the whole expedition set out in fine weather. They paddled to the tempo of the drummer and sang war songs as they followed the coastline. The Muchalat, under the direction of their strong chief Nissend, formed two lines of seven canoes each.

When they approached the enemy territory, orders were given to stay close to shore so they would not be seen. They landed and some of the warriors blackened their faces again. The next night was set for the attack, and the united warriors succeeded in landing on the island where the principal village of the Kyuquot was situated. Until midnight they stayed in their canoes and were very silent. The attack was made easier because there was no moonlight. When the signal was given the canoes went quickly toward the village and four hundred warriors jumped ashore under the leadership of their chiefs and rushed forward. The attack would have been successful had they not been seen by two fishermen who saw the canoes rapidly approaching their village. They jumped into their canoe and shouted warning, "Weenah!" meaning "strangers!" or "danger!" This warning took effect like magic and in a few seconds, even before the canoes reached the shore, the cry "Weenah!" was taken up from house to house and the Kyuquot sprang to arms. The fight began at once, since the attackers did not find the inhabitants totally unprepared, and the Kyuquot defended themselves with great bravery. Soon the rattle of gunfire was heard over the cries of the wounded and dying, while the houses started burning and lighted up the frightful scene. The Kyuquot yielded part of their village and concentrated themselves around the chief's house. The chief, well aware that his head was wanted, barricaded the house with boxes and anything else he could find. His roof started burning, but it was controlled. Setta Canim at once realized the situation and attacked the house with desperate rage, accompanied by his two gunbearers, but he was unsuccessful, for here he faced the concentrated force of his opponents. The left wing forced their way into a few houses and killed the occupants, but as a whole the attack was a failure because the victims were not surprised in their sleep and killed.

The lack of success was made clear when the Muchalat were the first to withdraw from the burning village and return to their beached canoes, showing no inclination to fight any more. This brought about the end of the fighting when other groups began to leave and the village gradually was emptied of attackers. Setta Canim tried another attack on the chief's house, but he was deserted by his own people and so he retreated.

The proud departure led to a sad return; the warriors from all the villages went home depressed and downcast, but most of all the Clayoquot. Two days later they arrived home to find their wives awaiting them out on the rocky promontories. As the warriors neared the beach in sullen silence the women realized that the expedition had failed and started to wail and sing mourning songs. They had cause for this, because their losses were eleven dead and seventeen wounded, really too large a sacrifice for the thirty-four heads of slain Kyuquot and thirteen slaves they brought home.

After the return a few victory feasts were held, and the heads of the enemy were displayed in the village until later, when the scalps were given to the victors and some warriors selected for their bravery were raised to higher rank and received more important names. But the attitudes of victory soon disappeared and the village of Clayoquot lived in fear that the powerful Kyuquot might attack them in bloody revenge. With this also came a break in their relationship with the Muchalat, whom they blamed for the disaster of their expedition. Daily rumors came that the Kyuquot were moving toward an attack on the village with an impressive number of canoes, and Setta Canim was so in fear of his life for being the originator of the attack that he did not leave his house. The fear was carried so far that the village was fortified and a good supply of food was stored ready for a siege. It was several years before the Clayoquot finally lost this apprehension.

On 12 January we began our way south, arriving at Barclay Sound in a few days, when I made my last collecting visit at Ucluelet, where I bought many things. Three days later we landed in Victoria. From there I returned to San Francisco and completed the first part of my journey.

7

A Visit to the Koskimo
and the Coast of
the Strait of Georgia

I found that I had to start my journey again from San Francisco on 20 February 1882, sooner than I had planned, reaching Victoria in three days. I was asked to visit again the Koskimo and Quatsino, the "longheaded" Indians, and become better acquainted with them. I was to inquire whether a number of these Indians could be persuaded to come to Europe for anthropological studies, the patron of this scientific inquiry, Mr. Carl Hagenbeck in Hamburg, providing the funds. This did not hinder me, because I had purchased all kinds of ethnological objects on my previous visit. The *Otter* brought me to Fort Rupert, where I was cordially greeted by my Indian friends. The place looked very different from its aspect in the autumn, for the whole tribe of the Kwakiutl Indians were gathered here for an elaborate feast with dances. At such an occasion chiefs tried to gain prestige by giving away all they possessed, and at this time also quarrels were settled and complaints heard. Conferences were held. The leader of all the festivity was a chief of the Kwakiutl who lived at Fort Rupert.

I naturally took up my residence again with my old friend and host Mr. Hunt, the manager of the Hudson's Bay Company post, and at once rented a sloop and engaged his two sons as my companions for a trip to Quatsino. On the evening of my arrival I attended a large Indian dance festival. Many ceremonies were included in it. First the common people came, later the important Indians and chiefs, and last the head chief. Along the walls were benches for the large audience, and in the middle of the house a large fire was burning that lighted everything including the people. Opposite the entrance the singers and musicians gathered under the direction of a leader, most festively dressed and with feathers in his hair, who recited the first words of a song which the chorus then picked up. After the head chief arrived, the largest drum was carried carefully, with a measured gait, four times around the fire. Then it was brought in front of the musicians and lowered almost to the floor, but on the fourth time it was set down.

At one spot in the house were hangings made of canoe sails that hid a small stage. From behind the curtains there suddenly appeared ten ceremonially dressed women, who danced around the fire and then disappeared. When this had been completed the curtain was suddenly let down again and we witnessed a wonderful drama.

A long line of masked dancers, representing animals, deities, and devils danced together. Here we saw a bear dance with a monster that constantly clapped his great jaw, then a wolf and an eagle clung together and danced the circle. It lasted only a few minutes, then the curtain was put up again and some musicians we could not see made a hellish noise with pipes and flutes. When the curtain fell again the whole dancing corps, which I think belonged to the Nemkis [Nimpkish], danced again to the music of the unseen flutists.

The second part of the festival consisted of the customary Indian dances without masks. At this point the head chief left the gathering to return to his house, where there was also a large dancing festival taking place. He had invited me to attend this festival also, so I went with him. His guests were the Nakortok Indians who lived on Seymour Inlet on the mainland a little north of Fort Rupert, and the host invited them to dance.

Before they began another unusual ceremony took place. A young girl from Comox, an Indian village at about the middle of the east coast of Vancouver Island, was persuaded by the chief to dance a solo. She did this in a peculiar way, used in many Indian dances. The dance involved no turning of the body but was based on a swaying hop, changing from the point of one foot to the other. With this the arms were extended so that the right hand was diagonally at head height and the left was pointed backward. The art of this dance is in the control of the fingertips, which tremble. While the girl carried on this dance with great skill she was accompanied by ten Kwakiutl women who performed a different dance. After the dance was over the girl received a new name from the chief, which I was told she must use until the next year, when she would perform another dance and get another name.

Fig. 26. Double-faced mask: closed, sea monster; open, human face. Kwakiutl.

Now the dances of the Nakortok also started with a dance by a young girl accompanied by a number of women, and later there were general dances. Between them was a dance of a single Hāma'tsa and a shaman from the Nakortok. The latter, though young in years, seemed to have great respect from his tribesmen; and he did possess unusual talent, which kept his audience spellbound, and was known for having achieved an unusual number of cures. He gave one sample of his ability during the feast.

When the dances were over, a helpless invalid was carried in on a mat and set on the floor. The shaman undertook to cure him. First he had to demonstrate, according to Indian practice, that he had power over the natural world by performing some sleight of hand tricks. He picked up a small stone from the ground and asked into what substance he should transform it. There were many suggestions, so he rubbed the little stone between his hands and chanted a ritual as he moved around the fire. At a certain moment he dropped the stone on the ground unnoticed and showed his empty hands; at the same time, a large stone was thrown onto the roof of the house by his helper. The Indians believed that by his magic he had put the stone through the boards of the roof.

Even though this trick was very simple, the people believed that the shaman had the power to throw a stone into the heart of a person, who would then die without fail. This belief was so firmly fixed that they believed if a shaman said to one, "In a few days you will die," he would consider himself doomed and in a few days die of fear.

The missionary Mr. Crosby told me of an incident. A young eighteen-year-old Indian from Nanaimo on the east coast of Vancouver Island, north of Victoria, who was an excellent scholar at the mission school and had become a Christian, one day jokingly teased a shaman. Offended by this the shaman said to the boy, "You will die in six weeks!" The young man was so shocked that, not trusting anyone, he withdrew into himself and finally lay down and became sick. In several weeks the missionary heard the true story, but all the efforts he made to persuade the young man that the medicine man had no such power over life and death did not influence the superstitious youth, who believed that the shaman had thrown a stone into his heart. Perhaps the boy could have been convinced if there had been another well-recognized shaman who would have undertaken the maneuver of extracting the stone and really shown him a stone. But this did not happen, and the poor boy died out of fear even before the six weeks were over.

Let us return to our Nakortok medicine man. After he had finished the first test of his power he took a piece of shredded bark into his mouth and chewed it up, with everyone able to see his movements between his lips. He then took the bark out of his mouth unnoticed and replaced it with a small glass ball. I am convinced that not one of the Indians was aware of the exchange, and murmurs of wonder came from the audience when they saw him take the glass ball from his mouth. Then he exchanged these two objects again and brought out the

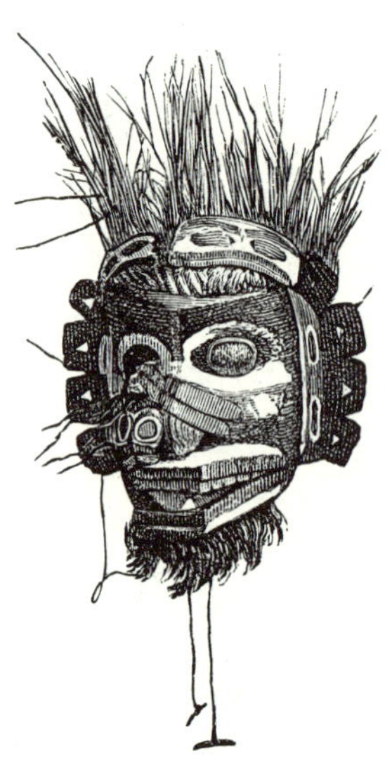

Fig. 27. Dance mask with movable lower jaw. Nimpkish Kwakiutl, northeast coast of Vancouver Island.

cedar bark. This was now used as medicine and was then given to the patient as a cure. The medicine man had evidently been told that he must impress me with his ability at magic, because every time he performed his exchanges he stood directly in front of me. Meanwhile it was getting very late, and since I hoped to leave early in the morning I left when they carried the patient out. I never did find out whether he was cured.

The next morning the wind prevented us from leaving, so I had a free day, which I used in an extraordinary fashion. I had lived among Indians so long that they began to consider me more or less one of their people, and for some time it had been hinted that I should give an Indian feast. It was clear that this was a kind of begging, a way of getting return value for their hospitality. But for me it had other importance, for in order to be able to purchase valuable objects from them I must have a good reputation with them. With the help of my friends I bought two boxes of pilot bread and some molasses, since these were favorite white man's food among the Indians. The feast was arranged in the usual Indian style, consisting of eating, singing, and dancing. I allowed myself the hoax of appearing as an Indian, with the help of a wig I once wore at a masked ball in Paris and an Indian mask, so that evening my friends did not recognize me but thought I was an Indian from elsewhere. After the feast I was given the ritual of receiving an Indian name from the head chief at Fort Rupert. From now on I was called "Sull-qutl-ant," which means "one who runs from one star to another."

This newly made "Indian" had to pay a high price for the honor. When I was trying to buy a few good pieces I was loaded with a large amount of trash that I had to accept and pay for. When the weather improved I left the next day.

There are only three villages where the "longheads" lived —the people whose heads were pressed into this deformed shape during infancy. These were Newette, northwest of Fort Rupert, and Koskimo and Quatsino on the west coast. We sailed to the small island on which Newette is situated, but there was not a single person there. They had taken advantage of the good weather and gone out fur seal hunting. In the evening they returned, having had fairly good luck, with some canoes bringing back four skins apiece. My plan of buying ethnological objects was not successful, because the people there were still carrying on their old customs and dances, so that none of the masks and regalia could be bought. The few objects I did secure were very costly.

I was also not able to persuade any of these people to come to Europe with me. Here, as well as in the other villages named, the women in particular are the ones with deformed heads.

Fig. 28. Cedar-bark neck ring of medicine man. Fort Rupert.

The next day we continued our journey; at noon we passed Cape Scott, the northern tip of Vancouver Island, and toward evening anchored near the entrance of Quatsino Sound, since the tide was too strong to enter. It took until the next evening before we could come close to the village of Koskimo, where my old friend, the son of Negetze, known as "Wachas," greeted me with his wife, who is the chieftainess of Koskimo and Quatsino. The next morning my little boat was overrun with Indians who all wanted to sell me any purchasable object for a dollar, half a dollar, or a quarter. Generally this was not a good deal, for many pieces had little value and the masks were not well carved. The Koskimo do not happen to be great dancers.

Fig. 29. Portrait of "long-headed" woman. Kwakiutl, Koskimo.

But I was successful in my other enterprise by getting the promise of Wachas and his wife that they would go to Europe with me, and that made others consider it also. Since I knew that an Indian might change his mind ten times over, it was necessary to arrange for our departure as quickly as possible. Wachas said he would need four days to get ready because he

would have to give a potlatch before he left. This also involved
me, for in order to remain in their good graces I had to buy
many pieces I really did not want in my collection. It was necessary to engage women because they had the best-deformed
heads. There were several young women of marriageable age
who wished to marry the men of their choice. The young men
were also willing, but they did not have the few dollars needed
to buy token gifts for the parents of the girls. It was clear that
one young couple had decided that the trip to Europe should
be their wedding trip; so I paid the money necessary to make
their union legitimate.

The group engaged grew to three men and two women.
Along with us was George Hunt, the dealer, who brought his
wares along. As a result of my transactions several hundred
dollars flowed into Koskimo, and the people spent this money
at once for the wares brought by Hunt. He had not brought a
large enough supply, so he sent a messenger by the land trail
back to Fort Rupert. This led through the deep forest I had
covered twice not so long ago. It was a piece of bravado to
undertake this in the bad weather, and the people of Koskimo
protested against sending one of their people on such a hazardous trip and threatened vengeance if their man was lost.
Fortunately the man returned with some bruises and cuts but
no other trouble.

In the meantime Wachas had held his potlatch, and my five
Koskimo were ready to depart. Before this happened William
Hunt and I made a "fishing and hunting" trip that was not for
that purpose; we went to the old cemetery near Koskimo,
where we got three exquisite deformed skulls to rescue them
for scientific purposes. In our haste I hurt my hand on the
bone of a mummy and it bled profusely. We had scarcely
stowed the skulls in the canoe when two Indians appeared
who had followed us out of curiosity to see what we were
doing. As soon as I saw them I shot at some sea gulls flying
by, and this satisfied them. So we managed to get our booty
on board unnoticed.

Even though I had spent much money in Koskimo and given
innumerable presents to my five engaged Indians, the attitude
of the people was not friendly. The whole tribe declared that
such a long trip was full of uncertainties. They believed one
of the Indians who was once on board a sailing vessel that
went around Cape Horn and took a whole year. The result of
this was that before we left, one of our party fled.

Even against the wind, on Friday 24 March I started out
with my two pairs of "longheads." For the sake of company
and because their children would be gone so long, old Negetze
and his wife accompanied us on board. We had hardly started

Fig. 30. Carved head of a
woman; used in ceremony
when woman is sup-
posedly beheaded.
Kwakiutl, Koskimo.

when a canoe filled with men approached us and demanded that I give up the second woman in the party. She wept and clung to her young husband, whom she did not want to leave. When the Indians began to threaten me I lost my patience and ordered them to leave my boat or else I would throw them overboard. This worked and soon we were rid of the troublesome people and started our trip unhindered. In the evening we anchored in a small cove in Quatsino Sound to wait for better weather.

George Hunt tried to cheer the frightened Indians with singing and dancing, but this really had no effect. The next day we sailed into a very deep inlet where we were protected from the southwest storm and decided to stay there until the weather improved. Our provisions had been reduced by the feast, to which I had invited the entire village of Koskimo. All we had in fair quantity was dried fish, tea, and molasses. It was necessary to add to the supply by hunting and fishing, so we moved to the mouth of a large river where there were ducks and shellfish.

At this place we were visited by the parents of the younger Indian girl, who begged her to come home. But she was properly married by Indian custom to William Hunt, the interpreter, and was not inclined to leave him. She reminded her parents that they had received seven beautiful blankets—at my expense—from him as a wedding payment, which they had accepted, and that she should at least go with him as far as Fort Rupert. She could then return home by the overland trail if the separation was necessary.

The next day we sailed again, but not in the direction I wished—around the north peninsula to Fort Rupert—but south to the outermost village of Quatsino Sound. This was done according to the wishes of the wife of Wachas, Negetze's son, whom I had considered the one who knew my plans the best and agreed with them. Mrs. Wachas felt she had to go to Quatsino to take ceremonial leave of her relatives there.

The welcome extended to us at our landing there did not further the enthusiasm for the great trip to Europe. Her uncle made the statement that she would be the most celebrated representative of the "longheads" in this distant land of the white people, and then he jumped up and threatened to shoot her if she went. After the uncle had received a few presents, he became calmer and said she could go, but he knew that he would never see her again.

With all these difficulties it is not surprising that I had a little quarrel with George Hunt, the leader of our trip. I have often stated that I did not consider the Indians great heroes at sea. And George Hunt, in spite of being half white, was not

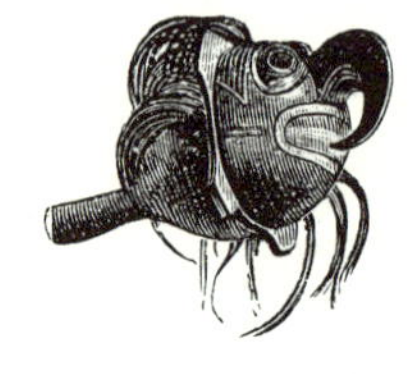

Fig. 31. Dance rattle of Hāma'tsa. Fort Rupert.

an exception. This showed itself when we crossed the open sea because there was little wind at Quatsino. Here we hit a high sea that made all my companions seasick. People who have had experience with this dilemma know that one concentrates on just one desire: to get off the ship and go to shore. So George Hunt, and even more so the other travelers, who now faced many days with the sea in this condition, with the boat wallowing in the waves like a rocking horse, accused me of having no plan for the trip and insisted that we should go back to a protected harbor before we all drowned.

The whole company united, as far as they could with their seasickness, to agree with him. This did not please me because we had idled long enough in "protected harbors," so I took matters in hand and controlled the boat alone.

We traveled for a day and the next night, safely passing Cape Scott, the fearsome point at the northwest corner of Vancouver Island, about three o'clock in the morning. As we went along with closely set sails in the dark night, the little canoe we carried was washed away, adding more agony to my already hopeless companions. The storm Hunt had predicted came in the morning, and we were forced to seek shelter in a small harbor. In the afternoon the weather improved and the travelers had recovered some of their courage, so we sailed to the neighborhood of Newette by evening. From here to Fort Rupert was only a short distance, which could be done the next day in spite of the southwest storm that was gathering.

In Fort Rupert I moved from Scylla to Charybdis. My traveling companions, even though they were about fourteen days away from their home village, felt themselves closer because of the overland trail. The people at Fort Rupert stressed this to make them realize how easy it would be to desert me. The underlying reason for this was their envy of the "longheads" because of the enticing offers I had made them, which the Fort Rupert tribe wanted to share. As for myself, I would have been satisfied with an exchange if the Fort Rupert people had had deformed heads, which was not the case.

The Fort Rupert Indians continued to remind my young couple of the difficulties of their trip this far, stressing how much worse it would be for a whole year to go to Europe, when they would be rocked on the sea and be seasick without a break. What helped me with these people was that I had told them that to reach their destination they would travel with me on the railroad across the North American continent and for less than two weeks be on a large steamer that was not disturbed by the waves; it also helped that old Mr. Hunt agreed with what I said.

Now I could begin to see that the distrust the Koskimo had

raised against me was beginning to subside. Then suddenly five Indians from Koskimo arrived at Fort Rupert and declared that their chief Wachas and his wife must return because the whole village was in an uproar. The next night, before I could give them an answer, Wachas and his wife left without even saying good-bye. The other man also left, so that all I had with me was his weeping wife. Now that the expedition had dissolved itself I no longer needed my interpreter William Hunt.

My next obligation was to pack the large amount of ethnological material I had bought for the Berlin Museum so that I would be ready for the *Otter* on 16 April at three o'clock in the morning for the trip to Victoria. We were in Victoria the next day.

A few days after my arrival, when I was still busy shipping the collection, I received an order from Berlin to board a whaling vessel to the Bering Sea and collect on Diomede Island. I telegraphed at once to San Francisco and received the information that in the month of June no whalers go to the Bering Sea. This gave me a little respite, which I used to go up the east coast of Vancouver Island around the Saint George Strait [Strait of Georgia].

On 2 May I left Victoria and landed the same day at Cowichan Bay, where there is a village of the same name. Among the Indians living here the most important are the Quamichan. I visited their village and found few ethnological pieces, since all had been bought by a previous collector. My guide was a Catholic missionary. In wandering through the village I saw a fine old stone weapon in the possession of an Italian collector, which later came into my collection, although on this first occasion the price was too high. North of Quamichan is a small "Copper" Island [this is "Kuper," the name of a person, not Kupfer, "copper"], and on crossing over I was greeted politely by Mr. Robertson, the local missionary. The next morning I visited the village of Pinalekaht [Penelakut], which had a rather large population. Unfortunately, almost the entire group was away at an Indian festival on the mainland directly opposite near New Westminster. The ethnological possibilities here did not seem very plentiful, since the population had become Christians and masks and regalia for dances were no longer used. Here as well as at Cowichan and Saanich the Indians had a little agriculture. The soil is very good if it can be cleared. In the evening I was again at the home of Mr. Robertson in Village Bay and spent a very pleasant evening in his company. The attempt I had made that afternoon with the help of a few Indians to find some skulls and burial goods in an old Indian cemetery was not very successful.

Northwest of Kuper Island on the east coast of Vancouver

Fig. 32. Double-faced mask, both human faces. Kwakiutl, Fort Rupert.

Island is the Indian village of Chimenes [Chemainus], where I arrived at noon the next day. Here also the whole population had gone to New Westminster. I bought a blanket here made of dog wool, the first I had ever seen. After several hours I went to Nanaimo, where I also found very little. The next morning in some houses along the Nanaimo River I found four old horn wedges or axes used to split tree trunks. A short distance from Nanaimo is the summer village of Juklutok but even there I found nothing.

In the vicinity I found an old Indian burial place I had noticed in passing. I engaged an old French resident to help me examine the graves. The good man charged me high pay, but on account of fear of the Indians, did nothing. The total results were several wooden masks that were nailed on some grave boxes.

The next day a little steamer took me from Nanaimo to Comox, which is about fifteen English miles to the northwest, still on the east coast. Here the Indians were also away traveling and I was disappointed in not getting any of the stone arrow points I had hoped to find. I had been told that the farmers of this area often found them and threw them away as worthless. Since the whole east coast of Vancouver Island is under strong white influence one finds some settlers in every village. In Comox there was even a hotel, whose host, Mr. Patrick, not only greeted me with pleasure but also helped me with my plans.

Comox is the southernmost outpost of the Kwakiutl, who are more centrally located at Fort Rupert. It was therefore interesting to investigate two old Indian burial sites near Comox. With the help of Mr. Patrick I obtained a few skulls but found nothing else in the graves. In the second cemetery there were grave boxes which, in customary Kwakiutl style, were twenty to sixty feet up in the trees. The Indians had taken the trouble to cut off all the lower branches of the trees so that it was impossible to climb, so we attached a rope to an arrow and shot it over a branch near a box and pulled a strong rope over the branch. On that we climbed up.

It happened that the box we selected contained a body without a head, but that showed that it was an important person. It was probably a warrior who was killed in combat and his head taken by the enemy. This was also done by the Indians at Alberni.

About fifty miles north of Comox, deep in the mainland, is Bute Inlet, east of Knight Inlet, already described. Bute Inlet was my next goal. The Indian in whose canoe I was to make the trip across a broad body of water had his whole family with him, a wife and four children, who traveled beside him

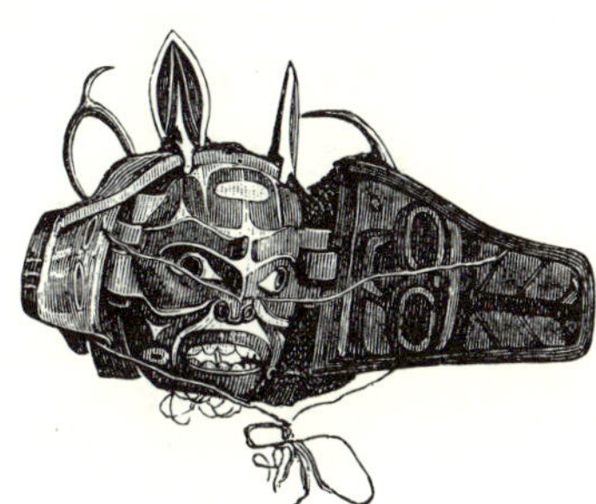

Fig. 33. Double-faced mask: closed, deer head; open, human face. Kwakiutl, Newette, Vancouver Island.

in a smaller canoe. There was a fresh northerly breeze that did not seem dangerous but might have been difficult for the small canoe. The woman seemed capable and thoroughly in control of the situation. She sat immovable at the tiller, which she held in a firm hand while the waves poured over the little canoe. Her long black hair fluttered open in the wind, and the salt water ran from her face and body. As the waves threatened the children they raised great cries, while the youngest, only six months old, was on its mother's back with its eyes and mouth wide open with fear when it seemed that the waves would overwhelm the canoe. She was a brave woman, this Indian mother, who kept beside us on the whole trip, after we shortened our sail to help her. Toward evening we came to Clayamen, an Indian village on the mainland of British Columbia opposite Comox, south of Bute Inlet. Here too all the Indians were gone.

The next morning we went north along the coast, and by evening we reached the Indian village of Malaspina. The whole collection here consisted of a stone arrow point and a lance. There my canoe man, who knew a few words of English, told me of a beautiful stone monument in the vicinity. But time was getting short, since I had to get the next steamer to "Frisco," the local name for San Francisco, so I gave up the trip to Bute Inlet and returned to Clayamen. Since the weather was fine but still, I paddled all day in order to make more progress and arrived at Clayamen with blistered hands. Here I found a little Catholic church that had been built for this village and the neighboring one of Clahus [Klahoose].

I set out as quickly as possible for the trip through the Strait of Georgia and arrived the next day at the village of the Seshelt [Sechelt] Indians. The population consisted of one old woman. There was a store there belonging to a Chinese merchant who was very friendly. In two days I reached Victoria, and on 23 May I was again in San Francisco.

8

In the harbor of San Francisco lay the schooner *Tiurnen*, which
had been chartered by a company of gold prospectors to take
them to Alaska, and I secured passage to Fort Saint Michael.
I knew that I could not complete the trip I had planned within
the year 1882, so I had to arrange to be absent for another half
year. After receiving money by telegraph from Berlin I deposited the larger portion with the Alaska Commercial Company, for which I received a letter of credit, and took the
remainder for equipment and travel money.[17]

Unfortunately it was already late in the year and the majority of the shipping for Alaska had left San Francisco. Loading the steamer dragged on until the middle of June. The prospecting company with which I was planning to travel north
originally consisted of two parties, one of which withdrew and
decided to go in July to Point Barrow to establish a meteorological station to which the United States had committed itself
in a large plan for polar research. The other party was made up
of five prospectors with Mr. Edward Scheffelien [Schieffelin]
who with his brother had a fortune of half a million dollars.
These men had spent several years in Tombstone, Arizona,
where they had made this fortune. They were so well conditioned that they had no qualms about the sudden change of
climate in unknown Alaska if they could make another fortune in gold. The prospectors expedition as well as mine was
to start at Fort Saint Michael and go up the great Yukon River.
For this purpose they had had built a very flat little steamer
fifty feet long, with a capacity of ten tons and a draft of two
feet. This craft had a single paddle wheel at the rear. The purpose of this steamer was to take the men and all their equipment and supplies up the Yukon. They offered me an opportunity to have the boat I would equip in Alaska brought
effortlessly to my destination towed behind their steamer,
which was being carried on the *Tiurnen* as a deck load.

While I was in San Francisco during this last trip I made the acquaintance of the brothers Drs. Aurel and Arthur Krause from Berlin. Both had a commission in 1881 from the highly respected Geographical Society in Bremen to make an important scientific trip to the Tschuktschen [Chukchee] Peninsula in an open whaling boat and go from East Cape on the Siberian coast to Bering Strait and gather valuable information. They spent the winter on the Northwest Coast of North America and were separating because the leave of one brother had expired. The other brother, Dr. Aurel Krause, went north as far as his time permitted to continue his work. I had hoped, but in vain, that I might meet these gentlemen again in Alaska.

Our departure from San Francisco took place at noon on 13 June 1882. There was a large crowd on the wharf, who expressed their good wishes by cheering and waving handkerchiefs. We had decorated the ship and the small steamer on its deck with flowers and other trimmings, and great hopes swelled the breasts of all as we were towed slowly and majestically toward the Golden Gate. "On to the Yukon!" was the cry.

If anyone had mentioned at our departure that before three days were over all our happy prospectors would be wishing we would turn back, he would have been ridiculed. And if anyone had prophesied that almost five weeks would pass before we set foot on dry land again, he would have been called insane.

The broad surface of the "still" Pacific ocean was in constant motion, and the wind was so stormy that often for days we could not steer a course—in fact, often we merely rocked in the same spot. Perhaps no other ocean in the world deserves the reputation of causing so much seasickness. The day after our departure every passenger on board was more or less seasick, and it was no consolation to them that within sight several other ships were rising and falling in the mountainous waves.[18]

At last, on 10 July we came near land south of the Alaska Peninsula close to the Shumagin Islands. When it cleared the next day we finally saw land when we were three hundred miles away from Unalaska. Twenty-four hours later, in a northwest wind and thick fog, we came to Tigalda Island and spent the night zigzagging between it and Unimak in the pouring rain. During the day we sighted the southern tip of Akun, and in spite of rain and fog went through Akutan Pass between Akutan and Unalaska. This is the pass customarily used by ships coming from the south into the Bering Sea.

Since we had to clear our ship at the American customs, we went to that port first. Who could have been happier than the prospectors, when after thirty-three days at sea, three times as long as it takes between Europe and America, they could see that there was still dry land on earth? Our steamer was still four miles from land when three impatient passengers let down a boat and hurried to the shore. We anchored in Unalaska Bay at one o'clock in the afternoon and went ashore at once. Our first visit was to the Western Fur Trading Company, whose head agent, Mr. Stauff, greeted us pleasantly. Later we called on the customs agent, the only official living here who was married to an American; the others were all single. Last we went to the Alaska Commercial Company, whose agent was Rudolf Neumann.

Who would have expected an invitation to a ball taking place that evening? This was a regular ball that occurs every Sunday night. "And the ladies?" we asked. There were plenty of ladies in stylish, elegant clothing entirely of European make. They wore flowers in their hair and on their silk dresses and danced with confidence and endurance. These ladies were from the Aleut population, which in Unalaska had especially mixed with the Russians. As an unusual physical trait the Aleut have very sloping shoulders. The two Russian priests came to the dance also, bringing their families, which did not prevent the Aleut women from smoking their cigarettes between dances. Altogether we did very well at our dance, even though the dance orchestra consisted of a kind of barrel-organ with paper note rolls that repeated at ten or fifteen bars while the dancers continued merrily in their circles. The conversation with the ladies was carried on in Russian. The entertainment continued until one o'clock in the morning.

North winds and rain prevented our departure, and the majority of the passengers were only too happy to stay in this frontier of civilization, for they knew that within a few days they would be in a region of Alaska where life was very uncertain. We had a chance to visit the warehouses of the company and were surprised to find how many things were available there. But one must realize how few articles there were of modern use. We were told that the natives here earned much money in sea otter and fur seal hunting and that they spent it at once on European goods.

At Unalaska I became acquainted with Mr. H. D. Woolfe, a correspondent for the *New York Herald*, a well-educated and traveled man who had been in China and has seen Alaska. Such a trip as I was making as "ethnologist of the Royal Berlin Museum" excited him, and he proposed that we make the expedition together. I agreed and had no cause to regret it, for Mr. Woolfe was a pleasant, tireless helper on our journey of several thousand miles.

Fig. 34. H. D. Woolfe, correspondent for the *New York Herald* and Jacobsen's traveling companion, in Eskimo costume.

On Tuesday, 18 July, at five o'clock in the morning we left Unalaska in fair weather, and by evening we were still in sight of land. There the wind changed and a storm from the west northwest brought cold, raw weather, giving us a taste of the Arctic dog days. The next day was calm, and we spent the time fishing. Evidently we had not observed the ceremonies necessary, for we did not catch a single fish. I took the occasion to bid good-bye to the south and allowed myself the pleasure of a bath in the sea, which naturally in the middle of the Bering Sea and near Bering Strait was a little frosty and reminded me of the time I ploughed barefoot through a snow-covered path in an Indian village on the west coast of Vancouver Island. Shortly after this we passed Saint Matthews Island and the next day Saint Lawrence Island, and on the 24th we were at the entrance of Norton Sound with Cape Nome opposite Fort Saint Michael and, to the south, the miles of estuary—the great Yukon River. One gets some idea of the volume of water this river carries when one sees it spread across Norton Sound, and of the speed with which it goes out to sea from the masses of driftwood. The great current and a southeast breeze made our movement very slow. It was a test of patience again for our prospectors because the coast seemed clear but behind us was a dark bank of fog. We zigzagged between Golovnin Bay and Fort Saint Michael until on the afternoon of 25 July we came to anchor. Here I was again at the beginning of a great adventure which would lead me through much desolate and unknown territory.

9

**Fort Saint Michael
and the Entry into the
Yukon River**

As we approached the harbor of Fort Saint Michael we saw another schooner on the same course. It was the ship *Leo*, which had left San Francisco ten days after us, but with good winds had traveled more rapidly. It went to Golovin Bay, west of Norton Sound, to leave some prospectors, then set out for Point Barrow, the northern point of Alaska, to deliver some of the personnel of the International Polar Research station that was being set up by the United States.

It would have been a great opportunity for me to go with them to this far northern point to visit the tribes there, but Lieutenant Paul wanted to leave the following day and I could not have equipped myself in such a short time. We anchored at Fort Saint Michael at seven in the evening and went ashore, where we found all the passengers of the *Leo*. We became acquainted with the second agent of the Alaska Commercial Company, Mr. Neumann, since the head agent, Mr. Lorenz, was on a trip on the upper Yukon River.

The arrival of two ships like ours at such a distant place as Fort Saint Michael aroused much excitement, because this was the only way they could pick up the news of the world in the past few months. So it is not surprising that it was past midnight when Lieutenant Paul invited us aboard his vessel for a farewell because he would be away from all civilization for many months. The sun had risen at two o'clock in the morning of 26 July when we left the Polar Research personnel after many toasts and speeches. After a brief rest I quickly started to prepare for my trip.

In the meantime the prospectors were also preparing their gear to go into the interior of Alaska as soon as possible. With the help of a hydraulic lift the little steamer was taken from the deck and lowered into the water, and all their gear was packed on it, including a large skin-covered Eskimo rowboat [umiak]. I also was loaned such an umiak by Mr. Neumann of the Alaska Commercial Company and engaged as interpreter Petka, to whom I was forced to pay a high wage, according to local standards. But the man was trustworthy and familiar with the region because he had worked in the same capacity for Mr. Nelson of the Smithsonian Institution on a previous trip.

In order to get some idea of the scale of prices for artifacts I bought a few pieces from the local people and came away with the feeling that trading would be quite successful. A few days after our arrival in Fort Saint Michael the plan for the expedition was arranged by Mr. Schieffelin, who would be aboard the steamer with a few companions, while the rest of the prospectors and their luggage would be in the first skin boat, followed by Mr. Woolfe, Petka, and I in my skin boat. In this order the steamer would tow us all. We proceeded up the river for 900 English miles during August 1882.

The chain of stations and trading posts the Alaska Commercial Company had established on the mainland and the surrounding islands resembled those set up by the Hudson's Bay Company in British Columbia. As was mentioned before, the headquarters of the Alaska Commercial Company are in San Francisco and many of the principals are Germans. The company obtained a monopoly on fur seal hunting in Alaska, for which they had to pay the government a fee for each animal taken. Since it was their duty to see that the fur seal was not exterminated, they had a yearly quota. The islands of Saint Paul and Saint George in the Bering Sea are the only ones the fur seal visits for the purpose of mating. The Aleut inhabitants do the actual hunting. In addition to this, almost all the Aleutian islanders hunt the sea otter. The Alaska Commercial Company has trading posts both on the west coast of Alaska, where Fort Saint Michael is the headquarters, and on the south side in Cook Inlet. On the mainland there is considerable trade in skins, and there are trading posts 1,800 miles up the Yukon River which are serviced by two small steamers. In the south there are two stations on the Kuskoquim [Kuskokwim] River and the Nushagak [Nushagak], five in Cook Inlet, and even Prince William Sound has one. For the last of these Saint Paul on Kodiak Island is the main establishment. The station at Unalaska serves the posts on many Aleutian Islands. At each of these places there is a white trader who receives the skins from the native hunters and transacts other business. Under his control are a number of half-breeds who travel around during the winter to collect skins in outlying districts and are used as workmen as well. The Alaska Commercial Company has several sailing vessels and three larger steamers that bring the trade goods each year and take skins back to San Francisco. In recent years the influence of the company has been extended by the building of a salmon cannery on Kodiak Island. Among the skins handled in this trade are those of caribou, various marten, polar bear, red and black foxes, brown, black, and grizzly bears, lynx, wolverine, beaver, hares, rats, ermine, and other rodents, fisher, and so forth. The majority of these skins go to the big fur market in London. In recent times other products have also been exported from Alaska—namely, walrus tusks, salted salmon, and herring. In San Francisco the Alaska Commercial Company has a small ethnographic and zoological museum worth seeing. This exhibition is the result of the interest the company has had in the support it has given to scientific travelers and collectors, which they also extended to me and for which I am most grateful. I might also mention here that a large portion of the traders and agents are Scandinavians and Germans.

After I had written my farewell letters to Europe, I took a Russian bath before leaving, as is the custom of the country. The equipment for these baths is the same at all the company's stations, as I will describe it now. The bathhouses are usually built in the Russian style; in the first place, they are airtight so the steam will not escape. In one corner of the bathing area is a large stone stove that is heated with wood at the beginning of the bath. On the burning wood are laid a number of fist-size stones that soon begin to glow with heat. When the wood has burned down the oven door is closed, and one can no longer leave the space. Then lukewarm water is poured on the stones, and soon the room is filled with steam. The bathers sit naked on wooden benches and stay about half an hour. Then they go into the next room and dress. One feels fresh and clean after such a bath, and I used one whenever there was an opportunity. I believe these baths are part of the reason that the inhabitants of Alaska are generally so strong and hearty and that there is little illness. It would be very difficult to get medical care in such a large area.

The Eskimo of northwestern Alaska have an aboriginal bath of their own which involves not steam, but hot air. The baths, which resemble those of the Romans, are set up in villages that are near wood, either driftwood or a growth of trees. In the Eskimo villages there is a dance and festivity house called kassigm, kassigit, or kashim. These are built quite differently from their dwellings and are half underground. There is no door, but a tunnel to a large cellarlike space underneath the planks that are the floor of the house. There is a round hole in the center of the floor through which the visitor enters the festivity area. Benches are built against the walls. During a feast the space is lighted with ten to thirty stone and pottery lamps on separate stands. When used for baths the furnishing is different.

The planks of the floor are removed so that the cellar space and the principal room are all one. A fire is started on the floor of the cellar, which is about four feet deeper than the house. There the bathers undress and place themselves, lying on the benches. The bath assistants, who are Eskimo women, hand each bather a bowl of snow. For those delicately inclined toward European ideas of cleanliness this type of bath is not recommended. But for the Eskimo, whose way of life brings much uncleanliness to the body, so that it sometimes encrusts the skin, soap is replaced with the natural liquid of his body, urine, to melt the snow in the bowl, and with this he washes his whole body. While this is hygienically not recommended, it does clean the skin and open the pores. A release of hot air finishes the bath. The women assistants tend to their business with no attention to the unclad condition of the bathers. As a token, some wear a small string which they feel serves the purpose of signifying modesty. To protect themselves from the heat the Eskimo wear a cap made of birdskins. Another device is a kind of respirator, a ball woven of fine grasses, which they put in the mouth with a small wooden plug as protection from the smoke of the fire. Add to this the use of small bunches of the grass as towels and we have all the conveniences of the Eskimo hot air bath.

On the last day of July a large skin boat with twenty persons of both sexes arrived at Fort Saint Michael from King Island and brought many ethnographic objects with them, all of which I bought. The young women wore nose rings and had tattooed chins, like most northwest Alaskans. I could make these purchases with money, whereas in the interior I also had to have trade articles. For this purpose I had bought a certain amount of goods at the Alaska Commercial Company and depended on the advice of Mr. Neumann in their selection.

We departed from Fort Saint Michael at five o'clock in the morning on 3 August 1882 after affectionate farewells from the new friends made during our short visit. The way to the mouth of the Yukon was along the coast, then we entered a long canal between the coast and the island, reaching its end in six hours. Our little steamer had to carry, in addition to its own weight, two heavily laden skin boats and needed fuel often, for unlike the ocean liners it could not take on enough for a whole journey. In fact, it could not take on enough for one day, so it was necessary to stop often for firewood. Coal would have been better because it would have given more power for the same weight, but one cannot always count on getting it, so we had to depend on wood. In the tundra and treeless regions on the coast of Alaska one looks in vain for trees for this use; but often piles of driftwood on the coast can fill the need. All northern rivers bring large amounts of driftwood, which the wind and the tides pile up for the inhabitants to use.

Chopping wood became a daily task beginning with the first day. Near the mouth of the Yukon there was so much driftwood that we landed only twice a day when the little steamer went to the shore and was tied up. Like a commando attack, each man grabbed an ax and went to work, which all shared. Those who could not easily handle an ax searched for good pieces and carried the cut wood aboard.

When driftwood was no longer available we found some sizable trees growing right on the banks of the river. We looked for dead trees, since they were easier to cut to size than green wood. I observed that there were many "crippled" trees with large knots, and wondering about this I took a little tree with me to send to Berlin so that it could be examined scientifically. The cutting of wood caused an irreplaceable loss for me when one day a tree did not fall as expected and a part of it fell on my chest and shattered beyond repair my pocket watch, which I had had for a long time. The loss of my faithful timepiece made me live in Eskimo fashion for the remainder of my stay in Alaska, for a full fourteen months determining the time by the sun and stars during the long Arctic winter. At last on my return to San Francisco in the autumn of 1883 I could again possess a watch, for there was no place where I could purchase one sooner.

When we reached the end of the canal, where we had successfully cut a load of wood, we went ahead for the comparatively short distance to the southwesterly estuary of the Yukon, not expecting any difficulty. But the east wind blew the waves from behind and our little steamer was not prepared for this, as we discovered later; since the wheel was well in the back it interfered with the steering and the boat zigzagged. So Mr. Pettersen, our pilot, took the expedition into the mouth of the little Pikmiktalik River where the ebbtide grounded it.

This unexpected delay lasted until eight o'clock the next morning in spite of attempts to get the ship loose, in which we were joined by some Eskimo from Pastoliak who were interested in trading. In the evening they came in several kayaks and offered us fresh salmon, whitefish, ducks, and geese which we of course bought. When we were afloat again we stopped to chop wood for two hours in the morning, and after we started, an hour later, we entered the Yukon by a northeasterly estuary.

**The First Experience on
"the Great River"**

The greatest river in America that empties into the Pacific Ocean—here in its northern portion being the Bering Sea—is the Yukon, whose length Schwatka reported as 2,043 statute miles (1 statute mile = 1.62 km). It has many outlets, of which the Kusilwak is the largest. The floor of Norton Sound has been raised to such a level by the silt the river deposits that it is difficult for ships to pass. The next largest river in Alaska, the Kuskokwim, lies south of the Yukon, and between these two rivers there is a stretch of tundra, a wide-open area often covered with water, which at the flooding of the Yukon becomes part of a great delta.

The name Yukon is not used by either the white inhabitants or the natives, who simply call it "the great river"—in their language, "Kwik Pak" [Kwikpak]. The village or tribal names of the native inhabitants of this region usually have two syllables and end in "miut." So the people of the lower Yukon or Kwikpak are Kwikpakmiut. North of them, between Norton Sound and Kotzebue Sound, are the Malemiut; to the west of them on Prince of Wales Peninsula on Bering Strait are the Kawiaremiut; and south of the Yukon and on the lower river south of the Kwikpakmiut live the tundra people, who have no special name. Their neighbors on both sides of the lower Kuskokwim River are the Kuskokwimiut. These are the Eskimo tribes on the west coast of Alaska from Bering Strait to Cape Newenham. In the same manner the southern coast of Alaska is populated with Eskimo tribes. South from Cape Newenham the eastern neighbors of the Kuskokwimiut are south of Nushagak Bay; on Kodiak Island are the Kikertagmiut, and north of them on Cook Inlet are the Kenaiski. I do not know the names of the inhabitants of the Alaska peninsula. These people of the coast of Alaska, including those on the northeast where I did not visit, form a great ring around the Indian population that lives in the central area, generally known as the Ingalik. The boundaries of these groups often cross each other and areas are sometimes occupied by a mixed population.

Since I had decided to accept the opportunity offered by Mr. Schieffelin to go nine hundred English miles inland, it was necessary to forego my plans to make some purchases in order to conform to the wishes of the prospectors for a joint expedition on the upper Yukon with Nuklukayet as the goal. From this point I expected to go downstream and visit every Indian and Eskimo village in order to buy or barter for ethnographic objects, and I later did so.

Our entry into the northeastern mouth of the Yukon or Kwikpak, which led to the Upun [Apoon] branch, took place on 4 August 1882. At three o'clock in the afternoon we passed Kutlik [Kotlik], a trading post of the Alaska Commercial Company located on this branch. In a heavy rain we continued until midnight, and during this time we did not pass more than two or three Kwikpakmiut villages, each of which had only two or three houses.

The first evening and night on the Yukon River brought us a foretaste of a plague that would follow us the whole summer—the plague of mosquitoes. It is no wonder that all travelers in the tropics or up in the north immediately mention the nuisance inflicted by these bloodthirsty insects. One can overcome dangers, and against ambushes one can protect oneself with vigilance; accidents can often be prevented or lessened by energy and quick action; one can overcome all kinds of situations, but against the relentless pursuit during waking and sleeping carried on by mosquitoes, which are constantly replaced by millions of new ones, there is no defense. It is no help to try to seal the tent by pulling in the sides and placing stones and other heavy objects on the inside so that one feels certain one has won against them and none can penetrate the tent. What help is it, I ask, when after two or three hours of sleep one tries murderously to kill every mosquito in the tent and still is awakened shortly with new bites, the tent again full of mosquitoes and one's body covered with painful bumps that make one look like he is recovering from smallpox? A mosquito does not stop biting until his body is completely filled with blood; when one is squashed it makes a square-centimeter spot. No philosophy protects against mosquitoes!

We started out again at six o'clock in the morning on our trip upriver and stopped from nine to eleven o'clock to chop wood. Since the river is very wide, a storm approaching from the southeast endangered our tow and forced us to lie by in an unfavorable location. The rain poured down as we huddled under the boat tent, where we enjoyed the geese, ducks, and salmon we had bought the day before at Pastoliak. The uninhabited region between Fort Saint Michael and the mouth of the Yukon has a growth of grass that serves as a breeding place for millions of birds, among them the rare emperor goose; at our present moorage these birds furnished us some welcome entertainment. The next morning the situation had not improved. The storm continued, bringing high waves and if possible even harder rain, and we realized that it was impossible to proceed. Neither the delta nor the river had been charted, and it would have been of little use anyway because the strong current and the many small tributaries shift year by year; so we had to depend on our pilot's general knowledge to find the right channel.

Since we decided that it was impossible to continue on the main river because the waves were battering our three craft, we turned around and went downstream again until we came to a narrow channel that flowed in the same direction as the main stream, and then we steamed upstream again. We had the good fortune to have found a side channel of the Yukon and not, as might easily have happened, to have come into a little tributary that would later peter out and force us to turn around.

But to come to a decision and to carry it out are two different things, for we did not reckon with the capacity of our little steamer. While we were going downstream both small steering wheels gave out, being exposed to crosscurrents, and the vessel ran wild. In order not to run onto the bank we had to stop, and so our tow floated downstream in complete disorder until it reached the tributary mentioned above. Here again it took some maneuvering to bring the three units of our transport into the proper order and let us proceed through the channel. This peaceful traveling lasted only three hours until we reached a storm-whipped broad arm of the river, where we encountered pouring rain and tried to keep in motion as a defense against the mosquitoes. Finally, at about three o'clock the following afternoon we could continue on our way. We steamed along the left, or south, bank of the river without interruption. After our first pause for woodchopping we saw several places where the sandy bank had been torn away by high water. Here the layers of soil of which the bank consisted had been cut perpendicularly, and in these fresh breaks it was possible to see the displaced character of the successive changes. It was wonderful to see in various places about eight feet below the surface the stratifications of glaciation and further earth layers below. One can see here that in the far north the glacier ice, among other factors, played an important role in the building of these strata, and I believe this is also true farther to the north toward the pole. The banks of the Yukon which showed this stratification were not without vegetation, but they had the characteristics of the tundra and the delta, with small meadows and brush. It makes it clear that the glacial formations cannot be derived from last winter but are much older, perhaps many years older than the oldest vegetation on the banks.[19]

On the afternoon of 7 August we came to a side channel called the Tuenirok. Here we cut wood near a Kwikpakmiut village and then entered an area of higher riverbanks that began about ten English miles below the station at Andrejewski [Andreafsky]. The delta and the tundra ended. The tundra is broken here by occasional hills, among others the lone standing Kusilwak, south of the principal mouth of the river and more than fifty miles southwest of the five inactive volcanoes I later visited. Like the landscape at Cape Vancouver and Cape Romanzoff, at the place where we now arrived hills rise about five hundred to eight hundred feet.

At eleven o'clock at night we reached the trading post of the Alaska Commercial Company at Andreafsky. Like most of the posts of this company it is situated where a post had been erected by the Russians before 1868 [1867] when they had possession of Alaska. Since these posts are all very much alike I will describe this one.

There are always several houses and buildings. There is a well-arranged store, carrying the traditional manufactured wares used in trade with the natives for their furs and all the other goods obtained from them. There are living quarters for the trader who manages the station and also for the workmen, and a bathhouse, always present in Alaska and previously described. Finally there is a high cache for supplies such as dog-food, sleds, and dog harness. The inner rooms of the house are all beyond the reach of the dogs. Around this entire settlement there used to be a high wooden stockade as protection against the nightly attacks by unfriendly natives, but recently, since a more peaceful relationship has been established between the natives and the company, many holes have developed in the fence. Outside this settlement a number of native families usually live to enjoy the scraps from the table of the white people.

The trader who manages the post usually has from two to six assistants who are half-breeds of natives and Russians. In the winter when the trading journeys take place, after the thermometer has fallen to $-40°$ or $-60°$ F the half-wild dogs are captured and harnessed to the sleds. The sleds are loaded with white and colored cotton goods, powder, lead, percussion caps, tobacco, matches, knives and beads, and so forth—in short, something of everything that might please an Eskimo or an Indian and delight his lady. Then the journey begins over the frozen inland lakes, bays, and rivers, over hard frozen sand and glistening snow, until one reaches the next village twenty-five to thirty miles away. Here a lively trade ensues as the trader's goods are bartered for the furs the natives have collected. During the journey usually ten to twelve dogs are used on one principal line from the front of the sled so that they pull two by two, while the lead dog goes alone at the head. This dog constantly turns his head to look back at the driver, who indicates by hand movements or by his whip handle which direction he should take. A good lead dog is worth much more than an ordinary dog, for often he even responds to the call of his master and guides the sled in the desired direction. But there are also poor lead dogs who must be guided by the whip at every turn.

Every trader on the Yukon has from six to ten sleds, and for these he needs forty to seventy dogs. The animals are called wolf dogs and are the same as those used for sled dogs in Labrador and Greenland. One cannot claim that these animals are spoiled with fine tidbits of food. If the natives are regarded as not particular about their food, their dogs are even less so. The regular winter food for dogs is raw frozen fish, and if it is necessary to strengthen them for a journey they get a soup of fish with oil and seal fat. The dogs are very greedy and there is scarcely anything that can be grasped with the teeth that they will not attack. One has to take great care with them or they will eat their harness and the skin boat covers and even tear fur clothing from people. I once awoke in winter to find one of my dogs trying to eat my boot off my foot. In giving them rations, care must be taken to give them equal amounts and to see that the dog that finishes first does not rob the others of their food. Some gulp their food in seconds and then attack the younger animals. If care is not taken to protect them, they will suffer from malnutrition.[20]

On good ground one can cover thirty to fifty English miles in twelve to sixteen hours. The average day's journey would be about twenty to twenty-five miles. When we reached Andreafsky in the late evening on our steamer-towing expedition we were greeted by a tremendous howling of the dogs that belonged to the post. We had to stay longer than we expected, for during the next two days we had to pull the skin boats out of the water. These umiaks are very peculiar craft, for they consist of a keel that is in three parts, running the full length of the boat and supporting a large number of ribs to which the gunwale is attached at the upper end. A cover of skins sewed together is stretched over this frame. If one keeps these boats, which are called woman's boats in Greenland, in the water for as long as a week, the skin becomes very soft and stretches like rubber. If one should step on this, instead of staying on the boards in the bottom of the boat the skin might stretch with one's foot about six inches beyond the side of the boat. This is very apt to happen on the walrus hunt, and if many steps have been taken on the skin cover the boat must be put ashore, turned, dried, and oiled again.

We unloaded our boats, which took all morning and attracted swarms of mosquitoes, then we retired to our tents, which we even sewed shut against the pests, and spent several hours napping. While the boats were drying we also added to our provisions. At the same time the port was visited by two skin boats that had come down the river from Nulato in ten days and were going to Fort Saint Michael. After the covers of our boats were thoroughly dry we carefully rubbed them with oil and set our departure for the next day. But at three o'clock the next morning when we were ready to put the boats in the water we found that we had not considered the presence of the local dogs, who had chewed the skin covers. When the damage had been repaired we reloaded and departed at seven o'clock.

Our pilot Mr. Pettersen [Peterson] accompanied us a short distance, then gave up his post to a young half-breed. On the way we found a deserted fisherman's hut, which we demolished and took aboard because of the scarcity of wood. In the evening we reached the village of Razbolniksky [Razboinski], which the Eskimo call Ankasagemuit. Here the plague of mosquitoes was so terrible that we stayed in our boats and anchored in midstream. In the evening three natives came to us in their kayaks and sold us ducks, geese, and caribou meat.

At four o'clock the next morning we started out again in a storm from the southwest with rain. In the morning we came to a little stream where we could be protected from the waves. While we were cutting wood I saw the tracks of a bear, and taking my gun I followed them, but to no avail.

11

Being Towed up
the Yukon, Fighting
Mosquitoes

The delta of the Yukon ends a short distance above Andreafsky, where there is a short outgoing stream from the Yukon that flows diagonally across the low tundra and empties into the sea between Cape Romanzoff and Cape Vancouver. Geographical research concludes that the whole tundra between the Yukon and the Kuskokwim is really an extension of the delta that has been developing in this region for thousands of years.

After a relatively quiet night we left on Friday, 5 August, at five o'clock in the morning and traveled until ten, when we paused to chop wood. However, we did not get away easily, for as soon as we raised the anchor our steamer grounded. All our efforts did not move her, even though we were helped by some Eskimo living there. It was impossible to move the boat, so we unloaded her enough so that she floated again. We then reloaded and were on our way, but this accident cost us a whole day. As we continued we passed a long chain of mountains which showed on their steep banks the remains of thousands of former Eskimo houses. These are supposed to have been occupied by Eskimo who were river pirates, whose united strength allowed them to capture any boat coming on the river and force the occupants to live with them. I think I will try to find out more about this on my way back, for among these extraordinary ruins are supposed to be about one hundred dance houses. The legend has led many astray, and I will report on it later.

After passing three more villages we came near the trading post of the Alaska Commercial Company at Mission, but because of lack of firewood we could not get there that evening. The next morning we came to the post, and while my companions cut wood I visited the Kwikpakmiut who lived there and bought many very interesting ethnographic objects, including stone axes, spear points, and bone carvings.

The station, Mission, is the midpoint of the Russian missionary effort on the Yukon and northwestern Alaska. As the Russians settled in Alaska, missionaries were called for their duties to the officers of the Russian colony. As time went on and more natives on the Aleutian Islands and Cook Inlet, on the lower Yukon and Norton Sound mixed with the Russians, the missions became more important and an effort was made to convert them, until gradually a network of missions was spread with the trading posts. When Alaska came under American control the Russian officers returned home, but the missionaries who liked this country stayed and continued their work, unmolested by the American government. They must be thanked for better-ordered lives among the Eskimo and Indians. The missionaries were under the jurisdiction of the Russian bishop, who lived in San Francisco and came to Alaska every year to inspire them. In July 1882, several days before my arrival, he either jumped or fell from the steamer *St. Paul* of the Alaska Commercial Company, and his body was later found in Norton Sound.

About an hour before we reached Mission the north bank of the river began to build up into steep promontories, which extended far into the river and created the first rapids, in which the water moved at about six knots. It took our little steamer *New Racket* great effort to bring us through the current. We exchanged pilots at this station and traveled until nine o'clock in the evening of the same day. We left again at five o'clock in the morning and before noon we had passed the first two villages of the Indians whom we had noted were called Ingalik by the Eskimo. In one village we bought an old cabin and cut it up for firewood.

When we continued on our way, we experienced a small adventure. Two Indians had attached their birchbark canoes to our towline and held themselves close to my skin boat. Through careless steering the canoes swung against the current, and since they were tied together they both filled with water and sank. We saved both men but would have endangered ourselves had we tried to raise the canoes. Little concerned about the damage, our strange guests made themselves comfortable on board until we stopped to cut wood. Then by chance a tribesman, an Ingalik, came along with several empty canoes he was planning to sell to the Kwikpakmiut. They went with him and helped handle his boats. By nine o'clock in the evening we had anchored and set up our tents in the boat, since the mosquito plague was so terrible.

The next day there was little change in the landscape; after passing two Ingalik villages where we purchased wood, and after we took another pilot on board, because the first did not seem very confident, we saw for the first time some black earth with a change of vegetation in the conifer forest along the banks. The river, here between two and three miles wide, was covered with little islets; the current had a speed of three to six knots, and the depth generally was about four to six feet, enough to accommodate a steamer. This was necessary for the trading post for the Ingalik at Anvik. Here was the mouth of the Anvik River, coming from the north and about an English mile wide. Since the Yukon River from the end of the delta up to Nulato flows from southwest to northeast and the coast of Alaska between Norton Sound and Cape Romanzoff is almost parallel, the distance by land from Anvik to Fort Saint Michael is about one-quarter of the distance by water. The Alaska Commercial Company exploits this situation in the winter and has established a route by dogsled that takes about two to three days. The agent at the trading post was a countryman of mine, a Norwegian named Frederiksen. He was not at home, being with the company steamer on the upper Yukon, and so his wife, who was half Russian and a sister of our interpreter, Petka, did the honors. In the evening we refreshed ourselves with a steambath, in which, because of the heat, there were few mosquitoes.

We had unloaded our boat again to dry it out and make necessary repairs. This time, remembering the Andreafsky experience, we placed a guard at the boat, for there were fifty or sixty dogs at the station. My attempt to purchase Ingalik ethnographic artifacts met with little success, since these people live at a lower plane than the Eskimo and have very little. I bought several "raw" pots that had been finished by them.

Since the routine of the following days was the same I will record the outstanding events from my diary:

17, 18, 19 August: stopped at Indian villages to buy wood and found that they had no ancient artifacts and few current ones. No driftwood here, so green trees had to be cut. One prospector injured his foot while cutting wood.

On 20 August we met the steamer *Yukon*, where we found Mr. Lorenz, the head agent from Fort Saint Michael, who had been 1,800 miles up the river as far as Fort Reliance on his annual tour. After returning to Fort Saint Michael he would start again, delivering goods along the lower Yukon, and go as far as Nuklukayet if the weather permitted. It was planned to have the *Yukon* winter in the same place as our steamer.

On board the *Yukon* was also Mrs. Lorenz, the educated and charming wife of the head agent, probably the first white woman to travel with her husband in this region. In spite of our need for haste we tied the two steamers together at a small island and gossiped far into the night. On board the *Yukon* there were a number of agents and traders, among them Mr. Frederiksen from Anvik and Mr. Mayo of Nuklukayet. The latter was born in Kentucky, and after leaving a broken family had an interesting life walking on foot through many states and cities, often trying his luck at prospecting. So eventually he came to Fort Saint Michael in 1881 and there saw a large sailing ship at sea for the first time. Mr. Leavitt, the signal officer at Saint Michael, was also aboard. Our conversation was a lively one, for in this group we were the ones with the latest news of the world.

At this time there was a change of personnel in our group with the departure of Mr. Woolfe, my companion, who decided to go downriver with the *Yukon* in order to be at Fort Saint Michael when the American revenue cutter *Rodgers* returned from its search for the *Jeanette*, since it would come into that port on its way from Wrangel Island with news of the expedition. He was correct in his reckoning, for he was there when the ship came in with the story, which they allowed him to send to San Francisco by their telegraph. I was sorry to lose him.

The next morning at three o'clock we parted company and continued our journeys. By noon we came to Nulato to the Alaska Commercial Company and also saw the post of their rival the Western Fur Company.

This is perhaps the place to make a few remarks about this second company. This competing firm, which also had headquarters in San Francisco, had the same routes. So long as these companies were competitors the natives received high prices for their furs and other trade articles. Finally only the Alaska Commercial Company remained when their rivals withdrew after losing a quarter of a million dollars. This happened in the spring of 1883 when the Alaska Commercial Company took over the trading posts of the Western Fur Company. When I was traveling on the Yukon they were still side by side. Here I want to say that the agent at Fort Saint Michael, Mr. Greenfield, was most courteous and helpful to me.

In the spring of 1882 Nulato had the misfortune of having a flood that destroyed both posts and almost crushed a steamer that was wintering there. The Indian settlements around the post were also lost. The Indians in this area are very secretive, since in April 1881 one of them killed a trader at night. The prospectors in the vicinity heard that the murderer was still living in Nulato and had not been punished and decided to lynch him. But the Indian fled to the woods every time he heard a steamer arriving and stayed until the coast was clear. This happened when we were there.

On 22 August we stopped from eleven o'clock to one o'clock

to take on wood at an Indian village where all the men were away hunting; so ten women, not because of greediness for money, but with laughter and joking, helped us carry the wood on board and enjoyed the biscuits and molasses we gave them afterward.

In the afternoon we went through our third rapids. An hour later the steamer's rudder was damaged by hitting a deadhead [sunken log]. It took until the next afternoon to make repairs. The next day we saw another interesting example of the ravages of the ice age on the banks of the river. This day we had to stop at five o'clock because of lack of fuel.

The morning after we passed several Indian fishing villages, we stopped at eleven o'clock to cut wood and went on at about two o'clock, anchoring at another fishing village in the evening. The next fishing village remained in our memories because of the amazing Indian we saw running around like mad and jumping with threatening poses. He danced furiously like a crazy person, swung his cap around and threw it on the ground as long as he was in sight. The Indian pilot and steersman we had with us told us that the Indian was trying to bewitch the steamer to make it sink into the ground. Our vessel did not respond and steamed majestically past the high Hotlotulei [Hotlina] mountain range, whose tallest peak showed the first signs of the coming Arctic winter.

The fishing on the Yukon is different in many ways from that of other parts of the Northwest Coast of America. As usual the natives build a wooden trap that projects diagonally from the shore into the river. The fish that come to it are led into an inner section where there are wicker baskets. Among the Ingalik I saw another kind. In each of fifteen to twenty birchbark canoes an Indian stood with a dip net six to eight feet in diameter on a long pole. These nets were sunk into the river, and while the net was being turned downriver by the current the salmon were swimming upriver toward it. As soon as a fish was noticed in the net, it was raised carefully and the fish taken into the canoe and clubbed.

On the lower Yukon nets made of nettle fiber were also used with traps. These nets were set into the water perpendicularly, floated with stringers of bark and set with sinkers along the bottom. When the king salmon swim against this, the fisherman in a canoe feels the impact and promptly raises the net and takes the fish into his canoe and clubs it. Sometimes these fish are very large and strong, weighing eighty to ninety pounds, but generally they are about half that. The salmon are very agile, and sometimes the fisherman wrestles with one until his canoe overturns. In good conditions the fisherman is able to get many fish at one time, which overloads his small craft, so that he fastens them to the outside. Pike are usually caught with a bone fishhook or with a small fish carved of bone as a lure, but they are also harpooned from canoes. In winter when the ice is five to seven feet deep it is a difficult task to clear the fish traps every day. At this time of the year many whitefish, salmon, eels, pike, and occasionally salmon trout are taken. The inhabitants of the tundra live principally on a little black swamp fish which occurs by the millions in inland lakes, canals, brooks, and swamps. I could never develop an appetite for this fish and used it only as dog food. On the coast many small fish of the smelt variety (resembling the Norwegian *loddes*), which were caught, are very nourishing, because of their fat.

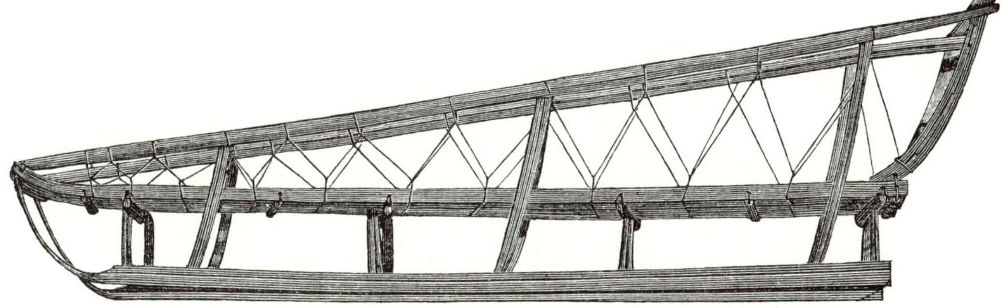

During the ice-free season the coastal tribes of Alaska live on sea mammals. In May and June many walrus are taken; in the fall, just before the bays freeze, white whales are captured in nets, the meshes of which are made of finger-thick walrus hide. This variety of whale has a tendency to remain close to the shore. The net was used because one section could be fastened on a rock and twenty to thirty armspans away it could be anchored in the water. The seal net was made partly of sinew and partly of modern spun cord. In January and February a variety of seals were hunted on the ice away from the shore. This was considered very dangerous because the ice is sometimes broken loose from shore by a storm and the cakes of ice are driven out to sea while the hunters are on them. There is a legend that Saint Lawrence Island at the south end of Bering Strait was settled by Eskimo who were driven out to sea in this way. For the Maklak [a large seal] hunt, both firearms and harpoons are used. On this hunt the Eskimo use small kayaks that are especially designed to be put on sleds, and in this way they can go farther out to sea and get seals that have plunged into the sea to get away. The principal food staple, however, is the dried and partially smoked salmon, which is prepared in large quantity. The family that does not prepare enough of this salmon, called yukala, is certain to suffer hun-

Fig. 35. Dogsled used by the Ingalik of the upper Yukon River.

ger before the winter is over. So these Alaskans are ichthyophagists in the true sense of the word—not just they themselves, but also their dogs.

This trip along the Hotlina range went along very slowly because we had to stop for five to six hours a day, cutting wood for fuel. On Sunday, 27 August, we arrived at Nuklukayet, happy that the towing job was over.

12

**The Return Trip
down the Yukon, with
Trading at Many
Villages**

Nuklukayet, an Alaska Commercial Company station, was the point at which we had decided to leave the prospectors, who at Mr. Schieffelin's decision expected to winter there. However, they intended to use the steamer *New Racket* for short trips to become acquainted with the country, as long as the weather permitted.

I had to curtail my stay at Nuklukayet because I had a nine-hundred-mile return trip to Fort Saint Michael and I wanted to catch one of the last steamers for San Francisco and ultimately to Europe. Before starting this journey it was necessary to unload the skin boat for drying and repairs. I ordered a sail to be made for it. On the trip upriver I had told the people in every Kwikpakmiut and Ingalik village where we landed that I would be back and would buy ethnographic artifacts they assembled. I began my trading at once at Nuklukayet, though the natives had very little that I could use and their prices were very high. The reason for this was that they lived in a rich fur-bearing area and at that time they could still get high prices from the two competing companies.

On Tuesday, 29 August, I started the return journey after friendly farewells from Mr. Schieffelin and his group. My crew consisted of Petka and an Ingalik who had steered the prospectors' skin boat. Since there was no wind for sailing we rowed in a strong current of the river and passed the village of Klokare at noon. The right northern bank from Nuklukayet to about twenty English miles above Nulato has steep cliffs about 1,000 to 3,000 feet high, and the left bank is almost flat except for the range of mountains at Nukakiet. We came to this village late in the morning and were received by a Finnish inhabitant, Mr. Kaheraien, who became our host. We left the next morning and soon came to Delsanorvit, the place where we saw the Indian shaman who tried to bewitch the steamer. I saw here an immense pike, weighing fifty to sixty pounds, which had just been caught. Later we visited the village of Makkatmekettan, but because of a strong wind we went aboard again. The population here was very hostile and overbearing, and I believe that the Ingalik we had on board stirred up his tribesmen against us. On the way I had stopped at a burial site and rescued a skull for scientific purposes, and it seems he told the people this in a language we could not understand.

The Ingalik, and the Kwikpakmiut as well, bury their dead in the following manner: four posts are erected to about the height of a man and on them is set the burial box, consisting of two rectangular boxes with a layer of clay between them to make them airtight. The inner box contains the body, which is covered with clay to protect it. The outer box is really the grave monument and is painted with red and black figures representing scenes of hunting and fishing in the life of the deceased. The red paint used in these paintings consists of some local clay, and the black is an artificial mixture of salmon eggs with some adhesive substance and pulverized charcoal. On the upper Yukon between Nuklukayet and Nulato I saw some grave boxes at burial sites that were partially set into the ground and the lids covered with piles of wood. At the burial sites one sees weapons and fishing gear on the men's graves and on the women's household utensils and clothing.

Continuing our journey, still on the same day we reached the villages of Norraden and Belase-karat. With northerly storms and headwinds we came the following noon to Nusaron and toward evening to Kommensita, without finding anything I could use. Here the Indians attacked us and threw away the wood we had just collected for cooking a meal on the shore. Our interpreter became very much alarmed and was sure we would be robbed of our possessions, which were very important to me. It was possible that their overbearing character might drive them to the extreme of murdering us and taking our goods, since they did not live in fear of revenge from the gunboats like those on Vancouver Island. They evidently wanted to commit this deed under the cover of darkness, so they followed us in half a dozen canoes. Petka steered us into a side stream where we camped in protective darkness and in rainstorms. We left the next morning without being followed, passed an Indian village about noon, and several hours later came to the mouth of the Kujikuk [Koyukuk] River. The wind changed to northeast and we could use the sail. As we approached Nulato we visited four villages upstream from there. We stayed only an hour in Nulato because of a favorable wind, and with that and the clear weather we continued until midnight. It was dark on the river, and since it was unfamiliar to

Fig. 36. Clay cooking pot. Upper Yukon River.

us we finally ran aground and camped overnight in the boat.

On 2 September at six o'clock in the morning we started out again. It stormed from the northeast, so we traveled fast. We visited two villages and bought articles made of bone, shell, and beads. In landing we broke a hole in the skin covering of the boat and spent the rest of the day bailing. In one village we visited that afternoon we found birchbark canoes, wooden dishes, baskets of birch bark, fishnets, and fish weirs. All the other utensils they had were of European, not American, origin. The northeasterly storm took us a long distance downstream. We found a deserted village and pulled our boat far up the bank to keep it from filling with water.

The next day we passed in quick succession Wetkelt-tokara, Kleitvit, Klaun-lokolte, and Kohara,[21] and in the last bought a few trifles. About six miles farther downstream our Ingalik pointed out a spot where mammoth bones had been found in a bank fifty to two hundred feet high. We stopped and searched the area, with success; after about two hours we found a large piece of the tusks of a mammoth, three molars, a vertebra, a joint, and so forth. These bones were not all in one place but were scattered along the bank, though they might have been washed in there when the river was flooded. The inner cores of the tusks were found at the mouth of a little creek. It is said that reindeer herders have found such bones in many parts of Alaska and call them "devil bones." In the spring of 1882 many bones were found at the site where we were.

In our haste to collect mammoth bones we forgot to tie the boat securely and it broke away into the middle of the river. Fortunately some Indians in birchbark canoes came along and rescued it for us, for which they were well rewarded.

At seven o'clock in the evening we reached Sakara. Here a famous shaman had died and was to be buried the next day. Many Indians had gathered to share in the funeral feast. Among the Ingalik as well as among the Kwikpakmiut the dead were buried after four days, and during this time no work was done. This relates to a story I will tell later. I had the unusual opportunity of seeing the corpse. He was dressed and seated in a crouching position on a kind of stool that stood on four posts driven into the ground. His back rested against two of these, and the other two supported his arms. The house was otherwise empty of furniture, and in it were the wives of friends and relatives who had come with quantities of food that was respectfully placed before the dead. It seemed as though the shaman, who had his eyes half open like a person in thought, were still alive and expected to enjoy the food. During this time nobody was allowed to enter the funeral house. The Indians remained outside in a serious ceremonial

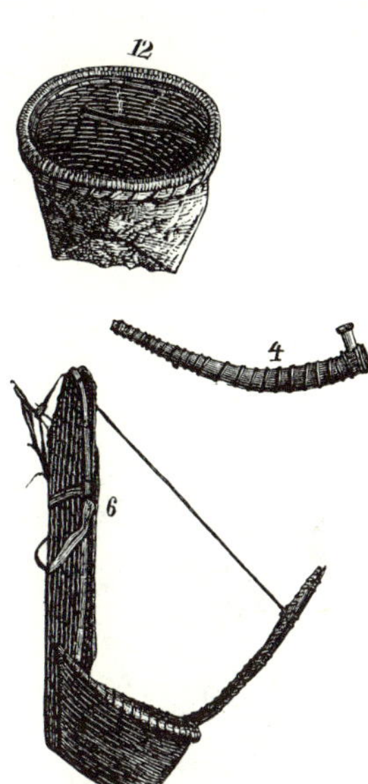

Fig. 37. Artifacts used by the Ingalik of the upper Yukon River: (4) pipe for tobacco, made of two pieces of wood lashed together, with a metal bowl; (6) baby cradle made of birch bark; (12) basket made of birch bark.

mood. No one laughed or spoke loudly. Unfortunately my time was too short to remain for the entire occasion. The only effort I made to buy ethnographic specimens from the people was fruitless. First they said they did not have anything, and later they said that because of the shaman's funeral they could not carry on trade. All complained about the current epidemic among them, which brought a very heavy cough. Many who had it lost their voices. They asked me for drugs to relieve this sickness, but since I had nothing of the kind with me I could not oblige them.

As we have so often realized that events do not occur singly but follow each other in quick succession, so on the same day when we continued our journey we encountered another Indian funeral. Toward evening we had landed at a village and I visited an Indian house to purchase some specimens when I found a motionless, stiff man seated in the middle of the room surrounded with food carried in and out by women. The sight was so realistic that I approached it very closely before I saw that the entire back of the head was a great bloody wound. The poor man had been killed by a grizzly bear which he came upon quite unexpectedly while he was in a canoe. He tried to shoot him with buckshot, and when he missed the bear upset the canoe with one stroke of his paw and killed the man with another. Another Indian then came along, killed the bear, and picked up his friend, who died in his arms. It was told me as a great curiosity that the head of the bear was almost white.

We continued another five miles the same evening, and since my companion, Petka, did not trust the Indians we camped outdoors. We started out again at six o'clock in the morning and came to a little village where almost everyone suffered from the illness mentioned above. The need for medicine became greater than ever. At this village I found an unusual instance of an Ingalik having two wives, although his tribesmen had the custom of having only one. A little below this village I put both my companions on shore so that they could go along the bank and look for mammoth bones. Meanwhile I stayed in the boat and paddled along slowly, occasionally stepping out to help in the search. We found a few remains, mostly molars. They had obviously fallen down from the riverbank, for they were covered with the same black soil that was visible in one of the upper layers. The Indians said that in the spring of 1881 the Western Trading Company had excavated four large, well-preserved mammoth tusks. In the afternoon we reached Anvik, where we were hospitably received by the wife of the manager of the station, Mrs. Frederiksen, Petka's sister. After we unloaded our boat and set it up to dry out we en-

Fig. 38. (1) Sock woven of basket grass; (2) hunting gear on belt. Ingalik.

joyed a steambath and the luxury of sleeping again in a house and in a bed.

Even though the Ingalik collection was limited in variety it finally added up to about two hundred pieces. Among them were bows and arrows and an iron lance with a strong wooden shaft, as well as modern hunting gear. The nets were generally made of moose and caribou sinew, and some were of nettle fiber. Caribou were hunted in winter in the deep snow, in which it was difficult for the animals to move. The Indians pursued them on snowshoes and killed many. The snowshoes, of which I purchased a number of pairs, are from three to five feet long and are made of a wooden frame divided into three areas by crossbars. A webbing of caribou sinew is woven within this frame, and the crossbars also serve as a base for fastening the shoe with leather thongs. Among the household utensils were oval wooden dishes with the rim ornamented in a kind of mosaic of little stones. The Ingalik, like the Kwikpak-miut, have special dishes for eating for both men and women. Among the Ingalik one finds many birchbark vessels as well as wooden water buckets and dippers. The buckets were carved out of pieces of wood that had been steamed and bent and sewed together with root and then had wooden bottoms fitted into them. These buckets have a wooden or bone handle. The dippers are made the same way but are smaller and have a handle on the side which is a continuation of the side itself.

The Ingalik make a good deal of pottery, principally clay pots for cooking and lamps. The pots are quite large and reach the circumference of half a herring keg. The gray clay is worked with the hands, without a potter's wheel, but with a stone or a piece of bone. Most of them have designs incised with a stick.

The Ingalik usually dress in jackets made of tanned moose-skin that is smoked a little after tanning to give it a reddish brown color. These jackets are decorated with beads and shells which earlier were trade items from Fort Yukon and Fort Sel-kirk through the Hudson's Bay Company or the Chilkat Indi-ans, who came with their trade goods as far as the Tanana River on the upper Yukon. At present the Alaska Commercial Company is supplying the articles. The other pieces of cloth-ing worn by the Ingalik—trousers, boots, and gloves—are not decorated very much. The natives between Anvik and Nulato make themselves clothing of salmon and other kinds of fish skin. These garments are worn especially during the wet sea-son in the autumn and spring and have the advantage of not getting stiff and hard in cold weather. The Indians make a kind of sock out of fine grass which they gather in summer,

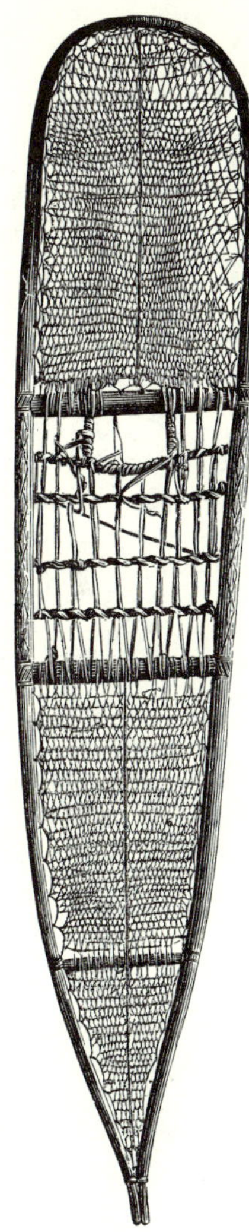

Fig. 39. Snowshoe used by the Ingalik of the upper Yukon River.

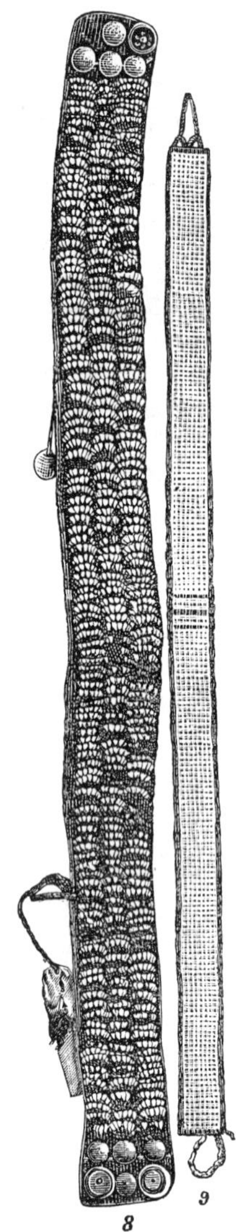

Fig. 40. (8) Woman's belt decorated with caribou teeth; (9) woman's belt decorated with ptarmigan quills.

and they make baskets and mats of the same material. Especially fine and useful are the canoes made of birch bark by the Ingalik. I have bought two models of these canoes for a special purpose for the Berlin Museum.

Our skin boat did not have an opportunity to dry out in Anvik because of the weather, but I had to continue our journey nevertheless. Now I bought everything that had any ethnological significance. Among the items were several well-preserved stone axes, a number of handsome masks, and a belt ornamented with caribou teeth. The Ingalik who had accompanied me from Nuklukayet left me here, and in his place I engaged another man for the distance to Fort Saint Michael.

Since the rainstorms from the west and southwest did not diminish, I left Anvik on 6 September and soon came to the village of Makkiem [Makak], whose Russian name was Barnassella. Here I bought several things, including stone knives, stone axes, and wooden dishes ornamented with stones which a native falsely tried to pass off as fossilized mammoth bones. A few miles below this village we met in midstream the steamer *Yukon*, on its way back from Nuklukayet. On board this time as captain was my countryman Mr. Frederiksen as well as two traders from the Alaska Commercial Company, a few half-breeds, and many Indians from the Tananah [Tanana] River, which empties into the Yukon above Nuklukayet. These Indians had undertaken the long trip to Fort Saint Michael just to see the great salt water. They were earning their free passage back by cutting wood for the engine. Mr. Frederiksen wanted to take me back to Anvik with him, but time did not allow this. Practically everyone on board, traders and Indians alike, seemed to be suffering from the illness found among the people we saw on the river, which seems to be an epidemic of coughing. We left the steamer and continued until after dark.

The last Ingalik village of any importance was Koserowsky, where we found a few old pieces. Some distance below the village we came upon an Indian burial ground, where I found a good grave box that is now in the Berlin Museum. In the inner box I found wrapped in a woven mat the mummy of a woman, her head covered with a cap of glass beads. The young Indian who was with us did not raise any objection to our taking these pieces. Soon afterward we left the territory of the Ingalik and entered that of the Kwikpakmiut.

13

The white settlers in Alaska do not make any distinction between the almost pure Indian tribes of the interior and the Eskimo population that lives along the coast. In fact, the entire population is often referred to as "Indian"; but when one wants to be specific, they are called by their local names, such as Kwikpakmiut, Malemiut, Kuskoquimiut. On the Yukon River the transition from one group to the other shows in the place names. So it happened that on the same day we left the last large Ingalik village and arrived at the first Kwikpakmiut village, called Kingerumiut. The epidemic was here also, and the demand for medicine was so urgent that I could no longer remain uncooperative, so I gave them tea and sugar, and finally when this ran out I tried black pepper to drink in hot water. This met with great success, and the people said it was strengthening and warming. While rearranging the load on board, I had the misfortune to drop my last revolver overboard and could not find it. On the afternoon of the same day we came to Takkjelt-Pileramiut, where there were only a few people because many had gone hunting. I did buy some very nice small pieces here, but they did not wish to sell me anything from the burial sites close to the village. On many of the Eskimo graves there were carved figures of the deceased, heavily decorated with beads, especially the female figures. One could see by the painting on the boxes what occupation the deceased person had followed in his lifetime. If he was a fisherman there were scenes of fishing, and if a hunter graphic scenes of the hunt. On the boxes were also masks of animals and spirits. It was distressing that these pieces could not be bought.

Later I passed two more small villages and camped on the riverbank late in the evening. At noon the next day we came to the large village of Eparsluit, a Russian name given it by Gregori Schapka in reference to a sugarloaf shaped rock six or eight miles away. An hour later we passed the station, Mis-

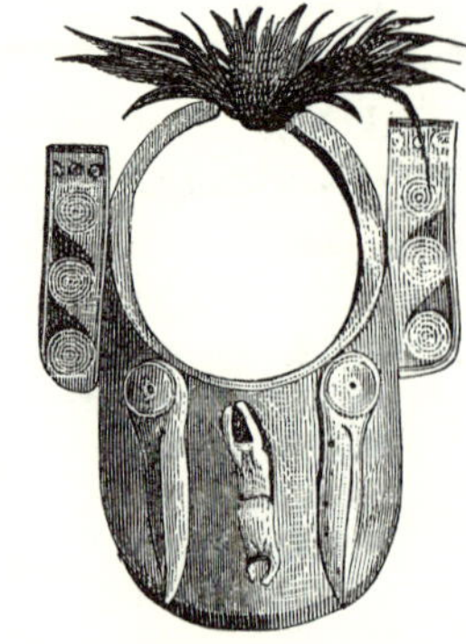

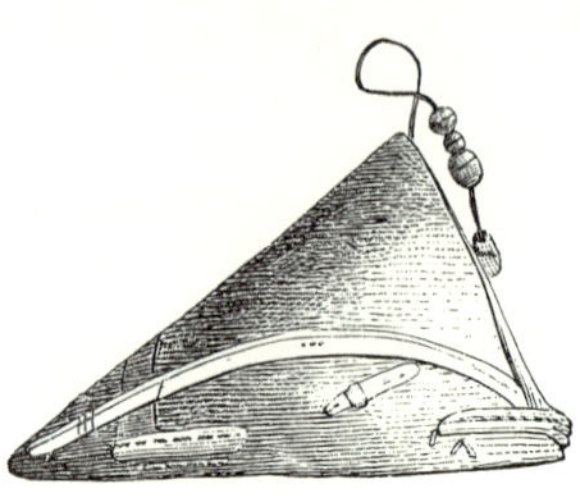

Fig. 41. Two hunting hats made of wood bent by steaming, decorated with carved ivory and the feathers of the parasitic jaeger. Used by Eskimo and Aleut. Lower Yukon River and Kuskokwim.

sion, already described (chap. 11), where we paused for a short time, and by five o'clock in the afternoon we visited Nunalinak, where I bought some good stone pieces. Toward seven o'clock we came to a mythological site where my Indians insisted on taking a side trip to see the place where a giant bird lived who attacked adults and carried them to his nest as food for his children. I was assured that on a nearby mountaintop were the remains of the nest and even bones that I would want to collect. I was convinced and pitched our tent for the night, then engaged a young Indian to take me to the next village, the site of the nest. By a forced march we reached the 1,500–1,800-foot-high mountaintop, which we could recognize from the distance as a steep towerlike structure. Because of my past climbing experience I succeeded in ascending the thirty-foot high rock that was supposed to be the nest of the giant bird, but there was not a sign of anything in it. However, the view of the landscape from here was worth the effort. An endless fine veil of golden fog was lying on the land between the Yukon and the Kuskowkim Rivers, while the small waterways and lakes lay on the land like a net.

It was already getting dark when we left this unforgettable sight and started back to the boat on the riverbank. My presence had become known and a number of people gathered and discussed my trip up the mountain with great eagerness. Their faith in the presence of this bird was not shaken by my not finding it, and some of the older ones insisted that in their youth they had seen the giant bird with their own eyes. It was also said that an Eskimo found the leg bones of an unusually large bird and gave them to a traveling scholar. This is supposed to have been Mr. Nelson, who was collecting for the Smithsonian Institution. On the way down from the "nest" we found fresh bear tracks, and the Indian carried an ax in a position from which he could split the head of an animal at a moment's notice. Neither the bear nor the Indian myths interfered with our appetite when we found a roasted goose ready for us.

The next morning we started early and came to the village of Ka-krome, where my purchases took an hour. Here again we were at a mythological site, which I mentioned on our journey upstream. One finds here along the rocks on the banks and down at the water's edge the remainders of houses for about four English miles. However this may be, it is certain that Alaska once had possibly fifty times as many inhabitants, but where the boundaries were between the Eskimo and the Indians would be hard to guess. We needed only an hour downstream to reach a village that is considered the border of the former populous area. I made a few purchases here and went on to Kjukkarremiut,[22] where the people likewise had gone caribou hunting, leaving the village to numerous dogs. They took their task of protection very seriously as we tried to hold them off while we walked through the village and back to the boat. We sailed away in a strong headwind and a thunderstorm, and we were weary and soaked when we set up our camp just above Dakketkjeremiut.

The Kwikpakmiut, like all the tundra people on the Kuskokwim River, buried their dead in the same way as the Ingalik, as I have already stated, in boxes set on four posts. On the lower Yukon the grave boxes are usually set on the ground and covered with stones and wood to keep the lid from falling off. At Cape Vancouver, the western coast of the tundra, I later saw a number of very high grave monuments, as much as twenty to thirty feet above the ground. One carried a wooden sculpture of a seal to indicate that the deceased was killed or drowned while seal hunting. Another carried a caribou for the same reason, and beside it were small human figures with eyes and mouths inlaid with walrus teeth. Unfortunately I did not frequently have the opportunity to see a good burial site.

The Ingalik and Kwikpakmiut legend that decrees restraint from all work for four days until the burial is the following: In a large village on the lower Yukon a very powerful man lived with a beautiful daughter. He was visited once by a man with his wife and son. They were unusual because of their dwarfed size, but word was spread that the young man was a great shaman. He substantiated the rumor and impressed the whole neighborhood with his remarkable cures. His host was so pleased that he gave the young shaman his beautiful daughter in marriage. A great misfortune occurred when the young woman died on her wedding night. The young groom in his sorrow ordered a very ceremonious burial and announced that no work was to be done in the village for four whole days. After this four-day period the body was buried and the young man and his parents left the village, never to be seen again.

At seven o'clock on the foggy morning of 10 September we landed at Dakketkjeremiut. Here my lucky period of collecting began, for in the villages of the lower Yukon there was much more to be found. I especially bought stone knives and axes. It was here that I discovered the fake reproductions the Eskimo made by carving stone knives of soft stone and boiling them in oil to make them look old. But still I found a rich collection in the village of Ankasagemiut, called Razboinski by the Russians.

Now my skin boat was so full of purchases that it was not sensible to camp anywhere in the neighborhood of a village because of the curiosity of the natives. We found a place the next night on the right bank of the Yukon, which we discov-

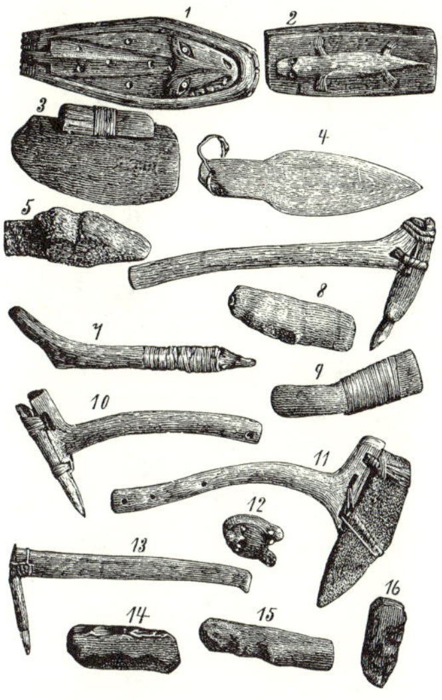

Fig. 42. Artifacts from the lower and middle Yukon River, where Ingalik and Eskimo meet: (1, 2) small trinket boxes, lids carved and inlaid with shells; (3) woman's knife with stone blade; (4) stone dagger; (5) stone ax; (6) hafted adze; (7) skin scraper with stone blade and wooden handle; (8) stone ax; (9) skin scraper with stone blade and wooden handle; (10, 11) stone adzes with caribou-antler handles; (12) snuffbox; (13) stone adze with wooden handle; (14, 15, 16) stone axes.

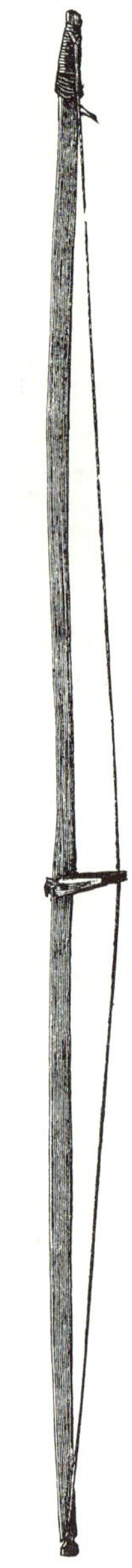

Fig. 43. Bow used by the
Ingalik of the upper
Yukon River.

ered had just lately been an assembly place for all the bears in
western Alaska, as the fresh footprints showed. It was very
late and even though my companions were afraid we stayed
and, rolled in our blankets, slept well in spite of bears and
wolves. We left at dawn with a strong wind against us, but
arrived at noon at Kingerumiut, where I also found a good
harvest. Since meeting any craft on the Yukon is an event, this
is written in my diary: "We met a number of natives from
Kusilwak on their way to trade on the upper Yukon. At noon
we met our former pilot Charles Pettersen, the station agent at
Andreafsky, who was going upstream in his schooner, carrying building materials. After half an hour of pleasant conversation with him we continued on our way."

A storm and unfavorable winds caused us such tiresome
paddling that we stopped very early for camp. We found a
little side canal of the Yukon for the boat and came upon a
grave monument on which a hunting scene was carved with
a bear pierced with an arrow, and beside it a post in imitation
of a bow. On the ground was a piece of an old stone vessel
which still showed bits of red paint and probably had been a
paint pot. The grave was evidently a cenotaph, since there
were no human remains, and I took it to be a memorial to
someone killed by a bear. Since this monument would be admired by many more people in the newly completed Royal
Ethnological Museum in Berlin than here on the banks of the
Yukon, and since it was made to be seen, I took it with me.

Still facing the storm, we started at dawn and arrived at
Andreafsky at ten o'clock in the morning. There was nobody
there, so we continued through the storm and waves, passing
two villages, and camped in a side canal.

The difficulties with the storm were compensated for by fine
weather the next day. Later in the day we began struggling
with the elements stirred up by the solstice, and late in the
afternoon we came to the Kusilwak River, the largest of the
streams forming the delta of the Yukon. We visited a village,
Nanowarogemiut, where the population was represented by
two old women, who brought a stone ax and a stone arrow
point. They mentioned an archaeological site, but I was in too
much of a hurry to start a "dig."

As we left we met a veritable cyclone, and we finally were
thrown against a fallen tree at the foot of an array of cliffs.
Our sails were torn, the rudder was damaged, and the steering
pole with which I had been trying to fend the boat off from
the rocks was broken. Night came on and we could see nothing of the landscape. At last we succeeded in getting one of the
Indians on the shore and could pass the boxes of artifacts to
him and fish out of the water the baskets, wooden bowls, and

other pieces that were floating around. The mammoth tusks were so heavy that we could not move them until I stepped out into the chest-high water to release the boat. This took the larger part of the night, and we were as wet as water rats. The storm had died down enough so that at least we could hear each other speak. We set up our tent and lighted a fire, for it was raining and snowing. We set the tent in a little green spot between the trees, and through the night gusts of wind tried to lift it like a balloon.

The next morning we found that we had come through the perils of the night very well. Our clothes were reasonably dry, and to our great joy we found that the skin boat did not have a single hole. When we got under way again we visited three Eskimo villages and came to Kotlik, an Alaska Commercial Company post where we spent the night. Early next morning we left the Yukon and cruised along the coast to Pastolik, a village of the Kwikpakmiut Eskimo. Because the water was shallow along the shore, I could not approach the village to make any purchases, but a message from us brought out six kayaks and I bought stone axes, lance points, and so forth.

By four in the afternoon we came to the very similarly named neighboring village of Pastoliak. Now that we were so close to Fort Saint Michael my Indian became homesick, so Petka insisted that we go as fast as possible to reach it. Regretfully I consented, for there were storm clouds on the horizon and there was no harbor along this coast. Less than an hour passed before we heard the howling of the oncoming storm that was approaching us. At first the wind was favorable for us and our boat acted like a whale, but it was no longer amusing when the waves poured so much water into our boat that we could not bail fast enough.

What to do? All of the Bering Sea was trying to pour into Norton Sound, and we were in the breakers. There was no alternative to allowing ourselves to be tossed onto the shore. We jumped out quickly and carried the boxes above the tide. It was more dangerous and difficult than on the Yukon, but it went reasonably well and we could even set up our tent, which we surrounded with driftwood until it looked like a block house. We got a fire going and finally the situation was improved by a dish of tea.

The next morning the air was clear, but the storm was still hanging in the south. The infinite number of puddles on the beach had all frozen during the night, and even our clothes felt wet and cold. I was very sorry for my poor Indians, and I loaned them each a pair of stockings to protect their feet from frostbite. The wind was more overland than at sea and the breakers were not high, so that we could load the boat. The

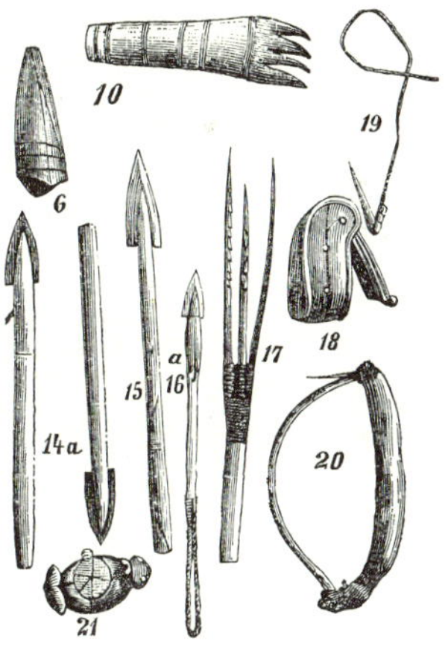

Fig. 44. Artifacts from the lower Yukon River: (6) wooden lance cover; (10) ice scratcher used for luring seals; (14, 15) stone lance points; (16) bone lance point; (17) trout spear; (18) wooden snuffbox; (19) wooden fishhook; (20) hook for carrying seal fat; (21) snuffbox in the form of a walrus lying on its back.

shore at Norton Sound would be a joy to geologists and geographers who wished to study the formation of a river delta from the clay and swamp deposits, but to us in loading the boat it meant wading and standing waist-deep in swamp with every piece we carried.

After this Herculean task was completed we started out and I noticed that my Indians were not as homesick as they had been before, though they seemed to have lost the interest in travel they had had. We passed Cape Romanzoff and put up our last two sails. The wind was right so that we cruised like a pleasure yacht, and although the waves were high at the cape we passed without danger.

After we passed the cape the wind became stronger, and after a council we decided to go as far as the Pikmiktalik River and to wait out the storm there. But when we came near, such a great desire rose in all of us to get to the end of the journey that we continued by sailing, rowing, and towing the boat on a line until on the same evening we were within ten miles of our goal. The next morning the wind was perfectly still, so that we towed the boat along the canal by the line. About noon we finally arrived at Fort Saint Michael; where Mr. Lorenz and Mr. Neumann welcomed us, and where a schooner lay in the harbor—none other than the *Leo,* luckily back from its trip to Point Barrow.

14

I had to find quarters in Fort Saint Michael, for I was planning to stay there for some time. My next tour was to the north, where I could go only in the winter months. The autumn is the least desirable time to travel in Alaska because of many storms, heavy rainfall, many snowstorms, and uncertain condition of the ground for the use of sleds. My next goal was to be on Seward Peninsula, where at Cape Prince of Wales I would be closest to Asia across Bering Strait; then I would go to Kotzebue Sound, which had not been visited by white travelers, and beyond as far north as possible. For this purpose I had ordered a number of sled dogs at Kotlik at the mouth of the Yukon, for later delivery.

The presence of the *Leo* in the harbor of Fort Saint Michael was a great help for my winter excursion, since before its departure for San Francisco it was going to the north side of Norton Sound to survey Golovnin Bay and would take part of my supplies. I would come back with them.

After the 1,800-mile voyage on the Yukon, one of my first needs was to get myself clean. Then I had to send a report to Professor Bastian in Berlin and write to my friends at home.

The next morning I visited the *Leo* with my mail and found that Lieutenant Paul and the captain had had a very good trip, without damage to the ship, and were well paid for their work by the United States government. His ship made the trip to Point Barrow without any "ice skin" and on the way obtained through trading about $3,000 worth of walrus ivory and baleen. On his trip to Golovnin Bay he was to collect some quartz and pick up a few prospectors who wished to go to San Francisco. Since the ship did not leave until the next day I hurriedly bought some provisions and other necessities and rushed them to be delivered at Golovnin Bay.

After all this business was completed I had to devote my entire attention to the collection, which I found in sad condition. Although the pieces were made in the Alaskan climate, they were not expected to go through two shipwrecks when, on account of circumstances, I could not give them the conservator's care they deserved. This I tried to correct.

The friendly cooperation I received from the Alaska Commercial Company gave me an opportunity to unpack everything, dry and clean the items, and tag each piece with its use and provenance. Petka helped me with this and stayed in my service for a little while longer. He was acquainted with the handling of skin garments, which I did not know, and also showed himself very skillful in packing, but he did not know the proper names of the Ingalik from whom we bought many pieces, probably because he was a half-breed. Regrettably, the real Ingalik who had traveled with us started for home immediately after we arrived at Fort Saint Michael. However, we finished our time-consuming task in one week.

It was now time for all kinds of hunting, and everyone, natives and whites, prepared themselves for it. On 28 September I went to the station of the Western Fur Trading Company and found that the agent, Mr. Greenfield, was arranging a large hunting party, including even his wife and their children and Mr. Leavitt, the signal service officer. They all seemed to trust the northern weather. Since I had nothing else to do I joined the party. The same day I rented two kayaks, light skin-covered boats made like those of the Eskimo of Greenland and Labrador, with the difference that those have the skin stretched in a gable shape in the front while the local ones are flat. The two kayaks were of different sizes; the principal vessel had three seat holes, and the smaller only one. We left in the afternoon and went to the entrance of the canal, where we met Mr. Greenfield's party, and after a picnic supper on the bank we spent the night in a number of tents.

In the gray dawn I went out with the three Indians I had engaged and slogged through the swampy morass along the banks, getting a single duck. The reason was that the tundra was already full of Eskimo from the neighboring villages, who were lurking in the lakes and lagoons and scared away all the ducks, geese, and ptarmigan. At eight o'clock we returned for the community breakfast, took down our tent, and left with the whole party, going farther down the canal. When Mr. Greenfield and his party camped at the end of the canal I took my two kayaks a few miles farther south along the coast, well known to me, and landed at the mouth of a little river. In the early evening hours we hunted again, and here in this less populated area we shot five ducks. We camped at this same place, even though a storm broke which again tried to make a captive balloon of our tent.

Storm, rain, and eagerness for the hunt did not let us wait for the end of the night, so we went out at dawn and stayed until noon. For that length of time we had little to show, for in our surroundings our bodies were the tallest objects in sight and the geese and ducks noticed us by our reflections in the small ponds where they were swimming. Also, we began to tire of the constant "sucking" through the swamp only to be seen by the "sky birds." We ended our "pleasure" and went back to the canal where the waves of Norton Sound almost foundered our large kayak.

Toward evening we arrived back at the mouth of the canal, dog tired from sitting in the kayak with our legs stretched out at right angles to our bodies. We set up the tent on the shore and spent the night there. The second hunting party had already started for home. We hunted again until eight o'clock in the morning and then also headed home.

The storm was still not over, but we figured out a maneuver to use its strength without endangering ourselves: we brought the two kayaks side by side and fastened them together with some boards. In this way they worked like the outriggers used in the South Pacific, supporting each other and preventing each other from turning over. Then we put up our tent pole as a mast and my rubber blanket as a sail, and the storm was so accommodating that we went through the canal at great speed!

There was just one problem we had not considered: the waves sprayed water into the hatches of the kayaks and we were not in a position to bail it out. We did not have the kamelikas that kayak boatmen usually wear. This is a waterproof jacket that is pulled over the head and covers the torso, then is fastened to the kayak opening with a ring that is laced to the kayak (the jacket is made of seal or walrus intestines). With this a person in a kayak can go through any kind of wind and waves. This is also found in Labrador and Greenland.

Since we did not have these, the waves soaked us until the salty water trickled down inside the kayak. To try to protect ourselves we used a panel of a feltlike grass fiber that had been torn loose from the shore to cover the front of the two boats, but as more and more water poured in we were in danger of sinking. When we reached Fort Saint Michael we were greeted with cheers because we were the last of the hunting party to arrive. If one is accustomed to the outdoors and from childhood has experienced wind and weather, these adventures are not injurious to one's health and do not disturb one; my European home lies about twenty English miles north of Fort Saint Michael in latitude and the weather is much the same. The results of the hunt were twenty-five ducks and five geese, half of which I shot. A warm meal and dry clothing was all we needed.

I am writing on 9 October, and I am celebrating my thirtieth birthday in meditation and reminiscence. I thought of my distant home and the responsibility I had undertaken for the Berlin Museum. I again was in one of those situations in my life when the end results could not be foreseen. The weather had calmed down, and there was no indication of any immediate frost. Since it was impossible for me to start out until the frost came and I could not order my Eskimo sled dogs to be brought from Kotlik, I was faced with perhaps several weeks of waiting, which is the most difficult situation for someone accustomed to action.

The next day I went on a little anthropological-ethnological expedition to an excavation on a nearby island (Whale Island), a rocky place similar to Helgoland, where a few landing places showed the remains of villages which, according to local hearsay, were about 150 to 200 years old. The remains of the houses in two rows near the landing places were easily recognized. The excavation revealed pieces of pottery, broken stone axes, lance points, stone knives, arrows, and bones of both land and sea mammals. These pieces did not differ from the artifacts I had been buying in the vicinity. To the left of the village and far above the sea was a burial ground. I opened a few graves and found the bodies so far decayed that it was impossible to consider transporting them to Europe.

The next day a letter from my former traveling companion, Mr. Woolfe, ended my period of inactivity. He had had the good fortune to secure the first reports of the research on Wrangel Island, which he sent to the *New York Herald*. While he was at Fort Saint Michael he went to the north shore of Norton Sound, to the east of Golovnin Bay, to Orowignarak [Ogowinagak] and stayed with a highly respected Eskimo named Eisak,[23] who was the agent and trader for the Alaska Commercial Company extensively, even as far as Kotzebue Sound. His house, in which his large family and several other people lived, had burned down, and Mr. Woolfe had injured his arm and hand. The letter stated that a new house was being built and that Eisak would like to have a fresh supply of trading goods from the company. Mr. Lorenz decided to send a boat with the necessary goods to Ogowinagak at once and for this purpose prepared my old skin boat that I had used on the Yukon.

My original decision to stay at Fort Saint Michael until the frost came was therefore cast to the winds. I offered to take the consignment as far as Golovnin Bay, since I had to go there anyway on my way to Kotzebue Sound. And since the region was within the territory of the Kwikpakmiut, I would have an opportunity to make my collection from them more complete, since I could land at their villages.

My suggestion was accepted, but I almost failed to go on this trip because of an incident that endangered my life. In the summer Mr. Lorenz had a cow sent from San Francisco to furnish fresh milk for his family, but in the winter fodder could not be provided for the animal, so it was decided to slaughter it and the job was given to me. In the eyes of the Eskimo this horned, cud-chewing beast looked like a terrific monster. So I had a Russian throw a rope around her neck so I could stab her in the base of the neck in toreador style, but the Russian became frightened and dropped the rope. The enraged cow lowered her horns and came to attack me. Just in the nick of time the fatal blow was delivered, and that evening we had steak for supper.

When everything was ready for the journey I engaged a young Eskimo named Kanojak, meaning "copper," and left with the good wishes of my friends on 15 October in my old skin boat that had already carried me 1,800 miles from Fort Saint Michael. We landed the first evening in the Kwikpakmiut village of Kikertaok [Kikertarok], where we spent the night in the kassigit (dance house).

The next morning the weather forced me to stay there, so I spent my time making some purchases. Among them was some unusual fire-making equipment formerly used; it consists of the two well-known pieces of wood, one of which is held vertically through a bow drill, with its horn bit in a hollow of the second board, and rapidly moved to and fro until the pulverized wood first creates some smoke, then bursts into flame. After my return to Berlin, when I unpacked my collection, Mr. Woldt, the editor of the account of my journey, asked me to demonstrate this. I brought it to a bright fire from which the men present lit their cigars.

Among other things I acquired in Kikertarok was nephrite, a kind of green stone that arouses great discussions in anthropological research from many parts of the world. Later I found examples of this valuable stone used in practical utensils by the Eskimo. I will discuss nephrite later where it is necessary. Among the artifacts made of nephrite were two drill points, and other artifacts included stone axes and harpoons. Long visits in these villages were not very profitable, since the Eskimo take these only as occasions for the most shameless begging. The next day I continued my journey but had to make a side trip. In addition to the Eskimo Kanojak, I also had on board the Eskimo who brought Mr. Woolfe's letter to Fort Saint Michael. He had to walk the last miles of the trip. He left his kayak in the vicinity of Kikertaok, and we found the boat near the house where an Eskimo family had just made themselves at home to join the hunt for the especially large variety of seals.

We continued on our journey along the coast the next morning, making a sharp turn to the north. Since there was almost no wind we tried the method, often used in Alaska, of tying a line to a skin boat and pulling it along the shore, getting along much faster than if we were paddling. My two Eskimos were not good oarsmen. We now approached the last of the Kwikpakmiut villages, Unalaklik [Unalakleet]. About ten miles before reaching there I noticed a sizable outcropping of coal. About noon we met an Eskimo named Saxo, well respected by the Alaska Commercial Company, who annually makes a trading trip for the company to Prince of Wales Peninsula and Bering Strait and also across the strait to the mainland of Asia for trade with the Chukchee. Saxo is a large man with tremendous body strength and is one of the handsomest Eskimo I know in Alaska. He is friendly to the whites and is known for his courtesy and helpfulness. He has this respect in spite of the fact that he has committed a number of murders. They happened in this way.

Saxo was born on Sledge, or Aziak, Island at the south end of the Bering Strait and moved in the early 1870s with his younger brother and several relatives to Unalakleet for his permanent home. An Eskimo named Arnakpeik was a smuggler of Siberian whiskey and was known to have killed Eskimo and Indians after he had gotten them drunk. To be more invincible he gathered around himself a bodyguard of young people who followed his orders. To prove his absolute invulnerability he acquired an iron cuirass from a whale hunter. He boasted about it and ordered his bodyguard to shoot him. When this happened Arnakpeik was not injured. He became so bold that he decided to become the most important power in Alaska.

One day he became very angry at the Alaska Commercial Company and let it be known that the next time he came to Fort Saint Michael he would burn down their trading establishment. Mr. Rudolf Neumann, with whom I stayed, was the agent, and he set a day and night watch on the buildings. One day a small flotilla appeared with Arnakpeik and his fellow murderers. When they were still a musket shot away Mr. Neumann sent a messenger saying that if he did not leave at once he would turn the large cannon on them. Arnakpeik assured him that he had come only to trade, but did turn away.

Since he did not feel powerful enough to defeat the Alaska Commercial Company, he decided to terrorize the Eskimo in the neighborhood and tried to force them to become partners with him. One day when he was drunk with his Siberian whiskey, a few Ingalik came to Unalakleet on their way home on the overland trail. In order to gain possession of the goods the Ingalik had obtained in trade and distribute it among his retainers, Arnakpeik decided to kill them and included in his plot Saxo, with whom he had been living in peace, enjoying his hospitality daily, and not fearing any chance of betrayal on his part. When he told Saxo the plot and the latter refused, he threatened to kill him himself. Since Saxo knew that Arnakpeik kept his word in such matters, there was nothing he could do to protect himself but kill him first. So he went outside and returned with a sharp ax and split Arnakpeik's head open. The men in the house did not dare move except for the twenty-year-old son of Arnakpeik, who tried to escape. According to the Eskimo laws of revenge it was the son's duty to kill his father's murderer. When the son was bending over to go through the low entrance of the house Saxo aimed an ax at his back, which cut his spine and killed him instantly. This gave Saxo control of the situation, and he has remained feared and respected. The relatives of Arnakpeik have often tried to kill him, but he has become a kind of desperado who is ever watchful and sleeps with a revolver under his head. Since it was impossible to touch him, there was an attempt last winter on his younger brother.

We met Saxo and his brother when they were setting up a seal net about ten miles from Unalakleet. The frost that started a day or two before I left on this trip and brought with it some snowfall became heavier, so that we found six inches of ice at Unalakleet. Since it seemed risky to continue the trip in the skin boat, I decided to leave the load here and stayed overnight. Unalakleet is generally an unruly place, and we had scarcely an hour of sleep, since the people occupying the space with us did as they pleased; one started singing, another carried on a loud conversation with his neighbors, many coughed in a frightening manner, children screamed and cried, and the women were constantly doing something. In addition, the dogs howled from time to time.

The next morning I made an effort to continue the journey, but the ice conditions were very unfavorable in spite of improvement. The shallow water grounded us within a mile of the village. We sat firmly on a sandbank and worked several more hours, standing in ice cold water, trying to float the boat again. When we realized it was impossible, I walked back to the village and borrowed three kayaks and returned to my boat. It took several more hours to unload the heaviest pieces and float the boat again. The Eskimo were freezing pathetically, so out of pity I lent them several pieces of clothing. In addition to our other troubles the waves from the east came into our open boat, soaking us. This water did not run off, but froze until our clothing was stiff. This was my farewell to the Kwikpakmiut territory and my entry into that of the Malemiut who lived between Norton Sound and Kotzebue Sound.

15

After overcoming the difficulties of the sandbank we sailed until four o'clock in the afternoon and arrived at the first village of the Malemiut, Igawik [Egavik]. It was very cold, so we boiled some coffee, and after warming ourselves we had a favorable wind, but also more and more frost. It seemed impossible to get to the next village because the coast was covered with rocks and clay. In the evening after it grew dark, the tide was so strong that it took much effort to land in a little cove. We camped there in the open and the cold was so intense that even though we nearly scorched ourselves in front from the heat of the fire, our backs were almost frostbitten.

In these circumstances it was pleasant to leave, which we did as early as possible in the morning. Since the wind came from the shore, loading was easier than the unloading the previous night. We put the boat on a towline again and pulled it along the flat coast, but the ground was full of stones, and that was hard on the skin boat, which was easily injured. It is always toward the end of a trip that the hardships pile up, and it seemed now that we might have to abandon the journey. In the neighborhood of Schaktolik [Shaktolik], another Malemiut village, we met two Eskimo who helped us pull the tow. The water was so shallow that the boat had to be held away from the shore and it still hit the ground. An English mile from Shaktolik the inhabitants of the village, who had heard of our coming, came toward us to greet us in the customary way and brought presents. Then a small board with a piece of ice on it was laid before each of us. I was given a pair of skin boots and several muskrat skins. Since I knew that this involved giving in return gifts of much greater value, I did not accept the honor of receiving these. When we were about to depart the villagers told us that the water at their village was even shallower and we could not land. It was obvious that for some reason they did not want us to visit their village. The people

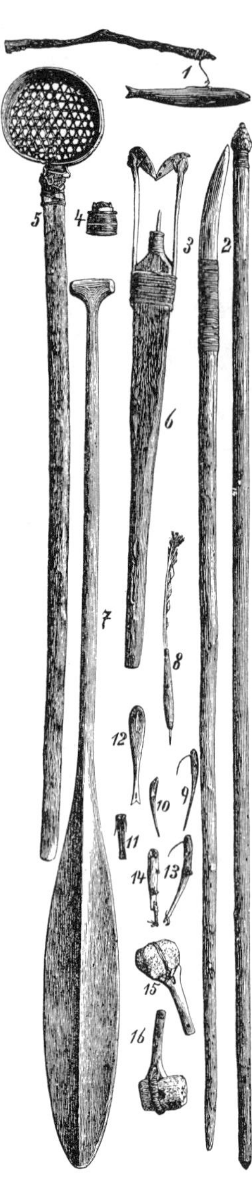

Fig. 45. Implements from the Kwikpakmiut and the Malemiut: (1) fish lure of mammoth bone; (2) lance with stone point; (3) ice breaker with stone point; (4) snuffbox; (5) ice scoop; (6) fish spear; (7) paddle; (8) gaming piece; (9–14) fishhooks; (15, 16) stone hammers with bone handles.

in this region are very superstitious, and as I found out later they believed our presence might be harmful to two sick children. To please them I camped on the banks near Shaktolik, but the poor children died soon after in spite of this. The frost, which had been limited to freshwater areas, now also moved to the salt water and covered the next bays with ice.

Reluctantly I accepted my own judgment and that of the Eskimo that the skin boat could no longer serve us, and I had to take all the goods to a little warehouse of the Alaska Commercial Company even though the agent was absent. I now borrowed a sled and three dogs in order to make the rest of the journey to Ogowinagak on foot. During the night a storm broke up the ice in the nearby river and I could not cross, so I spent my time hunting and shot eleven ptarmigan.

At last on the third day it was possible to go over the river with a sled. We took a little food and a few small things and bravely started on our march, coming to Unaktolik in the evening, very tired. I had left Kanojak, the Eskimo previously mentioned, to guard the goods I left at Shaktolik, and this left with me only the man who had brought the letter from Mr. Woolfe.

In Unaktolik we were given fresh fish to eat and slept well during the night, but in the morning we found that two of our three dogs were missing. After much searching we found the two curled up in the brush asleep. We continued to Iglotalik [Iglutalik], arriving by evening, and we were well received and again given fresh fish. It is an Eskimo custom after the evening meal to throw the wood, still burning, through the smoke hole in order to relieve the smokiness of the house. Usually these firebrands burn themselves out in the snow, but this night the sod roof began to burn and we had much trouble in putting it out. In Iglutalik I saw a very handsome amulet made of nephrite on one of the men, which I would gladly have purchased, but he would not sell it.

Here I borrowed two excellent dogs, and we started out in a big snowstorm coming from the north. At this point the east coast of Norton Sound turns left toward the north coast, so we shortened our journey by going diagonally across the frozen surface of Norton Sound and arrived at Kuikak. Here we made ourselves some tea and left the borrowed dogs. Now we were very close to Ogowinagak, which for some time had been my destination. The way there went around a few promontories where the ice of the storm had been swept away. Nothing hindered us and at five o'clock in the afternoon we arrived at the amply filled home of Father Eisak.

The occupants, as well as my former traveling companion, Mr. Woolfe, greeted me in a hearty manner, and the rest of the day was spent in exchanging experiences of the last few months. The house, as we had heard, was built and looked like a Norwegian peasant house, but it still had none of the partitions inside; so that gave Mr. Woolfe and me something to do in the next few days. Eisak began at once with his people to repair the harness for the dogs and the sleds to go to Shaktolik and bring the load I had left there to Ogowinagak.

It was always a puzzle to me why Eisak selected this place to settle. It seemed to lack all the necessary features for the Eskimo type of living, especially good hunting and fishing areas, the nearest being a small river quite a distance to the west. Eisak was forty years old and was born on Kotzebue Sound. His Eskimo name is Kaleak—in German, "a protector." He also called himself, as Eskimo often do, by a second name, Alok. In his youth in Kotzebue he had seduced the daughter of an important shaman and he fled here to Ogowinagak with her. She is his principal wife, and her name is Kuwaluk,[24] meaning muskrat.

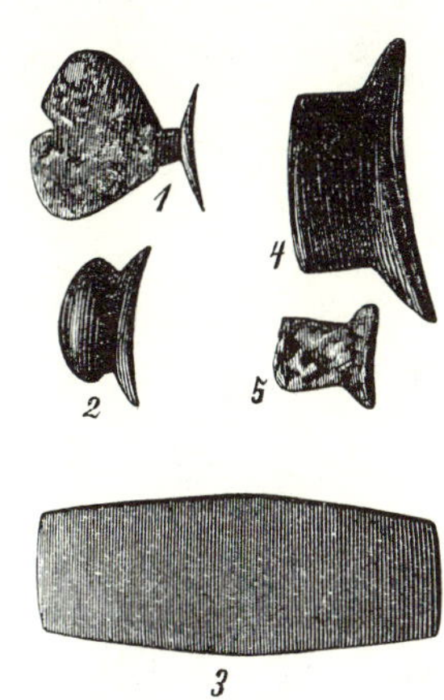

Fig. 46. Labrets: Malemiut and Kwikpakmiut, northwest Alaska.

I may be allowed to take this opportunity to count the number of people living in Eisak's household, for it is typical of an Eskimo dwelling:

Individual	Eskimo Name	Meaning of Name
Eisak	Kaleak, Alok	Protector
Eisak's principal wife	Kuwaluk	Muskrat
Eisak's second wife	Arnalukkik	———
Eisak's son	Kikertaurok	Island
Eisak's first daughter of second wife	Marschan	An edible root
Eisak's second daughter of second wife	Naunak	———
Eisak's unmarried adopted daughter	Sernak	Eagle's tail
Eisak's unmarried adopted daughter	Mayok	Steps upward
Eisak's adopted son	Kinjuran	Greedy for food
Eisak's cousin	Kajulik	Eel or tadpole
Eisak's adopted son	Kalurak	Hand net
Eisak's adopted son	Napaingak	Just grown up
Eisak's adopted sister	Awagarak	Hammer
Eisak's adopted daughter	Datluk	Snowshoes
Eisak's adopted sister	Tunraorak	Devil's woman or wife
Eisak's mother-in-law	Kijanuk	———
Eisak's two brothers	⎰ Kograk	———
	⎱ Akpak	———
A man, no relationship	Maktigelak	———

plus six to eight more persons of both sexes. It is obvious that this arrangement is not exclusively patriarchal. The mother-in-law of Eisak is a very resolute woman who once killed the woman she found with her husband and declared she would

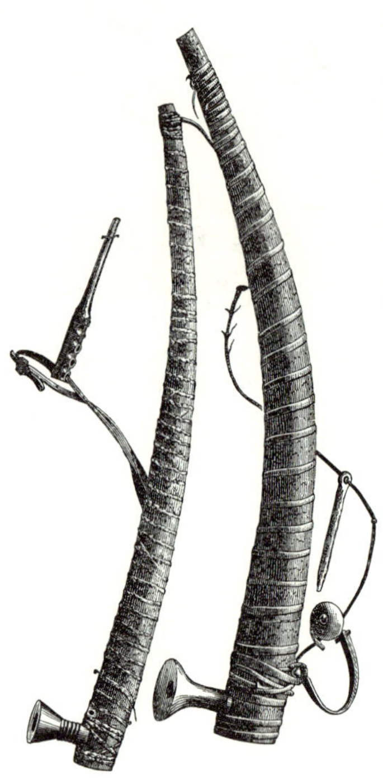

Fig. 47. Two pipes with wooden stems and bone bowls. Northwest Alaska.

do the same to every rival. It stands to reason that to feed such a large group was not easy, and makes it understandable that famine is frequent because of the length of the winter and because the only food available is what can be caught by hunting and fishing in the frozen sea. But I must also add that every Eskimo family is willing to share their food with guests, however greedy they are, as long as there is any food left. This works both ways, for it is also expected that former guests will reciprocate.

The day after my arrival four young Eskimo with two sleds and eight dogs went back the way I had come to pick up the load I had left at Shaktolik. In the meantime I busied myself in building a bunk bed for Mr. Woolfe and myself, for the sleeping arrangements in the house, side by side, were not agreeable to us. The usual Eskimo house had boards laid on the ground on three sides parallel with the walls and about six feet from them. This created a six-foot passage all the way around the interior walls of the house, covered with caribou skins and dried grass. This was the sleeping area for all occupants. They lay down beside one other with their feet toward the outer wall, and the boards were used to support their pillows. During the day the bedding was rolled up toward the wall and used as seating. The fire was always in the middle of the room, surrounded by stones, and food was prepared in large kettles. Usually the flames of the fire completely surrounded the kettle so that fish cooked quickly. The square skylight window in the roof was translucent, made of seal intestines sewed together, and was removed to let the smoke out when the fire was burning. The houses are built of driftwood, which is found everywhere.

My pleasure and efficiency in working were curtailed through a peculiar taboo put on me that can only be explained by the superstitions of the people. It was forbidden in the first days of my visit for everyone including me to use an ax or any other sharp instrument. This taboo evidently was applied so as not to drive away an Eskimo deity who was in the house before he could use his healing powers on Eisak's ailing son. This young man, who seemed to be on the way to recovery, used as his pillow a bag whose contents he kept carefully hidden. These were figures of this deity that had been given him by the shaman, who had been in Eisak's house quietly, without attracting my attention. He issued the taboo, although he was friendly and willing to help me in my work. The young man wore around his neck a valuable awl-shaped nephrite amulet about five inches long.

Eisak's principal wife, Kuwaluk, went off with a sled team to the river to get fish and came back with her catch after two days. During this time Mr. Woolfe took on the role of house-keeper and worked with the Eskimo girls in the house, play-fully learning the language. The preparation of our food was not so difficult, since we had the same food for every meal, consisting of "pancakes" made only of flour, water, and some fish oil. The sack of fish Mother Kuwaluk brought after a four-day effort did not change the menu radically. I was equally unable to change our food very much by hunting ptarmigan, since they were very shy.

My work on the house continued even without the use of an ax, and when I had completed five sleeping places the house began to have the appearance of those in my home rather than an Eskimo dwelling.

On the fourth day after our arrival the spirit came to the shaman in an evening gathering of the whole family, and he finished his cure of Eisak's son. The shaman began suddenly to roar like a sea lion and howl like an old dog while he ges-ticulated with his arms. He was handed a seal intestine jacket (kamelika). At the same time he took the valuable piece of nephrite from the patient's neck and wrapped it in a caribou-skin jacket, which he passed around so that everyone could feel it and be assured that the long, slim stone was in the package.

The Eisak family stared with open-mouthed wonder. In a secretive manner the shaman walked around the circle, blow-ing on the package and biting it. At last he said he was going to bend the stone sideways and then let everyone feel the rolled-up jacket again. It was a tense moment, as the faces of the family showed, for they believed that the life of the pa-tient depended on whether the stone amulet was bent.

Fortunately the shaman arranged it so that everyone could feel the jacket, then he shifted the stone again into its original position and it appeared completely unharmed. By this revela-tion the family knew that the patient would recover and they joyfully breathed more freely. During this performance I no-ticed that everyone was convinced that the stone was bent, only a young girl was not allowed to touch it and pulled her-self back from it. I discovered later that there was a taboo on women and girls during menstrual periods. They are also not allowed to use eating and drinking utensils with other mem-bers of the household, but have their own dishes.

Then, with many expressions of astonishment, the nephrite amulet was held close to the flame of the lamp and carefully examined for the slightest break. Now the shaman went into action with the wooden fetishes in his fur sack. First he brought out and showed a previously hidden figure of a wolf with the head of an alligator. This was put into the kamelika and held

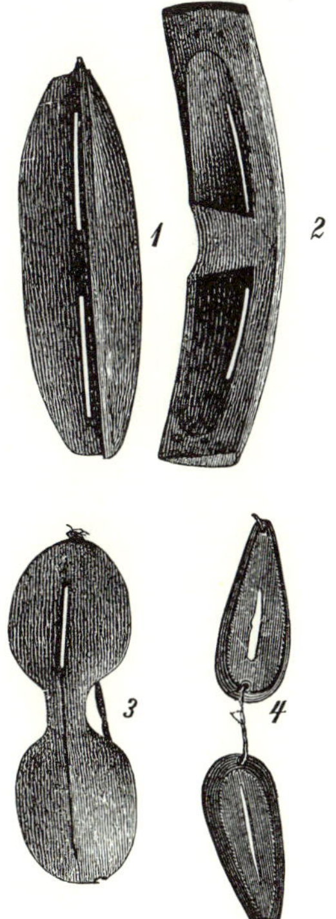

Fig. 48. (1–3) wooden snow goggles; (4) snow goggles made of mammoth bone. Northwest Alaska.

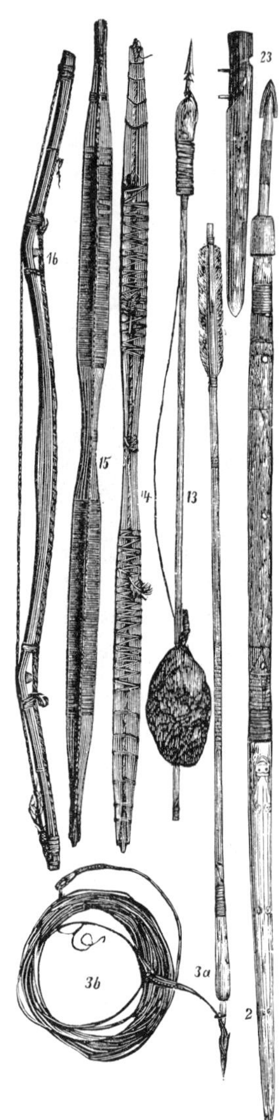

Fig. 49. Hunting gear from northwest Alaska: (1, 23) throwing boards for harpoons; (2) lance with double points; (3a, b) seal harpoon and line; (4) three-pronged bird harpoon, used at sea; (13) seal harpoon with bladder; (14, 15) front and back of bows; (16) bow from the Yukon area.

between the cupped hands of the shaman, who moved back and forth as though the image were plunging forward, then backward. At this point the shaman started bellowing again. Then he squeezed the figure and blew on its head and tail and slowly let it back into his sack.

Now the final act of this drama began with a representation of the spirit world. The old shaman took the kamelika and swung it in a circle, making a long-drawn-out sound, "Hui," at the same time, as though a storm wind was going through the house. Then he gave a few examples of ventriloquism, speaking in one voice far away and answering in his own voice. This was carried out with great skill and was done to impress the poor, ignorant Eskimo. Then the ceremony ended with some songs in which the whole family took part. Now the taboo on the use of iron implements was immediately raised and it was no longer necessary every morning to carry the fur tool bag outside and bring it back every night in order to work undisturbed.

Only one man who had been ill for a long time was forbidden to use iron tools. There was generally no healthy condition in the patriarchal household, for many young people and children had severe colds and suffered from racking coughs. It seems to me that the heavy fur clothing of the Eskimo does not contribute to conditioning the people to the raw climate of their environment. In this respect I believe that of all native people on earth the Indians of the Northwest Coast are best conditioned.

The vicinity of Ogowinagak is geologically very interesting. Eisak told me that there were hot springs and lakes not far away, and Mr. Woolfe also came to the conclusion that Prince of Wales Peninsula between Norton Sound and Kotzebue Sound is volcanic. He had observed to the southwest, several weeks before my arrival, a fiery glow like the eruption of a volcano.

Meanwhile the month of November was approaching, and I felt very comfortable in our new house, which no longer had the aspect of an Eskimo dwelling with its discomforts, especially after I replaced the seal-intestine window covering with a pane of glass. There were constant opportunities for interesting observations and also for necessary work; Mr. Woolfe was collecting Eskimo words, and I wrote in my diary or did some carpentry. Every evening Eisak and his wives and young people sang for us. The only unpleasant feature in this situation was the slow approach of the Arctic winter. A storm from the south broke up the ice and blew it northward so that the journey was impossible.

Then an Eskimo from Iglutalik arrived with a sled for a

visit. The man had been tending the grave of Eisak's father according to local custom and kept it in good order. Now he appeared to collect the presents due him for this service. For this reason he stayed not at Eisak's house but with Mrs. Barbara, Eisak's mother-in-law. So our host dressed himself in his best furs and laid several salmon, with berries and seal fat, on two wooden dishes, and his wife did the same. Then the couple carried these gifts in a ceremonious procession to Mrs. Barbara's house. First Mrs. Eisak went into the house and presented her gifts, then Eisak did the same. The visiting Eskimo ate the food in silence after making a kind of offering by throwing small pieces of food into the corner while the movement of his lips showed that he said something with the act.

By now my house carpentry had reached the point where I could lay the floor of the building. There were a few strong conifer trees nearby that could have been used, but the wood was too fresh and full of sap for this purpose. So I used the traditional material, driftwood, which the Eskimo brought me in great quantity. At this time the need for more food began to be a problem. We were living on dry bread baked with flour paste, which we euphemistically called pancakes, and tea and coffee. In spite of the snowstorm from the southeast we went hunting for ptarmigan, but on the winter snow their white plumage makes them difficult to spot and they were very shy. We bagged two.

The shaman who had successfully performed the cure at Eisak's house was still staying there, disregarding the shortness of food and even though his wife was waiting for him at home, perhaps because he enjoyed the entertaining company and hoped that from this group he might get another patient. But finally he left with no more fees for his services and probably had to face a lecture from his jealous wife.

At last our provisions arrived; because of the bad, windy weather that tore up the ice, the young men took ten days for the return trip and brought only three sleds, about half the supplies. This put off my trip to Golovnin Bay even further into the future. In spite of the storm and snow Kuwaluk, the wonder wife, went to the river again, but the weather hindered any fishing. The long stay at Ogowinagak was beginning to wear on us, and we cast about for entertainment. So one day we amused ourselves by papering the inner walls with old numbers of the illustrated magazines we had. It was amusing to find that we had a picture of Bismarck next to one of Sitting Bull.

Outside, the snowstorm had changed to pouring rain, and this put us all in a bad state of mind. It seemed that any kind

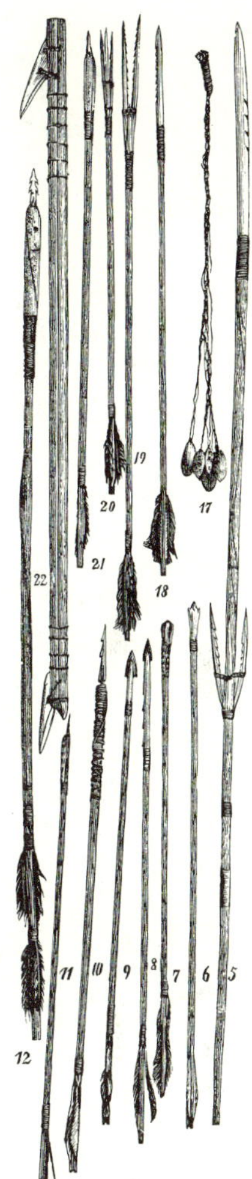

Fig. 50. Hunting gear from northwest Alaska: (5) bird harpoon used on land, with throwing board; (6, 7) arrows with blunt points for bird hunting; (8, 9) arrows used for bear, caribou, and other large game animals; (10) beaver arrow; (11) arrow for small seals; (12) arrow for larger seals; (17) bola for ducks; (18) bird arrow with bone point; (19) two-pronged bird arrow; (20) three-pronged bird arrow; (21) seal arrow; (22) boat hook used in kayaks.

of work was too much for the women and girls, and the dear things just let themselves be fed and entertained by us. But we could not spoil the relationship at this hour, and, since the trip we were to take with Eisak was being postponed, it was right that we should stay at his house; if a quarrel took place we would probably be out in the cold.

On 10 November there was clear weather and a breeze from the north that gave a little frost. I was laying the last planks in the flooring, which made the interior of the house warmer. Now we decided that I should make a sled, for I expected whenever it was possible to go to Golovnin Bay to get the luggage that was still there since the schooner *Leo* had brought it for me from Fort Saint Michael. Now the hunting for ptarmigan was more successful, and we had a good meal again. The excitement created by this good meal was further heightened by a supply of fish brought back by Mamma Kuwaluk. This also decreased the terror of starvation that the dogs faced.

Clearly we were on the threshold of good times. In order to make the house more comfortable we conceded to Eskimo architecture in making a little entrance lobby at the door so that the snow would not come directly into the house. As a reward nature provided us with two great phenomena—first, beautiful northern lights and, second, a fairly strong earthquake on 12 November at 9:15 P.M. The house trembled for a few seconds, and parts of it swayed. Since then all has been quiet.

Eisak explained to me later that there were often earthquakes in winter, but never in summer. He said that the local Eskimo have a legend that long ago there was an earthquake with a flood that covered the land, and that only a few people with their skin boats could save themselves on the tops of high mountains. So we find that the story of the Deluge, known so widely, also occurs in Alaska. Earthquakes in Alaska are sometimes so strong that the ice in the river breaks. They call an earthquake "Nunaaudlarok," meaning "the earth goes." The Eskimo believe that the earthquakes occur when a volcano erupts. They believe that the rocks mate and the rocks thrown out of volcanoes are the rocks' children.

The earthquake and northern lights augured well for my trip, which soon began and took me to the westernmost point of the New World, Cape Prince of Wales.

16

After several days of work we succeeded in putting the sled
made of birch wood together, without the leather straps it
should have had, but which could not be obtained until we
arrived at Golovnin Bay. After we had finished our preparations for the journey to Golovnin Bay word came from Unaktolik that the ice was holding well, so we set out with two
sleds, with five dogs on one, four dogs on the other. We
had just gotten under way when heavy snow flurries began,
which followed us until four o'clock in the afternoon, when
we reached Kjuwaggenak on the Quinekak [Kwiniuk] River.
There we found it possible to dry our wet clothing and rest
our weary bodies. Orre, the Eskimo from Fort Saint Michael
who had come with us, was at home here and we engaged him
to carry some of our gear through the loose snow to the higher
level because our sleds were weak, and so he accompanied us
with one sled and four dogs to lighten our load. The house in
which we slept that night measured only twelve by fourteen
feet and was occupied by twenty-five people, and we all slept
very well. The next day we covered only two miles because
we had to go down the Kwiniuk River to its mouth, where we
found an Eskimo dwelling. We were met here by a messenger
from Ogowinagak, who said that two sleds had come across
the peninsula from Kotzebue Sound to Eisak's house and would
like to return with us.

It now appeared to me that Eisak was not fulfilling his contract with me himself, when he sent one of his people to carry it
out. Our expedition then consisted of six men and one woman.
We stayed at the same place that night, but could not sleep
peacefully for a single minute on account of the noise made
by the children and the dogs, so we broke away at the first
sign of dawn. The trail took us in a west southwest direction
along the cliffs of Norton Bay, and though we could see far
out to sea, the ice on the shore was wide enough for ample

passage for our sleds. After a few hours we came to a place where the cliffs rose out of the water with no shore. So here we used a few cakes of ice as ferries, putting on one team at a time and rowing them in shallow water. At another place we had to use the sleds to build a bridge. It was toward evening before we finished passing through this troublesome spot. The cold was severe and the snow flurries became heavier. It made me very happy to find an abandoned house in which to spend the night.

This place, which is used only during March, April, and May for seal hunting, is called Cape Jungfrau, in Eskimo Newiarsualok. The following legend is connected with it:

The inhabitants of the region from Shaktolik to Golovnin Bay, namely, the people from the inner region of Norton Sound, which I have mentioned is called Norton Bay, came from the north, from Kotzebue Sound, and drove the earlier inhabitants partly south and partly west. The incoming Malemiut became enemies of the former population. Finally the Shaktolik pulled themselves together, and assembling all their warriors suddenly attacked the Newiarsualokmiut. In the ensuing battle all the latter were killed except a very pretty girl. She was sentenced to a cruel and gruesome death. After her captors had treated her shamefully, they tied her hands and feet to four kayaks and then paddled in opposite directions. This happened in front of this promontory, which now has the name of Cape Jungfrau.

This was also a point of decision for our journey, for here the open sea caused strong movement in the ice. We had to come to the decision that instead of continuing along the shore we would have to go over the high, steep mountains. We still did not find a favorable terrain, for after climbing the mountains we found thick brush and forest undergrowth, thickly covered with loose snow. It is hard to believe the difficulty this gave us when we had three men cutting the way with axes through the Arctic wilderness to make a trail and trample down a path in the snow. And so it went, up the mountains and down again. In the afternoon, when we were again climbing a steep mountain, a heavy snow flurry occurred, so that Mr. Woolfe, who was wearing snowshoes for the first time, dropped behind and lost sight of us. He went the wrong way, and we had to pause and shout his name to bring him back to us. When it became dark we built a large fire and cooked fish and made tea. Our night's lodging consisted of dry branches put down where the snow had been shoveled away. We were tired enough so that after drying our clothing we did not need to be rocked to sleep.

The next morning we became convinced that all our efforts

of the day before had been unnecessary. We could have shortened our journey by four hours. We consoled ourselves by
realizing that what happened could not be undone and continued on our way until the afternoon, through the woods,
where we found to our pleasure that the trail was not as difficult as it had been. Toward evening we came to a bare, rocky
mountainside that led down to Golovnin Bay. In the ravines
and the little creek beds there was short meadow brush. At
one of these places we camped at dusk, but there was no material for a fire, which we badly needed to dry out our clothes
and cook some food. As the cold became more severe, the Eskimo, without asking any questions, tore some boards out of
our sleds and tried to start a fire with them. Two of us waved
blankets over the little fire to help it get started. At last it was
possible to make some tea to warm us, with which we ate a
small amount of raw dried salmon.

The next day we passed a chain of mountains that ran from
west to east, and from its height we saw in the northward
valley a column of steam. There was a small lake with a hot
spring that the Eskimo had mentioned to us. Since I was the
first white man to see this natural wonder, I took the liberty
of naming it in honor of the director of the Royal Ethnological
Museum in Berlin, "Bastian Lake and Geyser." A lake with
hot springs lying northeast from this my traveling companion
named "Bennett Lake."[25]

I had taken only a small amount of provisions from Ogowinagak with us because I wanted to save them for my longer
journey later and considered the trip to Golovnin Bay just a
little trip. For the return trip I had depended on three boxes
of biscuit, four sacks of flour, and a few other things that Mr.
Hartz[26] of the Golovnin Mining Company had received for
me from the schooner *Leo* and was storing.

The icy cold night we spent here did not entice us into staying, especially since we knew that the end of our journey was
only a day's distance away. We rose long before daylight and
did not linger even to make tea, which in the circumstances
would have taken us three hours, if we had succeeded in making a fire. It was our good fortune that the snow on top of the
cliffs was hard and smooth so that we could travel quickly.
Toward noon the terrain began to fall off toward Golovnin
Bay, and our impatience to reach our goal led us to go faster
and faster until we traveled as fast as a train in a snow-covered
ravine. It was a mad trip, the kind that all expeditions some-
time take and usually complete without any undue accident.
And so it happened for us, even though I almost broke my
foot and one of the dogs was almost squeezed to death under
a sled. We arrived at Singek at three o'clock in the afternoon,

at the residence of Mr. Hartz on the shore of Golovnin Bay. Here we were received in the friendliest way by two Americans and were well fed by them, since we had not had any food that day. Mr. Hartz was away at a large Eskimo feast at Igniktok which had been going on for several days, attended by the entire surrounding population.

The opportunity to attend such a feast was ethnologically important enough that it should not be missed. Since my traveling companion, Mr. Woolfe, was very tired, I took one of the Americans with me. We drove to Igniktok in two sleds with thirteen dogs in a sharp north wind and frost, passing the villages of Singakloget and Ojaralik [Ojeralik]. On the way, as we were climbing the steep ridge of mountains, we met Mr. Hartz on his way home, and he gave us interesting accounts of the feast. At one o'clock in the afternoon we reached Igniktok.

It is seldom that one can find in the northern villages of Alaska a gathering of about two hundred Eskimo, enjoying feasting and ceremonial activities for a whole week. One of the principal problems would be the quantities of food necessary, and the second would be finding sleeping quarters.

As soon as we arrived we were invited to the feast. I was astounded when I went into the ceremonial dance house, called the kassigit. Around the walls, as in an amphitheater, were three rows of viewing places one above the other, on all four sides, as the architecture of the Eskimo houses permitted. As may be known, the entrance to the Eskimo house is through a round hole large enough so that a man can climb up from the bottom. On the bottom row against the walls the Eskimo women were seated; the second row was for the adult men and guests of honor, where we were taken. On the top row above us were the chattering children and young boys and girls. The dances took place in the square in the center around the entrance hole.

The drum was made of a large hoop like a tambourine, with translucent skin for a head; there was a handle, and the drum was used by striking the rim, not the skin. Today the feast started with an introductory song. Then the dancers, a number of adult Eskimo men and women, came into the empty center area and proceeded to remove their fur clothing and put on robes of white calico. Since the Eskimo did not use rattles like those found among the Indians of the Northwest Coast, they substituted long fish skin gloves, reaching to the shoulder and decorated with many beaks of the sea parrot, or puffin, which make a rattling noise as the dancers gesticulate. These gloves are held in place by lacing them to a shoulder band.

Even though we had not slept for several days and nights we prepared ourselves to return to Golovnin Bay in beautiful bright moonlight. Since Papa Eisak decided to stay here I had to satisfy myself to set out alone with one sled. My baggage was not heavy because I had bought very little at Igniktok. The weather was bright and clear and the snow frozen hard, so the trip was short and I arrived at the residence of Mr. Hartz and the other American prospector on the shore of Golovnin Bay at five o'clock in the morning.

Among the many guests at Igniktok there was one Eskimo from the village of Kawiarak [Kauwerak] in the far west on Prince of Wales Peninsula, who had made the long journey solely to attend the feast. Since he was returning, a remarkable opportunity opened for me to travel with him and become acquainted with his people. I had already discussed the possibility at Igniktok that he would pick me up at Singek. I spent a day skating with the American on the beautiful smooth ice around Golovnin Bay. When the Eskimo came he announced that he would leave the next morning. It was a risky undertaking, since I was prepared only for a short trip from Ogowinagak to Golovnin, and my supplies for trade were not enough for this extended journey to Kauwerak. And I had still not received the dogs I had ordered. So I had to call on the friendship of Mr. Hartz to borrow from him what I needed to supplement the material I had in storage from the *Leo*. Up to the present no white man had undertaken this trip westward on Prince of Wales Peninsula, so I received much advice and concern and was warned by everyone that under no circumstances should I go to the little village of Kingegan on Bering Strait, since the people there had a bad reputation as pirates.

Our expedition consisted of a heavily laden sled drawn by six dogs. On 25 November 1882 we rose early in beautiful moonlight and fine weather for traveling. We were joined by people returning from the Igniktok feast to Eratlewik, on the Fish River, which is about one-third of the way to Kauwerak. The trail took us to the northwest across the endless frozen surface of Golovnin Bay. Two of us helped pull the sled and, as is the custom, one walked ahead to examine the condition of the trail. We proceeded at a good pace and reached the mouth of the Fish River at daydreak. The river, on whose frozen surface we traveled, was so winding that our progress was slow. At one o'clock in the afternoon we arrived at a deserted summer house where we found that a party of three sleds had spent the night after a long day's trip. My people wanted to do the same, but that did not fit my plan so we started out with the remaining two sleds. It was a tedious

Some dancers wore head rings with one or two eagle feathers, and one very flashy dancer had a whole eagle tail attached to the head ring so that the decoration rose from his forehead. Many dancers carried eagle wings as fans, which they moved in a lively manner in a rest period and held close to the chest in dancing.

This feast was not a casual one, of which there are many; it occurred seldom and was an important occasion.[27] It was intended to honor a number of deceased and obliged the survivors to give away their possessions to those who had cared for the graves of these dead. After all the secrets of the costumes had been revealed to the audience, the drummer gave a signal to start a song in honor of the dead. In the song the heroic deeds of the deceased were recalled and praised, in a manner similar to songs I have heard among the Indians of the Northwest Coast. In the rhythm of the song and its accompanying drumbeat, the men began to move their arms and feet, stamping on the ground and spreading their arms in many fighting postures. The women remained in one place during the dance, constantly bending their knees and holding eagle feathers upright in their hands with a trembling motion.

After three dances with accompanying songs there was an intermission, which was filled with a festive meal. The entire group of women undertook the serving. The food was brought in wooden dishes, filled with dried salmon, black and red berries, salmon eggs, and so forth. As with all such feasts, the house was terrifically hot, and the odor from so many people dressed in fur clothing produced a great scarcity of fresh air. While the food was being brought in, the majority of the guests indulged in an extraordinary pleasure by taking off the fur garments from their upper bodies and devoted themselves—I cannot express this in more delicate language—to a search for vermin. Since so many people suffered from heavy coughs, without handkerchiefs and so tightly packed that there was no room to spit on the floor, they spit on the walls. The food which was served was not touched until small bits of it had been thrown on the ground as an offering, while the movement of the lips indicated silent prayer.

The lighting of the ceremonial house consisted of ten lamps set on high wooden stands. The lamps were principally worn-out iron frying pans with broken handles, but there were also a few pottery lamps that probably dated back to the period before the Russians and Americans came with their trade articles.

After the meal the skylight in the middle of the roof was removed and a drama of a very unusual kind began—the distribution of the gifts. There was so much to bring into the house that no effort was made to use the entrance hole in the middle of the floor, but items were brought in through the open skylight. The articles were fastened to a long line that the Eskimo slowly lowered. Every few feet another article hung on the line. Since the local Eskimo do not use the decimal system but count on their fingers and toes, limiting the count to twenty, the gifts were arranged in groups of twenty. While these articles were being brought in the assembled group sang. The words explained that now the possessions of the deceased would be distributed and that all present would get their share. With this, the deceased again were praised for the large fortunes they had assembled.

I made a list of the gifts that were distributed:

20	sewing kits of caribou skin	20	windows made of seal intestines
20	raincoats for children	20	sewing kits made of walrus throat
20	pieces of cloth		
20	kameleikas [waterproof parkas] of seal intestines	20	pairs of watertight gloves
20	pairs of boots	20	bladders for harpoon lines
20	pairs of small seal bladders	20	tobacco boxes
20	yards of colored cotton material	20	sacks made of salmon skin
20	shirts of cotton	20	bows and arrows for children
20	kayak mats	20	pairs of gloves
20	seal bladders	20	kameleikas
20	pairs of underpants	20	pairs of small boots
20	pairs of women's boots	20	pairs of children's boots
20	kameleikas	20	pairs of adult boots
20	sewing bags of salmon skin	20	harpoon points
20	cut straps of sealskin	20	harpoons
20	European knives	20	wooden dishes
5	large maklak (seal) skins	20	bird harpoons
20	bundles of dried salmon	20	bladders with bird harpoons, and so forth.

It took several hours to lower all this material into the house and almost the whole night to distribute it. There was no one in the gathering who did not receive something; even I was given a kameleika, a pair of boots, a sewing kit made of walrus throat, a bladder, and a maklak sealskin. Unfortunately all these articles were later stolen at Golovnin Bay. It was nearly morning when I went to my quarters to get at least one or two hours of sleep. Since all the houses in Igniktok were overflowing with Eskimo it was not easy to find a place, but the kind hospitality of the white people helped me.

In the early hours of the next morning I went again to the kassigit, where the festivities had already begun. One must understand that the Eskimo who were assembled there used these feast days to the utmost. This day was devoted almost entirely to feasting, and I could see what quantities of food and drink the Eskimo consumed. Vast amounts of dried salmon,

black berries, blueberries and mixed berries, seal fat, and whole sealskin bladders of fish oil. The meal continued for hours, and I noticed that our own group, that had suffered so much from hunger in the mountains, were among the best eaters. One cuts the seal fat into strips, puts them in the mouth as far as they will go, and cuts them off close to the mouth with a broad stone knife. I can guarantee that seal fat especially, when it has been salted for fourteen days, tastes very good, for I ate this in my home during childhood. Anyone who has eaten at big four- or five-hour modern banquets may remember that the festive board toward the end of the meal, even in our civilization, is not an attractive sight. One can imagine how it would look among the Eskimo, where there was no one to remove the remains of one course before another was brought in. It did not take long before the floor swam with fish oil and the seats, walls, and used dishes as well as the happy faces of the guests were covered with fish oil as though they had been painted with it.

As with the Northwest Coast Indians, the guests were expected to take home any food left over. Whole platters of food and seal bladders of oil were carried away from the kassigit, and when these had been removed the hosts gave the room a superficial cleaning by evening. The hosts consisted of five families that combined to give the feast to honor five deceased persons. A representative of each family officiated at the occasion. While the kassigit was being cleaned these five family representatives took on a very different role. The group consisted of two men, two women, and one youth. They declared that they had given everything away, and to show this they divested themselves of the clothes they had on and threw them outside the kassigit. When they had been driven to this ultimate act, suddenly new clothing was thrown into the kassigit by an unseen hand and the five promptly put it on.

Now that the responsibility toward the deceased had been completed, the last act of the occasion was lively. Everyone was invited to share in a song and dance festival. The people appeared in new clothing, and the drum led to a happy rhythm. The men who danced were stripped to the waist, but the women wore their customary clothes. In the dancing itself there did not seem to be much difference; the men stamped and the women bent their knees. During the dancing a man fell on the floor, but he quickly pulled himself up and left the kassigit. This and other parts of this Eskimo feast reminded me of the great feast of the Kwakiutl, who had the custom that if someone fell during a dance he was immediately killed by the others if he could not escape quickly. It was one o'clock in the morning when the dance ended.

Some dancers wore head rings with one or two eagle feathers, and one very flashy dancer had a whole eagle tail attached to the head ring so that the decoration rose from his forehead. Many dancers carried eagle wings as fans, which they moved in a lively manner in a rest period and held close to the chest in dancing.

This feast was not a casual one, of which there are many; it occurred seldom and was an important occasion.[27] It was intended to honor a number of deceased and obliged the survivors to give away their possessions to those who had cared for the graves of these dead. After all the secrets of the costumes had been revealed to the audience, the drummer gave a signal to start a song in honor of the dead. In the song the heroic deeds of the deceased were recalled and praised, in a manner similar to songs I have heard among the Indians of the Northwest Coast. In the rhythm of the song and its accompanying drumbeat, the men began to move their arms and feet, stamping on the ground and spreading their arms in many fighting postures. The women remained in one place during the dance, constantly bending their knees and holding eagle feathers upright in their hands with a trembling motion.

After three dances with accompanying songs there was an intermission, which was filled with a festive meal. The entire group of women undertook the serving. The food was brought in wooden dishes, filled with dried salmon, black and red berries, salmon eggs, and so forth. As with all such feasts, the house was terrifically hot, and the odor from so many people dressed in fur clothing produced a great scarcity of fresh air. While the food was being brought in, the majority of the guests indulged in an extraordinary pleasure by taking off the fur garments from their upper bodies and devoted themselves—I cannot express this in more delicate language—to a search for vermin. Since so many people suffered from heavy coughs, without handkerchiefs and so tightly packed that there was no room to spit on the floor, they spit on the walls. The food which was served was not touched until small bits of it had been thrown on the ground as an offering, while the movement of the lips indicated silent prayer.

The lighting of the ceremonial house consisted of ten lamps set on high wooden stands. The lamps were principally worn-out iron frying pans with broken handles, but there were also a few pottery lamps that probably dated back to the period before the Russians and Americans came with their trade articles.

After the meal the skylight in the middle of the roof was removed and a drama of a very unusual kind began—the distribution of the gifts. There was so much to bring into the house that no effort was made to use the entrance hole in the middle of the floor, but items were brought in through the open skylight. The articles were fastened to a long line that the Eskimo slowly lowered. Every few feet another article hung on the line. Since the local Eskimo do not use the decimal system but count on their fingers and toes, limiting the count to twenty, the gifts were arranged in groups of twenty. While these articles were being brought in the assembled group sang. The words explained that now the possessions of the deceased would be distributed and that all present would get their share. With this, the deceased again were praised for the large fortunes they had assembled.

I made a list of the gifts that were distributed:

20 sewing kits of caribou skin	20 windows made of seal intestines
20 raincoats for children	20 sewing kits made of walrus throat
20 pieces of cloth	
20 kameleikas [waterproof parkas] of seal intestines	20 pairs of watertight gloves
	20 bladders for harpoon lines
20 pairs of boots	20 tobacco boxes
20 pairs of small seal bladders	20 sacks made of salmon skin
20 yards of colored cotton material	20 bows and arrows for children
20 shirts of cotton	20 pairs of gloves
20 kayak mats	20 kameleikas
20 seal bladders	20 pairs of small boots
20 pairs of underpants	20 pairs of children's boots
20 pairs of women's boots	20 pairs of adult boots
20 kameleikas	20 harpoon points
20 sewing bags of salmon skin	20 harpoons
20 cut straps of sealskin	20 wooden dishes
20 European knives	20 bird harpoons
5 large maklak (seal) skins	20 bladders with bird harpoons, and so forth.
20 bundles of dried salmon	

It took several hours to lower all this material into the house and almost the whole night to distribute it. There was no one in the gathering who did not receive something; even I was given a kameleika, a pair of boots, a sewing kit made of walrus throat, a bladder, and a maklak sealskin. Unfortunately all these articles were later stolen at Golovnin Bay. It was nearly morning when I went to my quarters to get at least one or two hours of sleep. Since all the houses in Igniktok were overflowing with Eskimo it was not easy to find a place, but the kind hospitality of the white people helped me.

In the early hours of the next morning I went again to the kassigit, where the festivities had already begun. One must understand that the Eskimo who were assembled there used these feast days to the utmost. This day was devoted almost entirely to feasting, and I could see what quantities of food and drink the Eskimo consumed. Vast amounts of dried salmon, black berries, blueberries and mixed berries, seal fat, and whole sealskin bladders of fish oil. The meal continued for hours, and I noticed that our own group, that had suffered so much from hunger in the mountains, were among the best eaters. One cuts the seal fat into strips, puts them in the mouth as far as they will go, and cuts them off close to the mouth with a broad stone knife. I can guarantee that seal fat especially, when it has been salted for fourteen days, tastes very good, for I ate this in my home during childhood. Anyone who has eaten at big four- or five-hour modern banquets may remember that the festive board toward the end of the meal, even in our civilization, is not an attractive sight. One can imagine how it would look among the Eskimo, where there was no one to remove the remains of one course before another was brought in. It did not take long before the floor swam with fish oil and the seats, walls, and used dishes as well as the happy faces of the guests were covered with fish oil as though they had been painted with it.

As with the Northwest Coast Indians, the guests were expected to take home any food left over. Whole platters of food and seal bladders of oil were carried away from the kassigit, and when these had been removed the hosts gave the room a superficial cleaning by evening. The hosts consisted of five families that combined to give the feast to honor five deceased persons. A representative of each family officiated at the occasion. While the kassigit was being cleaned these five family representatives took on a very different role. The group consisted of two men, two women, and one youth. They declared that they had given everything away, and to show this they divested themselves of the clothes they had on and threw them outside the kassigit. When they had been driven to this ultimate act, suddenly new clothing was thrown into the kassigit by an unseen hand and the five promptly put it on.

Now that the responsibility toward the deceased had been completed, the last act of the occasion was lively. Everyone was invited to share in a song and dance festival. The people appeared in new clothing, and the drum led to a happy rhythm. The men who danced were stripped to the waist, but the women wore their customary clothes. In the dancing itself there did not seem to be much difference; the men stamped and the women bent their knees. During the dancing a man fell on the floor, but he quickly pulled himself up and left the kassigit. This and other parts of this Eskimo feast reminded me of the great feast of the Kwakiutl, who had the custom that if someone fell during a dance he was immediately killed by the others if he could not escape quickly. It was one o'clock in the morning when the dance ended.

Even though we had not slept for several days and nights we prepared ourselves to return to Golovnin Bay in beautiful bright moonlight. Since Papa Eisak decided to stay here I had to satisfy myself to set out alone with one sled. My baggage was not heavy because I had bought very little at Igniktok. The weather was bright and clear and the snow frozen hard, so the trip was short and I arrived at the residence of Mr. Hartz and the other American prospector on the shore of Golovnin Bay at five o'clock in the morning.

Among the many guests at Igniktok there was one Eskimo from the village of Kawiarak [Kauwerak] in the far west on Prince of Wales Peninsula, who had made the long journey solely to attend the feast. Since he was returning, a remarkable opportunity opened for me to travel with him and become acquainted with his people. I had already discussed the possibility at Igniktok that he would pick me up at Singek. I spent a day skating with the American on the beautiful smooth ice around Golovnin Bay. When the Eskimo came he announced that he would leave the next morning. It was a risky undertaking, since I was prepared only for a short trip from Ogowinagak to Golovnin, and my supplies for trade were not enough for this extended journey to Kauwerak. And I had still not received the dogs I had ordered. So I had to call on the friendship of Mr. Hartz to borrow from him what I needed to supplement the material I had in storage from the *Leo*. Up to the present no white man had undertaken this trip westward on Prince of Wales Peninsula, so I received much advice and concern and was warned by everyone that under no circumstances should I go to the little village of Kingegan on Bering Strait, since the people there had a bad reputation as pirates.

Our expedition consisted of a heavily laden sled drawn by six dogs. On 25 November 1882 we rose early in beautiful moonlight and fine weather for traveling. We were joined by people returning from the Igniktok feast to Eratlewik, on the Fish River, which is about one-third of the way to Kauwerak. The trail took us to the northwest across the endless frozen surface of Golovnin Bay. Two of us helped pull the sled and, as is the custom, one walked ahead to examine the condition of the trail. We proceeded at a good pace and reached the mouth of the Fish River at daydreak. The river, on whose frozen surface we traveled, was so winding that our progress was slow. At one o'clock in the afternoon we arrived at a deserted summer house where we found that a party of three sleds had spent the night after a long day's trip. My people wanted to do the same, but that did not fit my plan so we started out with the remaining two sleds. It was a tedious journey because in order to avoid going around a large curve of the river, we went crosscountry and had to chop our way through thick underbrush. There was a heavy frost that day so that our eyes were filled with ice, and wiping it off often tore at our eyelashes; in such a temperature a beard becomes such a heavy load of ice that all long beards are cut short.

It soon became dark, and since our destination was far off we had to leave our heavy luggage. At nine o'clock in the evening we arrived at the mouth of the river at Eratlewik, dead tired, since we had to help pull the sled for sixteen hours. We came at an unfortunate time, for there was a kind of epidemic of which two girls had already died and a number of others were sick. The basic human reaction to sorrow I have often seen in native parts of the world expressed itself here. The deep grief that had seized the relatives was expressed in the shaman's frequent order of a taboo that severely affected us, that we were not allowed to use a metal ax to cut wood for a fire. We had been without food or drink since four o'clock in the morning, so in response to our requests we received enough wood to make pancakes and boil water for tea. Excessive fatigue and the noise in the house kept us from sleep that night.

It was necessary to stay at Eratlewik while I sent off some of our people to get the pieces we had left behind the day before. It is the custom that there is no work done for four days after a death has occurred, especially with the use of an ax or a needle. This made it impossible to have my boots repaired, which had been torn the previous day. The fire for cooking our food was made of what branches we could pull off the trees with our hands. Frankly, one discovers in such circumstances what a useful material iron is!

The epidemic in Eratlewik was the same disease we had encountered two months earlier on the lower Yukon, in a Kwikpakmiut village where the whole population had bad head colds and coughs. In the evening a shaman came to the house and started an unusual cure of the sick girl. She was lying weak and listless when he wrapped a leather strap around her head, put a stick through it, and lifted her head high for a minute, then let it sink again. With this he carried on a speech with Tonrak (the devil), threatening him if he did not leave the patient and promising him some "tobaky."

My host at Eratlewik was an Eskimo trader named Kingaseak, whom I knew as the representative of the Alaska Commercial Company and had met at Fort Saint Michael during the summer. Among the people who lived here there was an old man who had a fight with a bear; the bear tore out his eye and disfigured his face, but he finally killed it with only his bow and arrows. I bought few ethnographic pieces because the people were very poor. In the course of the day all the people who had been at the great feast at Igniktok engaged in a strange procedure of washing their whole bodies in urine. I could not find out whether this was a cleansing after the feast or connected with the recent deaths in the village. Near Eratlewik there is a lead mine along the river which is run by the American prospectors.

When we left the next morning we headed northwest and went on the ice that connected the Eratlewik River with the Nerkluk. This river is quite deep and during the ice-free months is navigable to the mountain range which is the division between it and the westward-flowing Kauwerak, which empties into Bering Strait.

We found the Nerkluk was not completely covered with ice but was under a heavy blanket of snow that continued to grow with the daily snowfall on the entire landscape. We traveled the whole day along a shoreline thick with small pine trees, and toward evening, after leaving these trees, we came to a deserted summer house, Kelungiarak [Keluniak], which belonged to an Eskimo in Eratlewik.

At daybreak the next day we started out again, traveling upstream where we found vegetation in the afternoon, and toward evening we found another deserted summer house, Kaksertobage, where there was enough wood to cook fish and boil water for tea. The following night we could not sleep because of the cold—even our Eskimo shivered with it and tried to warm themselves up by dancing. Finally the extreme cold, about $-40°$ Reaumur, drove us to start the day at four o'clock in the morning. At first it went very well on the frozen river, but we came to open water so that we had to undertake the tedious task of hacking our way through the brush. The Nerkluk River rises from a little lake which we crossed, and at an altitude of 1,500 to 2,000 feet we found the watershed.

We climbed this height and at dark we reached the summit, an area covered with brush, so we set up our caribou skin tent and camped for the night. We were lucky enough to find wood to prepare our fish and tea, and this helped us endure the coldest night we had yet experienced. By this time my boot was completely torn and was filled with snow. To warm myself I put my finger in hot water and did not even feel the heat. At this point I cannot recommend a caribou skin tent like ours as the best for an Arctic journey. In the daytime the caribou skins are used to cover the sleds and at night for tent covers, and they have the advantage of not being attacked by the dogs, who will eat almost everything. But in this severe cold the caribou skin tent is not enough, especially if after weeks of strenuous activity the human physique has been weakened.

I used a double caribou-skin blanket as protection to keep my body warmth, whereas my Eskimo each had only one. It followed that this night we could not sleep, so we broke camp at two o'clock in the morning. Another of our problems was the meagerness of our provisions here in the mountains. We could easily be delayed by a snowstorm. We therefore made use of the bright moonlight to leave this inhospitable area.

The trail carried us through flat country, then over ten to twelve miles across the breadth of Dininek Lake, and again over flat terrain to the Maknek River region. This river flows out of the southern part of Dininek Lake and makes a large curve northward before flowing to the west. After hard work we reached the Maknek River at dawn. Our dogs, who had been kept on low rations and hard work, were exhausted. It was our hope that we could follow the Maknek River downstream in order to reach our destination with the least effort, but the winding river disappointed us.

Because of this we again started in the direction of Kauwerak through difficult country, and we reached a human habitation at dusk. I cannot describe how welcome was this little Eskimo settlement, Napariuseluk. There was a roof over our heads again and friendly people in the hut, as well as a fine-tasting meal with freshly cooked fish and a real warming fire in the center of the house. How happily we stretched out our half-frozen arms and enjoyed our food and then lay down on a warm bed! How we slept that night! But all this did not let me forget the purpose of my journey, and I found some good ethnographic pieces.

At daybreak we were on our way again, following the Maknek River but cutting off some of its curves by going overland. On the way, at one place where there were two houses, I bought a beautiful nephrite amulet; I had seen some on the way, but had never been in a position to secure one.

We now came into a region where I was a curiosity, for the people had never seen a white man. It was not surprising that they gave us directions and often ran along beside my sled for some distance.

The mountain range that formed the backbone of Prince of Wales Peninsula started at the cape of the same name and ran parallel to our planned route, but it stayed about a day's run farther north and followed the Maknek River with low hills and flat land. On the left there was a higher range that ran in the same direction, and at Port Clarence the river emptied into Bering Strait. The craggy tops of the mountains reached about 6,000 feet.

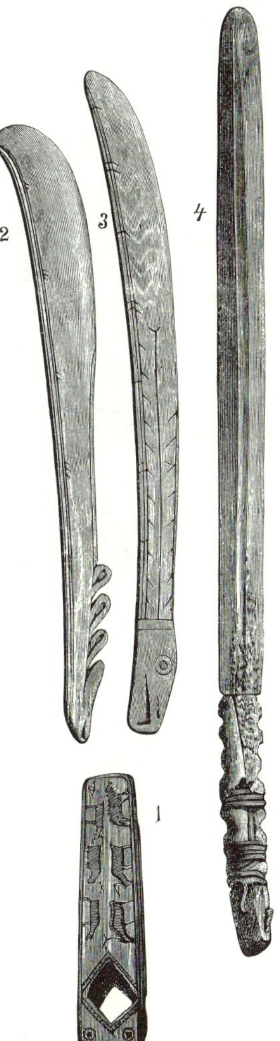

Fig. 51. Athapaskan and Eskimo artifacts: (1) arrow straightener made of antler or horn; (2, 3) bone knives, held in the hand while making a speech; (4) long bone knife used to beat the snow off clothing.

At three o'clock in the afternoon we reached our destination, Kauwerak, a village of five houses and a kassigit. One must add together the hardships since leaving Golovnin Bay to understand the extraordinary interest on the part of the inhabitants who undergo them in order to attend the feast in Igniktok. The Eskimo who traveled with us seemed to have realized the dangerous situation in which we found ourselves, for immediately after their return they gave a thanksgiving feast at which the drummer played and sang and made a speech in the way a shaman would do it. Beyond this, the opportunity was also taken to give a welcome to the three Eskimo who arrived at the same time from Port Clarence.

Since it would have been impossible to go to sleep I went to the kassigit to attend the welcome for the three Eskimo. It took several hours before the festivities began. The ceremony of welcome was as follows: the three men from Port Clarence came, one after another, through the underground passage into the middle of the kassigit; just below the opening the first one raised his hand and then withdrew it. Then he jumped with his whole body as quickly as possible through the hole. The second and third did the same. Each held a stick in his hand that had been especially shaped like a halberd for the evening. Then three ornamented Eskimo from Kauwerak came through the hole and danced to the beat of the drum and the rhythm of a song before the guests. The dance lasted until the dancers were exhausted. Suddenly the song and dance ceased and the three dancers asked the visitors a question that was not answered. Then the three Eskimo from Kauwerak sat down with their legs folded under them.

Now the second part of the ceremony began. An Eskimo woman from Kauwerak came through the opening and set a dish of food in front of one of the guests, at the same time pushing back the hood of her fur clothing and taking off the glove from his right hand, inviting him to eat. A second woman did the same with another guest and then a third. The guests from Port Clarence began to eat but did it so slowly that it seemed as though they would never finish. Then the traveling packs of the strangers were brought into the kassigit and set before them. Now the younger Eskimo from Kauwerak swarmed over the sacks and committed all kinds of havoc. They emptied them and with laughter spread the contents on the ground while they and all the people of Kauwerak laughed. Only the people from Port Clarence watched in grave silence. The meal the guests had eaten consisted of raw frozen fish, dried salmon with fish oil, and black berries. When they had finished eating and no one could make them laugh, the sacks were packed again and that was the end of the evening.

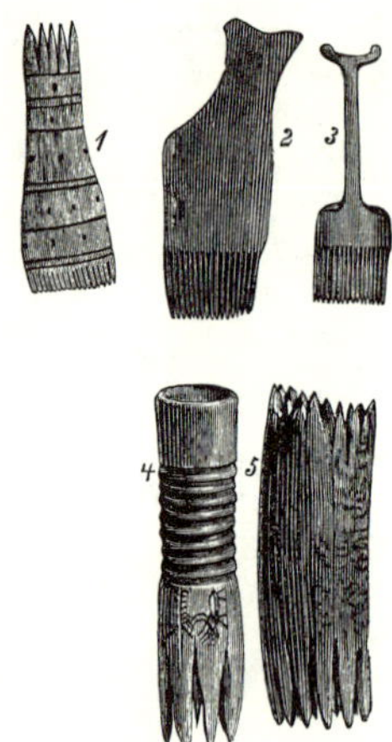

Fig. 52. (1–3) Combs made of mammoth tusks; (4–5) combs for cleaning caribou skins. Prince of Wales Peninsula.

I began trading with the people, but without much success, and was quite annoyed at their begging and aggressive behavior, which included examining me physically. It was impossible to prepare for our departure since for some unknown reason all work was taboo for the next few days. Our traveling boots all needed repair. On further questioning it came out that when the Eskimo return from a long trip they are not allowed to work for several days. As I was already very much annoyed by their behavior I paid no attention to the taboo and mended my torn clothing against their protests. When they saw that I was not giving in to their wish, they finally let me alone. My Eskimo, who was still weary, did not repair his clothing, and this delayed my departure. I also had to wash and dry my own shirt. Because of this bold ignoring of the taboo the people in a serious manner prophesied all kinds of misfortune in my coming trip.

I let them talk as they wished and left at five o'clock the next morning with five dogs and the same sled with which I came to Kauwerak and headed westward, for I wished if it were possible to go as far as Cape Prince of Wales. I took the oldest of my traveling companions with me, for in spite of his superstitions he was a sound and practical person. Shortly before our departure some Eskimo from the neighborhood came to sell some caribou meat, but even though my mouth watered for it, their prices were so exorbitant that I did not take it.

Our trail led us twenty-five English miles along Imarsok [Imuruk] Lake, which is connected with Port Clarence Bay and is part salt and part fresh water. It snowed almost all day and was so dark that we could scarcely see the lake. As usual we had to help pull the sled. Toward evening we came to the outlet of the lake into the bay and found there three houses in the village of Tukkerrovik. Our leader guided us so well that we continued to pull the sled until ten o'clock that evening, when we arrived tired and hungry at Singrak near Cape Prince of Wales. There were three small huts there, each not more than five feet across, but about five or six persons were sleeping and living in each one.

Even though it was late we were welcomed by the inhabitants with great joy, and all came in great excitement to see me. They handled me as if I were a wonderful animal. I bought a trout and gave it to an Eskimo woman, asking her to cook it for me, since I had had nothing to eat all day. She took it to her hut and was away for such a long time while I was suffering from hunger that I finally went in search of her. I found she had cooked it and eaten it! Fortunately I had some tea and biscuits with me so that I did not have to go to bed without anything. Weary as I was I could not sleep, because the Eskimo

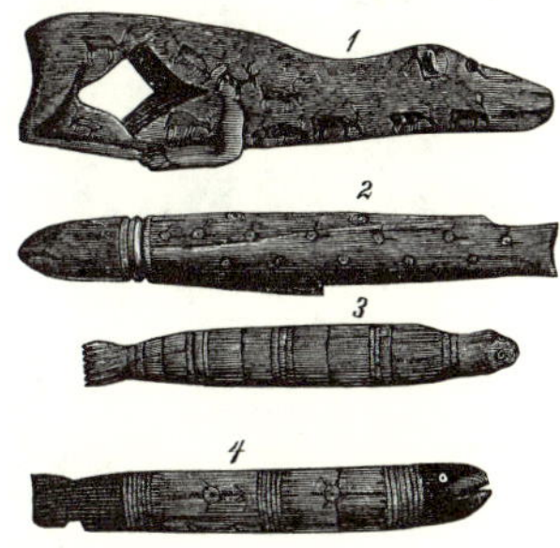

Fig. 53. (1) Arrow straightener made of caribou horn; (2–4) needle cases made of slender hollow bones. Prince of Wales Peninsula.

were so excited about my visit that they raised hell all night. These people have no idea of night and day, but everyone does what he pleases at any time.

The next day, 6 December, I was invited by the inhabitants of Singrak to the kassigit for a ceremonial welcome. Four different dishes, among them berries that had been boiled in fish oil, were set before me. Since I had been hungry for so long and while traveling was not particular in my choice of food, I had developed an Eskimo type of appetite that would have astonished those in other countries had they seen me. At last when I could eat no more I gave the remainder to my people. I remember now that I hardly noticed that the Eskimo women who served me were almost bald, a circumstance they shared with most of the inhabitants of that part of Alaska.

During the meal, preparations were made to entertain me with a ceremonial dance, and I saw in these dances many similarities to the actions of the Indians of the Northwest Coast, especially the west coast of Vancouver Island. In the first place the drum was not a skin stretched in a hoop, but a square box, which reminded me of my experiences on the Northwest Coast. The dance was started by three men with caps of eagle skin on their heads, wearing the familiar long gloves decorated with puffin bills. The song leader was an old bleary-eyed Eskimo who functioned by common consent. He kept count by holding a number of small wooden sticks in one hand and transferring a stick to the other hand at the end of each song. Even in his long life he evidently had not learned to count, for he examined the number of sticks in each hand after each transfer.

It appeared to me that this population did not outwardly resemble most of the other people in this area. Several of the men had heavy beards and all seemed to have a deeper skin color, broad cheekbones, and small, slightly slanted eyes.

In the evening of the same day another event took place. Six men and two women danced. The men's clothing differed from that worn at my welcome. They wore caribou skin boots and trousers, which came to the knees like those of the women in Greenland. The upper part of the body was bare except for a few ermine skins that hung on the shoulders and chest. They wore strips of wolfskin on their heads and one had a whole wolf's head skin. The women were not specially dressed but wore their soiled skin dresses. The dances of these Eskimo were different from those of the Malemiut. The legs were spread and the upper body was bent forward with lively gesticulation. A hand drum was passed around from one to the other, and each who received it performed a solo dance, whether he was in dancing costume or not. After the dance, food was brought to the kassigit and eagle feather fans were

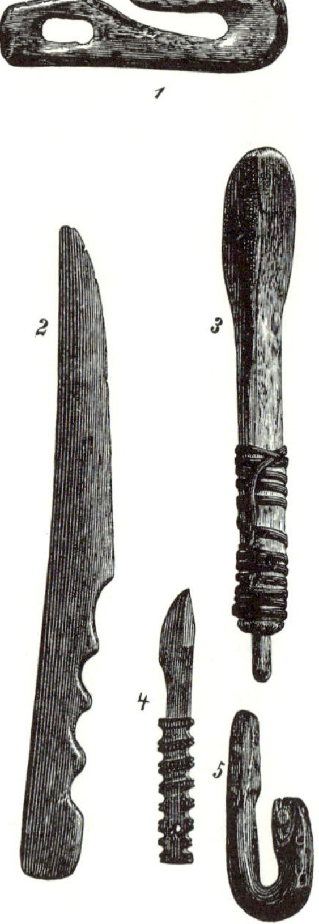

Fig. 54. (1, 5) bone blocks used in raising sails; (2, 4) finishing tools used in making boots; (3) tool for preparing lance points. Prince of Wales Peninsula.

used. After the meal everyone sat down on the floor, took off their ceremonial clothing, and put on their old clothes. After the close of the ceremony there was casual joking and everyone was sober, for they drank only water that the women passed around. That day the village received a visit from men on three sleds from Amelirok, which was on the opposite shore at Port Clarence. During the evening I decided to take a trip to Kingegan, which is even farther on Cape Prince of Wales, even though the people there have a bad reputation as thieves and robbers.

The next morning we started out at daybreak with a local man from Kingegan as guide, in a sled with ten dogs. The trail went along a bay with Bering Strait to the northwest. The mountains mentioned before, north where I crossed them, now appeared at a place where I had to pass steep, projecting cliffs right on the shore. The only possibility was to go out on the ice of the Bering Sea, but this could not be done with the sleds, for as far as one could see on a cloudy day the sea was covered with masses of loose ice that neither a man not a kayak could pass.

I looked over toward the west, where the coast of Asia was so close as to be visible on a clear day, but was now shrouded in fog, and we saw the impassable wall behind us that no sled could conquer. According to my local guide, the possibility that the ice would congeal in the months of January and February was not good. Since my supply of trade goods was very much depleted I could not have made extensive purchases. From day to day my small expeditions, which began at Ogowinagak to Golovnin Bay, continued to expand westward, so that it was inevitable that the moment would come when I could go no farther and could not risk the loss of the material I had already secured. So we returned to Singrak, where I still got a few pieces. I also bought a dog, since my Eskimo had only five. In the evening there was another dance at the kassigit, but I did not go.

17

The return trip began the next morning, and by noon we arrived at the Telegraph House, which was built here in 1867 by the Western Union Telegraph Company. There were expectations of telegraphic connections across the United States overland, then by cable to Siberia and through to Europe. The enterprise was bought by the Transatlantic Company and was discontinued when the Atlantic cable was completed. The lonely building on the shore of Bering Strait is well preserved except for the absence of doors and windows. I also found telegraph poles in a number of places in Alaska. The artistic Eskimo, however, made the telegraph wire into bracelets for their wives. We stopped at the house, which I had not noticed in the dark on my outgoing trip, to feed the dogs and then we went on to Sinaogak, where there are three houses, arriving there in the evening.

The next day we continued the return trip along the same route we had taken before. We went up the canal in severe cold and crossed to the big lake, where I froze my nose. In the evening we again arrived at Kauwerak, and this time I had no reason to criticize the people's behavior. I had given the Eskimo a lecture on their habit of begging, and although they could not understand the words, they recognized the gestures. We gave ourselves a two-day rest, during which repairs were made on our clothing.

On 12 December we started out again to Golovnin Bay; the count of pieces acquired on this expedition came to several hundred. The trail again went into the region of the Maknek River, where we visited the village of Errakwik [Eratliwik]. We had to endure a storm from the northeast with $-40°$ temperature the second night as we camped on the Maknek River in our caribou-skin tent. We had to fasten the tent by digging it deep into the snow to shut out the cold. We slept that night on top of our supply of meat. The dogs became aware of this and tried to chew their way through the tent, especially the dog I had just purchased in Cape Prince of Wales, who set the others a bad example.

The intense cold changed our breath to snow and frost until the inside of the tent was covered. We therefore rose before daybreak, climbed into the mountains, and crossing Dininek Lake reached the abandoned hut where we had stayed on the outward journey. It was a wonderfully comfortable rest. Soon the fire glowed and we cooked fish and fried pancakes in seal oil. For the first time in many days we were in a place where we were not freezing and in a house without children and screaming women, with no singing or carousing, and we slept only too well. In the morning we found that the new dog had totally devoured a pair of boots and a sealskin sack. Even though our rations were not too plentiful we had been feeding our dogs well, and it was not necessary for the dog to do this from hunger. And the prize of the whole affair was that he even ate the straw the boots were lined with.

The next day we continued east and spent the night in another summer cabin at Keluniak, where we feasted on the remainder of our fish and luxuriated with plenty of firewood. The next day after, we already received news from the region of Golovnin Bay. We met five men with two sleds who came from Eratlewik. These people came from the village of Kingegan at Cape Prince of Wales, which I did not visit, and it seemed at first that they wanted to carry out the bad reputation of the place. As we approached they raised their guns, and one man shot. But as we came toward them they appeared friendly and we conversed for a while. I obtained a few small pieces from them—among others, a bola similar to the ones from Patagonia. We parted as good friends.

At two o'clock in the afternoon, shortly after sundown, we had some snow flurries and soon came to Eratlewik, which seemed like a metropolis; for here we at last had a chance to wash ourselves and clean our clothing of the parasites that are a part of Eskimo life. We also did not have to satisfy ourselves with pancakes, but had a pound and a half of expensive trout, of which I ate several. The dogs also received a hearty meal. At five o'clock the next morning we left our pleasant shelter and set out on a severe day's march to cover the distance between us and Golovnin Bay and Singek, where a group of American gold miners lived. On the way one of our dogs became so weak that I had to put him on a sled, and we pulled extra weight, arriving dangerously weary.

The Americans greeted us warmly, and I must say that bacon and beans were never more welcome in an empty stomach. I also received a number of letters, including ones from

Mr. Woolfe, Mr. Lorenz, and Mr. Neumann. Also, the ten dogs and the sled I had ordered in the autumn from the mouth of the Yukon had arrived, but an Eskimo had borrowed six of my dogs and gone to Adnek [Atnuk]. My sled was broken, and I ordered it repaired at once and sent a messenger to Adnek to return with the dogs. I also paid my guide, who had given excellent service. He received about sixty marks and a quantity of lead, gunpowder, matches and other trade goods.

Since Mr. Hartz, the manager of the gold mining company, expected to send some people with sleds to Fort Saint Michael, to buy provisions and trade goods, I wrote letters to Mr. Lorenz and Mr. Neumann.

On 19 December, some people came to Singek from Igniktok, where I remembered attending the Feast for the Dead and the memorial giveaway, and I obtained some dog food from them, which seemed to be scarce everywhere. Since three more sleds came from Igniktok the next day, I could add to my supply. We were having storms and biting cold. At last my six dogs arrived from Atnuk in time for us to get ready for our departure the next day. But the poor dogs were not in good condition, for the Eskimo who borrowed them had not fed them properly.

We set up a little sled caravan that started out on 22 December from Golovnin Bay, going to the southeast. In addition to the two sleds from Mr. Hartz, the three from Igniktok joined us. The trail was not the same as on my first journey, overland to Cape Jungfrau, but with firm ice out into Golovnin Bay we did not need to travel the long way on land. A number of small incidents occurred in the early part of the trip, one being that I missed one of my dogs. I went on hoping that it was with Mr. Hartz's group, but when I found this was not true I sent an Eskimo back with one sled to find the dog while I continued with the others.

The second incident could have had serious consequences. Although the ice was firm in the inner part of the bay, as we went outward we found large weak spots over which I took my heavily laden sled. In the second when the ice broke, I jumped from the sled as it was sinking and pulling the dogs with it. My cry alerted Mr. Hartz's people, who had just passed over this spot, and with their help I lifted the sled back on the ice and we saved the dogs. I lost only part of my provisions in the accident.

Since the ice became weaker we directed our caravan to the shore and crossed the rocky peninsula that separates Norton Bay from Norton Sound.

Now it appeared that my sled had not been properly constructed because it fell on its side several times and was damaged in various places. It was even worse on the other side of the mountain on hard frozen snow. Here it took my entire strength to prevent my sled from turning over. The trail constantly became steeper and more frightening. It happened first to the Americans who were just in front of me; their sled upset so that one of their people was tossed in the air for several meters and fell headfirst. We thought he had broken his neck, but he was less injured than the sled was damaged. I tore along clinging sideways to my sled, warding off obstacles with my feet until I injured my foot, and then there was nothing for me to do but cling to the sled. It did not take long before we came to a clump of brush and the sled rushed into it and stopped. Since I could not go on with a broken sled I unharnessed the dogs and let them run to nearby Atnuk, on a trail they knew. We received help and shortly arrived in the village.

Here we found a feast of several days' duration, and since we were delayed for a few days in the repair of the sleds, we could attend parts of it. Like all Eskimo feasts it was attended by people from many tribes. It was not a dancing feast or a giveaway such as I had already learned to know so well, but it was to draw the mainstay of their food, the seal hunt. The feast is celebrated once every year and the women have the leading part in it.[28]

During the whole year the bladder of every captured seal was carefully stored in the Eskimo house until this festival, when they were painted in many colors, then brought to the kassigit and hung on a pole for the beginning of the celebration. The occasion started with a feast at which the men served the women. Every man coming to the kassigit had to carry in his hand a piece of a kayak, a light oar, a harpoon, or some such thing. An old man was placed close to an oil lamp and held a bundle of dried plant stems in his hand, near the flame; they were plants we call sloike (bear claws)[29] in Norway. Near the entrance a pole was erected and wound with a bundle of these. On entering, every man had to touch the piece he was bringing to the fire, then to each bladder hung on the post, and finally to the bundle of the plant. At the end of this ceremony all the young people from ten to fourteen had to undress. Then a woman came in with a bundle of raw frozen fish, which she threw on the ground. The young naked youths all rushed out for the fish to grab as many as possible. This wild scramble created great excitement with loud screams, as though everyone was trying to make as much noise as possible. After the youngsters were finished, the adults had their day. An object was set up as a target at which the men threw specially made small spears with wooden shafts, small iron points, and gulls' feathers at the butt. The Eskimo who scored the highest was greeted with loud jubilation. This game continued until two o'clock in the morning.

The following evening was ladies' night, when the women and girls came in and sat in concentric circles on the floor. Then one man after another appeared at the entrance hole, showing only his upper body, bearing a gift, and made a speech and sang a song. Then he raised the present high above his head and called out a person's name to receive it. The recipient went back to the walls of the kassigit showing his gift with great pleasure. After this ceremony the men also came into the kassigit.

The final ceremony and high point of the occasion occurred the next morning just when we were ready to leave. Several hundred festively dressed Eskimo men and women came to the beach carrying bladders. A fire was burning on the ice, which lit the group dramatically. Small holes had been cut in the ice and the people grouped themselves around them. Then the women stepped forward and, making all kinds of magical gestures and praying, pushed the bladders down under the ice with a stick. This ceremony was carried on in an earnest, sober manner because the bladders were a kind of sacrifice brought to the great seal, the Maklek. It was believed that if this were not done the seals would not come near the coast and the people would die of hunger.

We set out with our sleds along the cliffs of Norton Bay, but soon the ice became so bad that we could hardly make any progress. My sled, which is built comparatively high—too high perhaps—tipped over no less than six times that day. In the evening we reached Newiarsualok at Cape Jungfrau. After we had established ourselves in an Eskimo hut, a shaman suddenly came in and growled and howled and held his breath until his face was blue and his eyes bloodshot. Then he turned around and crawled out of the house. I never could find out the reason for his peculiar behavior, but I never saw him again.

An unpleasant incident occurred with one of our people. The Eskimo, Orre, who had traveled with me out of Fort Saint Michael, had given some difficulty in Singek; when I sent him to get the six dogs another Eskimo had borrowed in my absence, he went instead to a feast at a neighboring village. He also tried to take a sack of beans away from the Americans by putting it on his sled and covering it with frozen fish. So, sorry as I was about this, I had to dismiss him, which did not seem to bother him because he was close to his home.

On the first of the Christmas holidays we covered the short distance to Ogowinagak. It seemed as if the old shaman of the previous evening had conjured bad luck for us. Even though I had two Eskimo walking along on the sides of my sled to make sure it would not fall over, it broke down altogether. Fortunately there were empty Eskimo sleds at hand and I could lay my baggage on them. Three o'clock in the afternoon we were back in Ogowinagak.

Here I received my first news from the outside world. Mr. Woolfe had gone to Fort Saint Michael with three sleds to get trading goods for Eisak. Meanwhile, the Eskimo had made great inroads into my provisions. Perhaps it would have been better if I had gone directly on to Fort Saint Michael and gotten food. Eisak's house was full of Eskimo who were still here after a large feast that Eisak had given during my absence, for those who tended his father's grave. On the second day of the holidays the Americans went on with their sleds over the ice in Norton Bay, while I waited for my sled, which I sent to Unaktolik for repairs. During this time an Eskimo came to Ogowinagak from a neighboring river and told about the arrival of some Malemiut from the northern shore of Kotzebue Sound, in the village of Kikertarok.

These people came the next morning to our house and they expected later to go to Shaktolik for a feast. They were large, strong, well-built people, who wore labrets about two inches long, made of white marble. They brought sad news from the north in Kotzebue Sound and the Noatak River region, where there was famine because the caribou, their principal food, stayed away. They also related that during the summer the captain of a whaling ship, north of Bering Strait near Cape Hope, put an Irishman ashore who was a thief and very wicked. This man found himself among the Eskimo, who now fed and clothed him, for which he rewarded them with thieving and bad behavior.

The newly arrived Malemiut seemed to have a childlike innocence. While I was arranging the objects I obtained in my last expedition I always had two or three of them looking over my shoulder, watching every move I made, or they tried to look up my sleeves and began a close body examination. My desire to visit Kotzebue Sound, because I hoped to find many ethnographic objects, was strengthened by seeing these people.

On 1 January 1883 Mr. Woolfe came back from Fort Saint Michael and brought me as a New Year's surprise the information that the Ingalik of the middle Yukon, in whose territory I had collected several human skulls during my September visit, were now angry and had threatened the agent of the Alaska Commercial Company. There was also a rumor among the Eskimo that these Ingalik were going to come across the country to Ogowinagak to attack me.

I figured out that this rumor came from the Eskimo of the neighborhood so that they could take over my provisions, especially the gunpowder, lead, and so forth, to be prepared for the attack. The provisions Mr. Woolfe brought me consisted of a box of biscuits and bacon. The Eskimo from Kotzebue left that day to go to Shaktolik.

In between all these events I tried to find out from Eisak as much as I could about the customs and habits of the Eskimo. He told me, among other things, how his people carry out the birth of children. A little wooden hut is erected for the mother-to-be, in which she stays in summer or winter. She is visited by one or two women from time to time. When the birth is imminent the woman's abdomen is laced spirally from the top with straps of sealskin, and often if more pressure is necessary a stick is put through them. The mother kneels while the child is born. The child is washed in urine, and it is regarded as a good omen for a long life if this is done by a very old woman. If there are difficulties a shaman is called, as with all illnesses. The Eskimo women are very hardy because of their strenuous life. Eisak told me that once when they were traveling he had to call a halt while his wife was surprised by the early birth of a daughter. When the event was over Eisak and his wife put on their snowshoes again, wrapped the new infant in furs, and continued the trip.

Another Eskimo custom Eisak told me was that at sunrise and sunset work is stopped for about half an hour and then resumed. I had noticed this among the Eskimo.

On Tuesday, 9 January 1883, my sled finally arrived, but I could not see that its construction had been improved. The same day the Americans from Fort Saint Michael came back through stormy weather and brought me a message from Mr. Lorenz. Two days later I started my longest expedition from south to north across Prince of Wales Peninsula to Kotzebue Sound.

18

Our caravan was not small: Eisak had two sleds; Mr. Woolfe,
who was transporting trade goods to the north for the Alaska
Commercial Company, also had two sleds, and I divided my
ten dogs between two sleds. In addition were my guide, Ningawakrak, a tall, strong Eskimo from Kotzebue Sound, his wife
Allak, her fourteen-year-old half-sister Sewugak, and a boy.
All together we were nine men and two women. I expected,
with such a large group, to run into difficulties with food as
has happened on my previous trips, and I did not allow myself
to depend on the carelessness of the Eskimo, who never look
ahead to envisage future needs. It was this carelessness that
robbed me of my provisions, for the Eskimo had no thought of
my needs on the next trip. And also I had lost my trust in
Eisak, who showed little enthusiasm for making the trip to
Kotzebue Sound with me since the old shaman I mentioned before visited us one day in Ogowinagak and prophesied that of
Mr. Woolfe, Eisak, and myself, only two would return alive
from Kotzebue. This prophecy came true, because Eisak left
us long before we came to Kotzebue Sound.

Our trail first went from Ogowinagak eastward to the innermost part of Norton Bay, where we proceeded northward by
turning to the left at a right angle. The first night's quarters
showed how difficult it was to travel with so many people. The
house we slept in was large, but there were forty people in it.
We were lying close together, some even in the fireplace, so
that not an inch of floor space was visible. To add to this a
litter of young dogs who had been thrown out during the night
forced their way back in by the door, fastened with just a
leather strap, and walked over our faces and bodies all night.

I had engaged two Eskimo, Tatmik from Selawik and Akom-
meran from Norton Bay, with whom I started out again in the
morning after the sleepless night, while Mr. Woolfe and Eisak
stayed to buy some dogs. I reached the mouth of the Kujuk

[Koyuk] River, where we made ourselves at home in a village that was deserted while the occupants were away visiting. We had chosen the smallest house that would accommodate six people and started a fire when a sled came along with nine people from Kajak on the Kangek River [Kiwalik] in the north. They at once settled themselves down and naturally had big appetities. I had tea and pancakes prepared for them and they ate heartily, explaining that since they had only two dogs they had pulled the sled all day. The next day we selected another house for ourselves and shoveled the snow out to make it habitable. We had just finished when Mr. Woolfe and Eisak arrived. The latter again made great inroads on my supply of tea when I was trying to be very sparing. This really made me very angry, and I told Eisak that as long as I live I will never be silent when someone robs me to this degree. Eisak took this quietly.

A heavy snow flurry held us here another day in this corner of Norton Bay; so I used the occasion to buy some dried salmon from a villager who had just arrived. It could be used for soup for the dogs. Later I also bought some salmon eggs. This product, which is hard and heavy, cannot be eaten in the dried condition because if one bites it it is apt to make one's teeth stick together. But with water for soup it becomes the best dog food in the area.

The next day we were reminded that we were still in the neighborhood of Ogowinagak. Every time we moved from a village it was a signal for the visiting Eskimo to follow us as a source of food, and they pursued us like hungry wolves; at the third village they were waiting for us.

Their efforts were unsuccessful, because the next morning we left at daybreak and went north. Since I knew nothing about the trail we were taking and since almost all the maps of Alaska are incorrect on the hydrographic information between Norton Bay and Kotzebue Sound, the description of our journey may have some geographical interest. We followed the Koyuk River upstream and spent the night at Itlauniwik, where the Eritak River runs into Koyuk. Here Eisak began to remember the prophecies of the shaman, and a number of small incidents were brought about to make it easier for him to leave us. While we were preparing an unoccupied house for the night's shelter he suggested another place to stay. I bought a quantity of Arctic trout and blennies for the dogs, as I took every opportunity to add to our supplies. Since the food for the last few days had been frugal, there was danger that as we went north the dogs would suffer from hunger.

Eisak took this situation as a reason for not continuing the journey. He explained that the food for men and animals would

not be enough and suggested that we might have an accident,
like being killed by the Eskimo. In any case, it was clear that
Eisak did not want to go any farther, and his leaving would
relieve us of many people and so improve our food situation.

The news I received here in Itlauniwik about the inhabitants
of Kotzebue Sound was not very encouraging. The Eskimo
there, we were told, were having local fights among themselves; furthermore, on the Selawik River, which empties into
the eastern part of Kotzebue Sound, a murder had been committed; and finally among the western Kaviaremiut a number
of young people had been killed in revenge.

The next day I had a serious dispute with Ningawakrak, my
guide. While I was busy outside the house, Mr. Woolfe was
inside engaged in his favorite duty of commissary master, as
he sat by the fire and prepared hotcakes. He called to Sewugak,
Ningawakrak's wife's half-sister, to get him some more water
to mix the flour, and she ignored the request as though she had
not heard it. Thereupon Mr. Woolfe said that if she did not
get the water, she could not have any of the pancakes. At this
sad news she set off a howling scream and called Ningawakrak. He, probably thinking that the girl had been molested,
rushed at Mr. Woolfe and with his unusual strength picked
him up and held him at arm's length over the fire. Surprised
and helpless, Mr. Woolfe cried out so that I heard him and
came indoors. I released him at once, before the fire ignited
his clothing, and threatened Ningawakrak with severe punishment if he ever attempted another such attack. This solved the
difficulty and the incident was not mentioned again. Eisak,
who was still with us, now declared that our journey would
have a bad end and that he would not go any farther with us.

He actually carried out his plan, and the next day when we
started out he remained behind and returned with his son to
Ogowinagak. There were no other incidents with Ningawakrak, and he stayed with us as a knowledgeable and faithful
guide. Now we went ahead with four sleds and twenty-two
dogs upstream on the Eritak River, which flowed from the
north. Since the river was very winding and the few warm days
caused the ice to melt, our progress was very slow. In the evening we shoveled the snow out of a summer cabin and cut a
few trees to make a platform for our sleds out of reach of the
dogs. The next morning we left the Eritak and crossed the
watershed to Kotzebue Sound. The next waterway we found
was Pujulik Creek, which flowed in the direction of Kotzebue
Sound. From this point we had a good view over the mountains
that rose from the flatland with ranges in various directions.

In the west there was a mountain range of about 3,000 to
4,000 feet which, like our watershed, was bare of vegetation

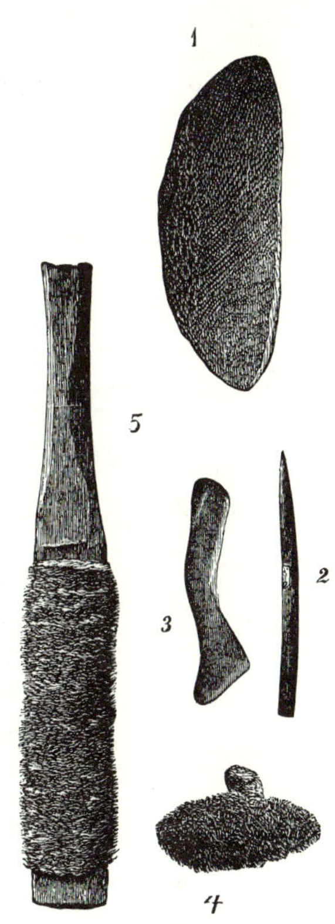

Fig. 55. Implements from
Kotzebue Sound: (1) clay
lamp; (2) instrument for
drawing designs on moist
clay pots; (3) tool used in
forming clay dishes; (4)
instrument for smoothing
inside of pots; (5) in-
strument for smoothing
outer surface of pots.

and extended in a northerly direction. Our guide told us that in the west these mountains run parallel to the rivers that empty into Kotzebue Sound. To the northeast of us was a long range of mountains where the Selawik River rises and empties into Kotzebue Sound at its eastern corner. In the far east our view of the mountains swept to the source of the well-known Koyukuk River, which empties into the great Yukon above Nulato.

We arrived at four o'clock in the afternoon at an Eskimo hut that would hold only five persons, so to accommodate everyone a tent was set up. On account of the scarcity of wood in this high elevation, it took us three hours to get our sleds into a position that would protect them from the dogs; nothing is more important on a trip like this, because the animals will eat the lines and often not even spare the sled.

Early the next day we started out to follow Pujulik Creek, and in three hours we reached a stately river that was not noted on our map and probably had never been visited by a white trader. We followed this river northward until it emptied into the Kiwalik River. I gave it the name Hagenbeck River,[30] but the Eskimo call it Unalitschok.

The difficulty with the sleds on the next day kept our progress down to only fifteen English miles, and in the evening we set up three tents for camping. The valley is about half a mile wide and heavily wooded, but the hills and mountains were bare.

The next morning we traveled downstream again and cut across many curves of the river. In the afternoon we made a brief stop to make some tea and then traveled in the dark, waiting for the moon to come out from behind the clouds. As we crossed the river I fell in before we reached Kajak on the Unalitschok River. We were well received by the inhabitants, who had never seen a white man before, but sadly these people did not have anything to eat themselves and could sell us no fish for our starving dogs. On account of the total exhaustion of both two- and four-footed travelers, we decided on a day of rest, which gave me more time to trade. I bought a beautiful piece of nephrite, two inches long, made into a labret, and I also found several stone hammers made of a mineral I did not recognize.

On the next day it was impossible to start out because of exceedingly bad weather. But even worse was the hunger that we all experienced together, since the fish were all eaten and my own provisions were almost gone and I was at my wits' end how to feed the group. The inhabitants of Kajak—that means the people in two houses, for the third was unoccupied

—tried to go up into the mountains to see if perhaps there might be some caribou they could hunt.

The next day we left Kajak and went to the Kiwalik River, into which the Unalitschok River empties. This river makes a great semicircle at its mouth that opens to the northeast and which we crossed on a rocky path. Because of exhaustion and hunger our dogs could scarcely pull the sleds through the deep snow, so I took part of the line myself and pulled so hard that I cut my hand. We did not come to the Kiwalik until it was dark, but we followed it until eight o'clock, when we arrived almost lifeless at Makakkerak, a village on the river. One of my dogs was so weak that we had to carry him. In Makakkerak we found just one house, but we all found room in it. Here food was so scarce that I could only get a little dried salmon for my poor dogs.

I did not really believe the famine that was mentioned about the Kotzebue district could be so severe. How wonderful it would have been to have for our use now all my supplies that were eaten at Eisak's house. In spite of hunger the weather forced us to stay a whole day in Makakkerak, and I did succeed in getting a few smelt for the dogs. I decided to leave my sick dog with these good people here, since I did not see how I could handle him in the next two weeks while we went to Kotzebue and returned. It was said that the famine was so great along the Noatak River that the people had even eaten their dogs. The poorest ones there live only by caribou hunting, which was very unsuccessful that season.

On Monday, 29 January, we set out again and went downstream on the Kiwalik River until we arrived at Eschscholtz Bay of Kotzebue Sound. On a point of land in the bay was an Eskimo house, Inuktok, where our guide lived. To get there we had a difficult trail on the ice, and our dogs' feet began to bleed. It was seven o'clock in the evening when we arrived at Inuktok. At last we found some fish and the dogs had a hearty meal. We stayed another day so that a good soup could be cooked for them. When they are driven to such hard work as mine have been, they need this at least once a week.

The inhabitants of Inuktok were well aware of the esteem they would receive from our visit and scaled their prices accordingly. I began to trade with them and bought several interesting pieces, for example, labrets. It seems that since I was the first white man to visit them they believed they should make a great profit from my visit and charged accordingly. Even their prices for the three days' rations for the dogs were high. I made a speech in language they could understand that

I would warn all white travelers of their prices—which I intended to do—but it did not have the least effect.

The month of January closed with a tornadolike whirlwind storm with snow flurries that developed during the night. In the morning I tried to go to a sled just a few feet from the house but could hardly breathe, and when I turned around I could not find the house. The dogs buried themselves in the snow on the protected side of the house and one could see only the tips of their noses. We dug them out and as a very special favor allowed them in the house. It was so bitterly cold that if this storm had caught us on the way it would have been impossible to save ourselves.

By morning the storm had died down enough so that at daybreak we could cross Eschscholtz Bay northward to get to the long narrow peninsula that extended northwestward into Kotzebue Bay. By noon we reached a little river called Arawingenak and spent the rest of the day in a small house there. My guide, Ningawakrak, was among relatives here. I noticed that the old Eskimo woman to whom the house belonged started to cry when she saw him. The voice of the human heart can be heard in all places and in all languages. The story back of this is that last autumn the old woman's husband shot a well-known shaman who lived at Selawik, only a few English miles away. Shortly after this the man became ill and his superstition led him to believe that this illness was punishment for his crime. He felt that he would never recover and so he really died of fright. The old woman's sorrow was renewed by seeing Ningawakrak, who was her husband's nephew. This sorrowful memory, however, did not prevent her from being a good hostess and preparing comfortable arrangements for us for the night.

Of the many places we wanted to visit in this region, the most important were nearby in the Selawik River valley. The river, which rises to the southeast of Kotzebue Sound, is well populated. It is connected with Kotzebue Sound through Hotham Inlet. This inlet has an inland connection with Selawik Inlet, a kind of bay above which there is a small lake not indicated on any maps. I named it J. Richter Lake after the chairman of the Committee on Ethnographic Collections at the Royal Museum in Berlin. Our trail led through the center of the long peninsula and on the ice of Selawik Lake to the village of Tuklomare, which lies between J. Richter Lake and Selawik Lake. The inhabitants were importunate beggars who crowded us so we scarcely had room to sleep. I succeeded in getting a large quantity of herring, so that for once my dogs had a really big meal.

The next morning we went a short distance up the Selawik

River until we came to a deserted house from which I could carry on my business. Since the house was full of snow, it took us three hours to shovel it out and make it liveable. While this was going on I sent out a sled to collect dwarf willows, with which we could start a fire. As soon as we had accomplished this the space began to fill up with Eskimo, whose greatest desire was to taste tea and pancakes fried in fish oil. The news of our arrival had evidently been spread like wildfire by runners, and our little house was full.

The next problem was the continual search for dog food, so I sent two sleds to Kajuktulik and had the pleasure of seeing them come back the next evening laden with herring. Then we sent out messengers to the neighboring villages, announcing that we would be at our house the next few days and wanted to buy ethnological objects and that Mr. Woolfe was buying skins for the Alaska Commercial Company. A lively business developed. My first purchase proved to me that one had to examine each piece carefully, for I bought a pretty pipe of greenstone that was not nephrite and a labret that proved to be colored glass.

The people were very aggressive and asked high prices and did not bring out as many ethnographic objects as I had been given to understand would be forthcoming. It seems that many of the objects of this type had already been purchased by Eskimo traders who took them to Fort Saint Michael, where Mr. Nelson bought them for the Smithsonian Institution. Toward evening I bought a few nephrite knives, labrets, and other pieces.

We had to keep trying to get the pushiest of the visitors out of the house. Mr. Woolfe bought several kinds of fox skins, some rabbit skins, and a pair of caribou boots. The next day the Eskimo who sold the boots came back and insisted on having them returned, throwing the trade goods he had received for them at Mr. Woolfe's head. Mr. Woolfe is not an aggressive person, so he returned the boots. This angered me so that I put on my leather belt in which I had a revolver and a large knife. The Eskimo, seeing this, quickly moved backward to the door and we never saw him again.

The next day the house was so full of Eskimo by daybreak that we could not move. Since they came to beg and not to trade, I took two sleds and drove to Kajuktulik to buy fish. The weather on this day, 6 February, was so mild that I traveled in shirtsleeves. In order to get to Kajuktulik I had to cross J. Richter Lake, which is five miles wide. This was another great day for my animals, for there was plenty of herring, and so I let them eat as much as they wanted. They were skeletons when we arrived and now they looked round and fat again. I bought two more sled loads and went back to our stopping place, which the Eskimo called Potogroak. When I arrived in pouring rain a sled came in right after me—one that I had sent out to announce my presence and my desire to buy ethnographic objects. The larger number of Eskimo, however, had skins, but the next sled came with objects. It was ten o'clock in the evening, but they wanted to start trading right away. I put them off until the next morning.

This time the trading was really worthwhile. I bought several nephrite pieces, stone axes, labrets, knives, and so forth. We used up almost all our trading material. After we had finished our trade, an Eskimo dealer for the Western Fur Trading Company came from the south, and because there was nothing left to buy showed his spirit of competition by offering high prices for skins. If he had come a few days earlier he would have spoiled Mr. Woolfe's business.

19

After we had concluded our business we started on the return journey from Kotzebue Sound to Ogowinagak and finally to Fort Saint Michael on 8 February 1883. The weather was fine in the beginning, so that we had a good trip from Potogroak over Selawik Lake to the previously mentioned long tongue of land. But since both my sleds were heavier than those of my companions I stayed a short distance behind them on the peninsula and had a hard struggle with a storm that came in from the south. We arrived at dusk at the Arawingenak River and village, where the sorrowing aunt of my guide Ningawakrak lived. During the night the storm developed into a hurricane with heavy showers, and since the roof of the house leaked in many places we were all soaked through by morning. I had to wring out my two blankets.

Our dogs misbehaved. Since there were no trees on the peninsula we had no material to erect a platform for our sleds. I had tied the fiercest of our dogs to the sleds with the idea that they would keep the others away, but this did not work. The dogs tore the sailcloth covers and ate a large quantity of herring.

This was our unlucky day! A storm out of the west roared with full force over the flatlands of Kotzebue Sound and violently hit the mountains of the peninsula. Disregarding this warning we broke camp, because our goal this day was a fishing cabin on the shore of Eschscholtz Bay. Our dogs did not want to go, but we forced them to climb over the rocky trail.

The same scene we had faced so often at the end of the day greeted us again. The cabin was filled with frozen snow, so hard that we had to break the back of the cabin to get at it. Toward evening the roaring of the storm was added to the grinding and cracking of the ice of Eschscholtz Bay and Kotzebue Sound, which was broken up as far as we could see. When our labors were completed we took possession of our cabin, which was about ten feet above the beach of the bay on a kind of island like a platform. We lighted a warming fire and prepared tea and pancakes.

I was drinking a beaker of tea and expected to go to bed very soon when our guide Ningawakrak went outside and returned in a moment crying, "The water is coming up!" I jumped up immediately and ran out of the house, followed by the others. In seconds the sleds were harnessed while the water of Eschscholtz Bay sprayed our faces. It was clear that after the storm a kind of spring flood took place, which was not unusual at the end of the peninsula where we were on the shore. The water had risen about ten feet in all, and in the last few hours no less than four feet.

We were all convinced that only the quickest flight could save us. It soon became apparent that the water was only one of our hazards, for the force of the hurricane and the biting cold threatened us if we could not find shelter. The only place I could think of and find in the black night was four hours' journey away, in the hut at Arawingenak. Without hesitation we rushed in the direction from which we had come yesterday over the snow-covered rocks and had the advantage of having the wind behind us. This saved our lives.

Late at night we reached Arawingenak, frozen and weary. How welcome the shelter felt now, which we had left happily in the morning. The inhabitants welcomed us with kindness and sympathy and as we told our story the "oldest people" of the area could not remember a similar occurrence and applied their Eskimo attitude to natural phenomena, saying we were unlucky birds [*Unglücksvögel*], and who knows what mishaps we might bring to the inhabitants of Kotzebue Sound. What can we do about it? It is a fact that soon after we appeared Nature behaved in an unusual way. These two incidents were related by the Eskimo as thunder and lightning are the act and the cause.

The night before, a sled from the Selawik River had arrived at Arawingenak on the way to Fort Saint Michael. He planned to go south, going overland to Makakkerak on the Kiwalik River. For this reason the owners of this sled heard nothing of the high water.

I regretted the next day, as happened so often on our trips, that I did not have a spirit thermometer. I could have established the fact that this day was the coldest I experienced anywhere in Alaska. I am certain that the cold that is endured in traveling by sled in Arctic Alaska, especially going over the mountains, is greater than any measurement recorded by the meteorological station.

The cold was so intense that we huddled around the fire in the cabin all day and were grateful for the plentiful brush available as fuel. It would not be surprising if all the broken ice in Kotzebue Sound and Eschscholtz Bay would again be solid if the cold lasted another night.

The second morning we left after the wind turned to the south and the sky was covered with clouds. We soon arrived again at the hut we had abandoned the night of the flood, and we stopped to determine the height the water had actually reached. We found the highwater mark at the roof, and we certainly would have drowned if it had overwhelmed us in our sleep. Now the water was much lower and Eschscholtz Bay had a layer of solid ice, over which we hurried and soon came to Inuktok. Here we heard many accounts of the storm, including the story that a heavy boat, turned over on a rack, was picked up and thrown far inland.

We would have gone farther that day if a snowstorm had not suddenly started. When we were in Inuktok the first time I bought one of their sealskin sacks of oil, even though they were low in provisions. Early in the morning we were awakened by a terrible noise made by the dogs, who were fighting and biting each other. Looking for the cause of this, we found to our horror that they had forced their way into the oil house and had devoured both sacks of oil. The oil spilled out on the snow and they ate it all, oil and snow. Sorry as I was that my small supply of food was dissipated, I regretted the loss of the Eskimo's part even more, for they were forced by this to move away. We paid them for the damages, which pleased them so much that they brought out a nephrite knife I had not seen before and allowed me to buy it. This knife is one of the most valuable pieces in my collection. It is set in a handle of wood, and although it has the shape of a pocketknife, it can be used in carving soft wood.

Even though it snowed constantly the next day we started out going southward up the Kiwalik River. The going was heavy, but we arrived at Makakkerak. The dog I had left there when he was sick had had good care and was well again through this good care and nourishment, for which I paid a good fee. The sled from the Selawik River, whose occupants spent the night with us at Arawingenak, was already in Makakkerak and waited there for us. I had heard some rumors about these people which made we try to get rid of their company before this. Our story was that a year ago they had cheated a trading company out of a quantity of merchandise. In spite of this they intended to go to Fort Saint Michael. What plans they had for further crime I will relate later.

In Makakkerak, days of more and better food began for us. We bought eight ptarmigan and also a good supply of dried fish. Since we were in a hurry we started out the next day even though it was still snowing. We left the Kiwalik River after two hours and crossed its large curve to the northeast. On the highlands the snow was better for the sleds than below. At dusk we came near Kajak, where I had the opportunity to see a rare phenomenon when a meteor with greenish rays fell close to us. It seemed to me it fell on a nearby hill. In Kajak the houses were empty, for everyone was away caribou hunting. We used the same house where we had been on the outward journey. The sled from the Selawik River also stayed and left, going southward, the next morning.

We decided on a rest day, since it was necessary to cook a nourishing soup for our hard-working dogs. We also had much to do in mending gloves and boots. I sent some Eskimo out hunting and they returned with some ptarmigan. The rest in this large and well-kept house was the most pleasant on the whole trip. My companion, Mr. Woolfe, had a surprise here. When we were here before he had bought a red fox skin and a caribou skin and had left them here for our return. The skins were not to be found, since probably the former owner took them back. In Inuktok an Eskimo sold Mr. Woolfe several skins and offered to keep them until his return, but in the meantime he sold them again to another dealer, then refused to give the sales price back to Mr. Woolfe. The natives, who believe that might makes right, take every opportunity to outdo a weaker white man. I often found that my energetic personality was my only protection from both the Eskimo and the Indians. In British Columbia this was aided by the respect the natives had for the cannons of the British gunboats. In Alaska the situation was much the same. I often told the Eskimo, when I saw they were trying to cheat me, that I would tell all my compatriots not to come to them to trade. If one can once support such a statement with a powerful physique one can establish a reputation and protection from fraud.

The next morning we set out but were surprised by a snowstorm coming toward us, which by dark forced us to set up our caribou skins as tents in the protection of a thicket. Despite the bad weather our menu for that night consisted of rabbit soup and pancakes. During the night the storm ceased, and in the morning we started out in beautiful weather as we left the river and climbed over the divide between Kotzebue Sound and Norton Sound. We again came to Pujulik Creek and found on the southern side, on the banks of the Eritak River, the cabin where we had spent the night four weeks before. We had a good meal again, with ptarmigan soup and other good things, while our poor dogs had to satisfy themselves with a more frugal meal. Our uncomfortable traveler, the sled from the Sewalik River, was here again with us for the night.

The longest single journey of this expedition was carried on two days after this, when we stopped at Itlauniwik and boiled soup from the remains of the fish for our tired dogs. We then took advantage of the bright moonshine and left at three o'clock in the morning in good weather with a north wind. We went downstream on the Koyuk River and reached its mouth at Norton Bay at the village of Kujuk at eleven o'clock. Toward evening we started out again and met Eisak's son, who was fishing, and spent the night with him. The next noon saw us back at our "Norwegian peasant house" at Ogowinagak after a trip to Kotzebue Sound and back, in thirty-eight days.

Eisak received and accepted accusations from us about his conduct: we had left a tin of biscuits at Itlauniwik for our return journey and he had used a large part of it.

We were very weary, but we could not allow ourselves much rest at Eisak's house, so we made the preparations necessary for the last lap to Fort Saint Michael in a day and a half.

Beside Eisak and his wife and son, a number of other Eskimo joined the trip, and our caravan included eight sleds and twenty-five men. After a strenuous journey over the ice in Norton Sound we came to Shaktolik late at night. In order to get rid of the disagreeable group of beggars that had attached themselves to our party, I went to an Eskimo house that had just been abandoned because of the death of a child. Even their longing for tea and pancakes did not overcome their fear of the presence of death. The only one who slept in the house with us was Ningawakrak, our guide.

The next day a snowstorm raged again, so severe that one could not see twenty steps ahead, but we were accustomed to such weather, so we prepared our sleds and started out. Even though the wind was behind us we had difficulty getting through the snow. On the way I stopped at a little house, for I knew there was a nephrite amulet there, which I bought for a high price, since it was a rare piece. We went along the coast so as not to lose our way. If we had not all been very anxious to finish the trip we would not have been able to keep on in the unfavorable weather.

It was the worst day of the whole trip. At four in the afternoon we were very happy to be in Egavik, the last Malemiut village where there was shelter. Soon we had a fire going and with a cup of hot tea forgot the day's hardships. The dogs relished the dried salmon I bought for them here. The weather was good the next day, and we spent the night in Unalakleet. We stayed out one more night at Kikertarok, and on Monday, 26 February, we were back at Fort Saint Michael.

20

In my six months in Alaska I had now explored the great land in three directions, using Fort Saint Michael as my central point. To the east I traveled 900 English miles, to the west, to the Bering Sea, and to the north, to Kotzebue Sound, and on these three journeys I collected about 7,000 ethnographic objects for the Berlin Museum. It was now necessary to go on another tour to the south, and I would probably leave Alaska without returning to Fort Saint Michael.

I stayed at Fort Saint Michael for three weeks this time. I found no changes had occurred and was greeted with a friendly welcome. The incident of my taking a skull from an Indian grave for scientific purposes and study, which I have already discussed, was still not forgotten, and the Ingalik had been antagonistic against a trader, who complained about this to Mr. Lorenz in Fort Saint Michael. He allowed a number of Ingalik from Nulato to come to the trading station, and with an interpreter I explained to them that this incident occurred more than one hundred miles farther upstream. Mr. Lorenz showed them a medical book with illustrations of the human skeleton, knowledge of which is necessary for exact medicine, and explained that white people are anxious to learn all they can about the subject. He said that skulls of whites are studied in the same way and that no white people get angry about this, but have great respect for the students of medicine. So they should go home and tell their people that they should not be angry.

This ethnological lecture had good results, and the Ingalik went home satisfied. I then began to register and pack my collection with the faithful help of the younger brother of Saxo, an Eskimo trader previously mentioned. I lent my guide, Ningawakrak, a large amount of trade goods for his next trip, which he was commissioned to use in making purchases for me. I could do this for him because I could give him credit on better terms than the Alaska Commercial Company.

Beside transacting this business, my physical condition was my principal concern. I took expensive steam baths and had all my clothing cleaned and washed, my boots and gloves repaired. I also placed my dogs in good care so that they would recover from their fatigue, for the trip ahead of us would be more strenuous than the ones in the past. Then I packed everything so that it would be ready to go to Europe on the first ship the following summer. I also wrote letters and reports.

While I was spending a week at Fort Saint Michael, Mr. Greenfield, the head agent of the Western Fur Trading Company, came over to Mr. Lorenz's house and said that during the night before his warehouse had been broken into and a large part of his trade articles taken. It was noted at this time that there was also one sled missing from the village—the one from the Selawik River that had traveled with us from Kotzebue Sound to Norton Bay. The man and his two Eskimo guides from Kotzebue were gone. Mr. Leavitt, the Signal Service Officer, offered to organize a party and follow him, and I was invited to join. One of the Eskimo was found in Fort Saint Michael, but he insisted at a hearing that he had not taken part in the theft and that he did not know the name of the other Eskimo.

The thief with his loaded sled had a twelve-hour advantage of us, but we traveled with a lightly packed sled and were well armed. In the darkness we arrived at Kikertarok, where we received the news that the sled we were following had passed through that afternoon. We continued in our way, feeling certain now that we would meet him in Golzowa [Golsovia]. It was so dark that we passed the village without seeing it, then turned back.

As we neared the place we held a council of war, and since we knew the thief was armed, we entered the next house. In the entrance an old Eskimo came toward us, who was embarrassed when we asked if the thief was in his house, but he said that the man had gone to the nearby kassigit, from which we heard a drumbeat and singing. We found that we had been on the right track at first and went back to the first house in the village. We ran in and found that the bird had flown by opening the skylight and climbing out. I ran onto the roof, but was too late.

One Eskimo who was left on watch with our sled stood during this time ready to fire if there was occasion for it. The thief, who did not know where our sled stood, came close to it and was seen by the Eskimo, who raised his weapon to hinder his flight. In the same moment the dogs noticed the stranger, and since they are trained to start as soon as some-one moves suddenly, they started to run. The Eskimo fell back on the sled, and before he could grasp the reins and straighten himself the thief disappeared in the darkness. As we later found out, the poor fellow, fearful that we were still after him, half-dressed as he was, ran for two days and two nights to the northwest over the ice of Norton Sound, and when he could no longer run he slept in the open on the ice. In consequence of this matchless adventure he was so far away that we were not in the mood to follow him, but we took his sled drawn by four fine dogs and loaded with his booty, and after lecturing the man who had given us wrong information about the thief's presence in his house, we went back to Fort Saint Michael.

When we arrived there, dead tired, we were laughed at by Mr. Lorenz and the other people for not bringing the thief with us. In the course of a hearing about the incident it became known that the Ingalik at Fort Saint Michael knew that this theft was planned but gave no warning because they were afraid the thief would take revenge.

This experience and the constantly increasing arrogance of the Ingalik and the northern Eskimo led the station agents of the two large trading companies to decide not to compete with each other any more. They decided that they would alternate days in dealing with the natives. In their agreement they also decided to lower the prices for skins by about one-third and no longer offer sugar as a trade item, so that this would end the Malemiut's use of it for making whiskey. This pact was agreed upon at a two-day visit of the families of both station managers.

So the time passed quickly, and I soon had my preparations for the trip in hand. After fond farewells from all the previously mentioned persons here and my traveling companion, Mr. Woolfe, I left on my long journey early in the morning on 18 March 1883. My sled was heavily laden with provisions for two months and many trading articles. It was pulled by thirteen strong dogs, who had to make a great effort to get through the deep snow. We went along the coast of Norton Sound, which I knew very well to the south of the Yukon River. My guide started to complain of all kinds of pains, so that it was impossible for me to move as fast as I liked to do.

We had to spend the night in a deserted house, and after traveling for an hour we came to Pikmiktalik, where I exchanged guides and started out again in really warm weather to Cape Romanzoff,[31] a place I well remember on my return from the Yukon River with my laden skin boat, which broke there. Here we set up our tent for the night while a storm was again gathering. My physical condition was not the best, and in spite of all the care I took I became snowblind and suffered great pain. Of course this could not delay the journey, so we started out in the morning against a heavy snowstorm and arrived at noon at Pastolik. Here I had an accident.

When I was entering the kassigit I missed a step and fell very deep into the lower floor. I hit my right shin on a stone that was under the entrance opening. It was lucky that I did not break any bones, but my foot became swollen and was very painful even into April before I could use it again. I must have made an impressive appearance, being blind and lame, when I came to the gathering that had been organized by the Kwikpakmiut of Pastolik who were friends from my former visit. They all came to trade and I bought a number of pieces, principally many dance masks. Even though my condition was not satisfactory and the snow and the storm had not ceased, I went ahead, especially because it was a short trip to Kotlik, where the Alaska Commercial Company had a trading post at the mouth of the Yukon River. Since I could not stand or walk I let myself be laid on the sled. We arrived there at noon, and the station manager, Mr. Kammkoff, was happy to see me. I received back ten of my dogs, which had gone to Kotzebue Sound with me.

He promptly treated my foot with warm baths, which gave me some relief. Even though I had been here twice before this trip I had made no purchases, but now I found a few pieces. My collection had increased on the way from Fort Saint Michael, so I packed it and asked Mr. Kammkoff to ship it to Fort Saint Michael for further transport in the spring.

I remained here the next day for this packing and for further treatments for my foot, which responded well. The weather also was not good.

My host was very familiar with the regions into which I was going and gave me long descriptions of the customs of the people, but all this unfortunately was in Russian, of which I understood little. His kindness did not end with these descriptions; when I was ready to go on the second day, he gave me one of his sleds and three of his people to go along. How welcome his directions were showed in the snowstorm we traveled in, when we could easily have lost our way. Our intelligent guide brought us to a village of three houses, Nunapiklogak, where we again spent the night in the kassigit.

The next morning we started out in stormy weather. The sleds sank deep into the snow and the dogs pulled very hard, but even with the help of the whip they could hardly move them. We were soaked to the skin and were happy to arrive at the Nanuwarok River at noon, where we were kindly received in the village of the same name. I bought several pieces.

I noticed that the natives here amused themselves with a game that I had learned in Golovnin Bay.

Four men played together, two sitting on each side of the entrance of the kassigit. Beside each party a board was put on the wall, on which a circle was drawn in charcoal. Each player was given a wooden spear six to eight feet long, with an iron point, feathered at the butt end. The competition was between the pairs of men on each side of the entrance. Two players on one side threw the spear, one after the other, into the circle of the opposite side. Hitting within the circle was scored with a small wooden stick as a marker. This game is useful for the natives, since it provides practice for seal and bird hunting.

I stayed in this place for another day even though the hut we occupied leaked so that we were constantly wet. Mr. Kammkoff's people returned to Kotlik from here, so we hired three men and a sled and set out. In spite of the horrible weather we arrived at noon on 27 March at Eratlerowik, where we had to stay. The houses here were half full of dirt and water; the population also left much to be desired. Even though there was plenty of fresh fish we were charged high prices. I bought a valuable piece of carved nephrite. Although our circumstances here were disagreeable, the terrific storm forced us to stay another day.

When we were on the way again my people wanted to stop almost every hour to make tea. I was anxious to move on, so when they stopped I kept going even though my foot hurt. My effort was rewarded by our arriving at Andreafsky at nine o'clock in the evening. On the way I broke through the ice and was thoroughly soaked. We arrived with only two sleds, because one broke down and came the next day. Mr. Carl Pettersen, the station manager, an old friend, greeted me and spent half the night talking.

I decided here in Andreafsky to give up going along the Yukon and to cross the tundra diagonally toward Cape Vancouver. My host, a Swede by birth, had made many trips in this region in the service of the Alaska Commercial Company and gave me a good description of the country and its people. During the summer the wide, flat tundra has innumerable lakes and ponds, as well as rivers, creeks, and many waterways, so that one can find one's way as with the constellations; but in winter it has one great majestic blanket of white reaching to the horizon, hundreds of miles of land and water, while the sky is usually hidden in clouds. There is not one rise of land in the whole great circle. Our own stature is the highest thing in sight. There is no tree or bush or house to show the way. The Eskimo huts are only a few feet high, and sometimes these are completely hidden by one night's fall of snow. A heavy snowfall can in a few minutes erase one's own tracks, and it is impossible to find one's way back to a sled. If a traveler wanders too long his dogs will bed themselves down in the snow and, soon being covered by it, cannot be distinguished in the landscape, and the sly creatures will give no sign of their presence. This happened to my host.

After I decided to cross the tundra in the winter, Mr. Pettersen promised me one of his traders to go along for the longer part of the trip to show us the way. At the same time I made some necessary preparations; I gave all the pieces in my collection that I still had with me, including the one my host gave me, to him to pack in a box and send to Fort Saint Michael at the next opportunity.

21

The Tundra Journey

My sled journey over the tundra began early in the morning of 2 April 1883. We made an impressive little train. My heavily packed sled with fourteen dogs was in the lead, then two sleds of Pettersen's with a total of sixteen dogs followed in the caravan. The first was my accompanying sled, which carried part of my luggage, and the second belonged to the trader who was going in the same direction.

The snow was hard and good for traveling, and the weather at the time of our departure was as favorable as one could expect at this time of the year. We went first along the Kwikpak or Yukon River until we left it and traveled along a winding little tributary. The tundra here already showed its peculiar landscape formations, namely the dotting of the surface with little ponds, and it was impossible to determine as we went along whether we were traveling on land or ice-covered water. The vegetation, while still in the vicinity of the Yukon, consisted of conifers and brush.

At one o'clock in the afternoon we stopped at a little Eskimo village, Kjokkaktolik [Chakwaktolik], which lies on a little stream of the same name, and made tea. For the chore of caring for our thirty dogs we engaged an Eskimo who continued with us to the neighboring stream where he had a cache of fish that he sold us.

Here we stood on the edge of the real tundra, which spread out like a sea before us. Only in a few places, as far, for instance, as at the Kusilwak River, was there a rise of land that dominated the scene. We spent the night in a village called Kaggan in the southwest corner of a lake of the same name. Only after extraordinary effort did we succeed in securing enough firewood to make tea. We realized that we were now approaching an area where the natives were so short of firewood for cooking that they were forced to eat their food raw.

Even on this first day it became clear that none of my people or traveling companions were sure enough of the direction we should take to act as our guide. Therefore we took with us a native who knew the area. In such level terrain it is an event if one sees any rise of land, but we were faced with five mountains which we had already seen the day before to the southwest. As we approached these five mountains we discovered that they were inactive volcanoes. I climbed one of the lowest ones, which rose steeply from the ground for several hundred feet. I found the crater wall decorated with parapets that circumscribed a crater about 300 feet in diameter, with a funnel 150 to 200 feet deep. The floor of the crater was covered with snow. The rest of the volcanoes that were in this area of four to five English miles were higher, up to 1,000 feet above the floor of the tundra. I named the group for the most famous Arctic explorer of our century, the Nordenskjöld group.

Our road led through the middle of this group, where we found many polar foxes. When we came out on the tundra it began to snow, and any hope of finding our direction was given up. According to the information of our guide there should be a house in the area, which we found after much searching. It was occupied by only one family, whose name was Akulerpak, and served as our shelter for the night. Unfortunately we found no food for our dogs.

The next morning we started off again in spite of the blizzard and were put on the right trail by our knowledgeable guide. However, this man soon left us and could not be retained by any promises. So we were dependent on our own judgment, and luckily I had a pocket compass with which we decided on a direction and followed it. On the way we found sled tracks, and following these came to the village of Kajaluigemiut. It is a community of six houses and a kassigit. Here we were obviously in a very poor area, for the natives seemed near starvation. We did succeed, however, after much bargaining, in buying a small sack of fish for our weary dogs. After I had secured a few ethnographic pieces we continued in our southwesterly direction.

Toward evening we arrived at Jukkak, the abandoned residence of a trader, where we spent the night. The place is on the west coast of Alaska at the mouth of the Jukkak River, at the outer point of Vancouver Bay, which reaches from Cape Vancouver deep into the tundra. From this point on I went along the coast.

Before we reached the Jukkak River, as we rode away with the sled we noticed a wolf that was perhaps just as hungry as our animals. He kept his distance so that it was not possible to shoot him. When we unpacked our sled at Jukkak we noticed that at the previous starving village a bag of beans had been stolen, but as great a loss as it was to us, I could not deny them this small addition to their food supply. Most serious for us was the fact that at Jukkak we also could get no food for our poor dogs. It was therefore very fortunate that on the continuation of our journey near Vancouver Bay we met an Eskimo from whom we bought a whole sled full of dried herring heads, which made exactly one meal for our dogs.

The trail now led along the north shore of Cape Vancouver, where we met the trader of the Alaska Commercial Company at the village of Nulleslugemiut, who was about to start on the same trip to Andreafsky. In this village almost all the natives had died the previous winter of an epidemic. The trader went back with us to Tununak, where we arrived at one o'clock in the afternoon and found ample food for our dogs. The range of mountains gradually slopes from 2,000 feet down to the level of the tundra.

My prospects of obtaining ethnographic objects were not favorable so far, since I could not get any dance masks because the widespread sickness of the natives had canceled the winter dances. However, it was possible for me to secure some other very interesting objects, among them several labrets. These probably came from Nunivak, an island a few miles offshire. The people of this region are about as filthy as any I have seen anywhere in the world. Related to this is the fact that at most places in the tundra there is such a dearth of wood that they almost never have any fire and do not cook their food; they live in miserable huts that in the spring are so damp inside that they appear more like a swamp than a dwelling for human beings. As one enters the tunnel to their houses one sinks to the ankles and wrists in soft earth. Even during the least dampness, water drips constantly from the ceiling of the hut on those sleeping there, so that by morning the covers are soaked through and must be wrung out. In addition, wherever these covers touch the arm or hand, a dark crust of slime develops that leaves a hard residue. In these circumstances the natives live in a miserable condition during the greater part of the year, so it is not surprising that illness wipes out whole villages. The character of the people shows this eternal want they have to fight; they are shy, cowardly, fearful, and obsequious, which may have been contributed to by the oppression they suffered in the past from the Russians.

But in spite of all this we found traits among them that indicated they formerly had a more highly developed society. For example, they erected unusual monuments for their dead and for victims of accidents. I saw several at Tununak. These consisted of carved figures, some dressed. The arms of these figures were made of walrus tusks. Beside them were models

Fig. 56. Child's bone doll dressed in fur clothing. Kuskokwim River.

of kayaks, bows and arrows, seals, and caribou, suggesting that the person buried there might have been killed while hunting walrus, seal, or caribou.

This also shows the artistic skill of these people. The kayaks they have on the south and west coasts of Alaska are of better form and carry as an ornament at the front end the carved head of a turtle. The gunwale of the big umiak or rowboat does not lie level in the water like that of the more northerly Eskimo, but lifts itself up like the prows of boats in British Columbia, with a graceful curve. The lances used for hunting and fishing are good in design and craftsmanship. An unusual sight is the young girls, many of whom attach wooden figures to their fur hoods. But it was not possible for me to buy any of this carved work because they were worn for many years. My purchasing was also very much curtailed by the previous visit of Mr. Nelson of the Smithsonian Institution, who had bought extensively.

At Tununak I received certain information about conditions on the tundra from the trader Aloska, who understood English quite well, that substantiated statements made by Mr. Pettersen in Andreafsky. There exist between the lower Yukon and Vancouver Bay two waterways through the tundra. One is supposed to be an "outflow" of the Yukon, which in many windings is so increased by this additional water that it flows through a lake; the other is dissipated in a straight line so that it is necessary to cross over stretches of land at two places in spring and at four places in summer when the water is lower. The second of these waterways enters the Yukon a few miles above Andreafsky and the other the same distance below.

After a pause of one day I continued my journey in a southerly direction. In order not to travel around the whole of Cape Vancouver, which projects far into the sea, I tried to cross the peninsula formed by the cape. After some hesitation the people with me decided to go along. The passage seemed very good, the snow was right, and so by evening we reached the village of Ommekomsiut. It is an unusual village in that there are two kassigits. I began at once to show my European trade wares and found tobacco and needles to be in great demand. With the exception of pretty hunting gear I could find nothing. In the kassigit, where I had established myself, the natives crowded around so that one could scarcely move. This situation was taken advantage of by a few thieving characters, who took our biscuits.

On a beautiful day with bright sunshine we set forth the next morning along the coast and arrived at Peimilliagaremiut, where we stopped to make tea and purchase some items. When we started out again I saw at about two o'clock in the afternoon the phenomenon of a sun dog in the most extraordinary form I have ever seen; a thin ring surrounding the sun, not in the usual vertical position from top to bottom, but horizontally. This line was crossed by another ring from top to bottom and so created two sun dogs. These last vertical stripes had rainbow colors, while the horizontal curve glittered like a fine thread of silver. The whole scene presented a beautiful sight not often seen; not that the sun dog is unusual in this region, for I have seen them often, but never such a sight as this. The statement is often made that the appearance of a sun dog foretells a south wind, and during my journey I can substantiate that; even on this day by evening a heavy storm with snow came from the south.

We arrived during the day at a peninsula where there was a large Eskimo village, Kikertaurok, which looked like a small town, since the numerous huts were surrounded by poles on which were drying nets that from a distance looked like flags. The village has two kassigits, one of them quite large. There was very little to buy here because there had been extensive purchasing for Washington.

The storm from the south raged all night and prevented us from leaving early the next morning. At noon we finally left and about three o'clock in the afternoon we passed the village of Nogemiut, then Kjikjingemiut [Chichinak], where we stopped for tea. After another two hours' run came to Pinjakpagemiut [Paingakmiut].

It was snowing and the whole landscape, including the sea, had been changed to a monotonous flatness where it was impossible to orient oneself. Our guide then lost his way, and we did not come to the village we expected to find. It was impossible to find any shelter, so we had to content ourselves with camping in the open. At dawn we started out again and we were fortunate enough, in spite of continuing snow flurries, to find a sled track that led us to the village of the Paingakmiut, which consisted of ten houses and two kassigits.

Our starved dogs strengthened themselves by eating to their hearts' content innumerable hornfish. Even though the poorly built kassigit had snow blowing into it, we made it our night's shelter, since there were unmistakable signs of more snow. This was very fortunate for us, because another night of camping in the open could have been a disaster for our party. My physical condition called for a little care, for my eyes pained me excessively in spite of my colored glasses and Eskimo snow goggles, and I was almost blinded. In this village careful searching turned up no ethnological objects to buy.

While we were sleeping in the kassigit and the storm was raging outside, a strange dog who had lost his way fell through

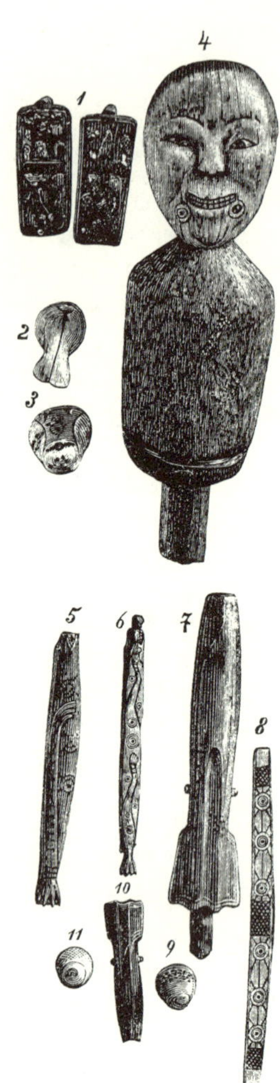

Fig. 57. Miscellaneous
pieces from the mouth of
the Kuskokwim River:
(1) bone earrings with
inlay; (2, 3) kayak
ornaments; (4) doll carved
of bone; (5–7) needle
cases of hollow bone;
(8) fastener for sewing
bag; (9, 11) kayak orna-
ments; (10) needle case.

the window in the roof of our underground hut, breaking the seal-gut covering. He broke his foot, and his howling, along with the wind and an avalanche of snow that came down after his fall, all combined to interrupt our sleep. At the moment nothing could be done about it, so I pulled my covers over my head and fell asleep again.

Naturally the next morning it was utterly impossible to continue our trip, since this type of weather usually lasts for several days. Another circumstance contributed to our staying—there was plenty of food for our dogs.

The women of this neighborhood had developed an unusual skill in decorating themselves with beads. The women, young girls, and even children wore beads everywhere, when possible even in their hair. The lower lips of the young girls were perforated in three places; the two end points held a labret, a small crooked bone fastened by a button-shaped end inside the mouth to prevent its falling out and on the outside ornamented with beads. In the center perforation there was also a very small bone with bead decoration. The septum was also pierced, and a string of small beads was inserted that hung down to the mouth. This little string of beads is also found among the Eskimo beauties on the lower Yukon and farther north among the Malemiuts. All these people also share the custom of tattooing the chin, except that in the south the two bands of tattooing are farther apart than in the north. The inhabitants of the tundra coast lived, at the time I was there, principally on hornfish and blackfish. In uncleanliness they competed with the population of the interior tundra.

The storm lessened during the day, so we prepared for our departure; but I refused, for good reasons, to start out without a guide, knowing full well that we could not make any headway alone. At first no one in the settlement would guide us, but when they saw that I was really in earnest a young man volunteered. In favorable wind and weather we started out and came next to the Eskimo village Kwikluk [Kwethluk], which lies on the coast. From here we turned in the direction of the second-largest river in Alaska, the Kuskokwim, which has often been mentioned.

The next community, which we reached about noon, was Orrutoremiut. The natives had no ethnological pieces of any importance except some bead ornaments with which the women bedecked themselves. On the same day we came also to three villages; Sintuleremiut, Sewartlaremiut, and Ameoraremiut. In this last place we slept in the kassigit that night. The advanced time of the year, 12 April, drove us on because I needed to dash across the river to Quigiorremiut, but I found nothing there. Not until we stopped at the next village, Noksiaremiut, did I find anything, and even there there was not much. There I met two Eskimo families that out of dire need spent the whole winter under a turned-over boat. They had spread skin blankets on the ground and had existed without fire all winter because they had no way of carrying out the smoke; consequently they also ate all their food raw.

We were lucky to engage a very skillful guide who kept us going in spite of violent snow flurries, and we came next to the large settlement of Kangerenaremiut, where I found the largest kassigit on the whole coast. Another indication of the wealth of this community was the many graves on which had been placed articles of all kinds—old guns, wooden hats, harpoons, lances, bows and arrows. We had a hard time finding our way and spent the night at the summer fishing village of Ilquigamiut.

In bitter cold and storm we fought our way the next day to Kulewarewialeremiut, where our excellent guide left us. We proceeded at once to Kukkaremiut and finally came with great difficulty to Klekusiremiut. Here we had to stay because of the storm. I saw two large grave monuments of wood. One figure represented a man whose body was painted red and whose mouth and eyes were inlaid with bone. Behind this figure a wooden wall was erected, on which all kinds of grave goods were hung. The natives of this area of Alaska live on the tundra in the winter, but in spring they come to the delta of the Kuskokwim to hunt seals. Later in the year when the salmon runs begin they spread out into the waterways. We found ourselves for several days in the funnel-shaped spreading mouth of the Kuskokwim River. The ice was no longer passable, so we had to spend several days traveling up the river to get around the bay. From Klekusiremiut we went, in spite of the storm, along the left bank of the Kuskokwim until noon, when we could finally see the opposite shore. Here we crossed the river and found, in some breaks in the ice on the opposite bank, the first signs of vegetation since we had left the Yukon.

The next village on this bank was Joktjitleramiut, a currently uninhabited summer fishing community of eight temporary huts. Here we lost our guide, who could in no way be persuaded to go any farther. As a farewell he sold me several very good dance masks he owned. Alone without a guide, we set out in the storm, on the left bank. The wind was so cold that I again froze my nose. We tried to follow the bank of the main stream, but there were many small tributaries, so we became confused and finally found it necessary to camp in the shelter of a small hill.

In order not to get further confused by the waterways, we decided the next morning to find our way to the main stream

again in spite of the rough ice along the bank. After two hours
of hard traveling we came back to the Kuskokwim River. In
the next village we engaged a guide who brought us in the
afternoon to the long-sought-for village of Mamtratlagemiut[32]
where there was a trading post of the Alaska Commercial Company. I was greeted by Nicolai Kamelkowski, a half-Russian,
half-Ingalik who was the agent there.

22

The great mountain range that runs from south to north for
the entire length of the North American continent ends, except
for spurs westward, on the left bank of the Kuskokwim River
and the tundra takes over.

At the moment when my trail led to the right bank of the
Kuskokwim I found myself at the border of the tundra and
entered the territory of the Kuskokwimiut, an Eskimo group
whose existence depends on the river along which they live.
The welcome we received from the station manager, Nicolai
Kamelkowski, reminded me of the fleshpots of Egypt and
brought me back to luxuries of which we had long been deprived—butter, fresh bread, reindeer roast, and so on.

My stay at this place was limited to two days because the
melting of the snow and ice cover was far advanced. It was not
the necessity of getting back to San Francisco that seemed urgent at this moment; I wished to take advantage of my being
in this region as long as the condition of the snow allowed
travel by sled. Therefore I was anxious to cover more of the
south coast of Alaska. It did not seem too daring at this time
of year to attempt to cross the high mountain range which
rises east of the Kuskokwim, since it was a certainty that in
the upper reaches of this range there would still be plenty of
snow for sledding. The only circumstance that made me hesitate to take this route was that this area had never been
crossed by a white traveler; but this urged me to continue
rather than restraining me.

My next job was to register all the objects I had secured
on the trip so far and pack them so that my host could send
them out to San Francisco on the first ship. In this way my
baggage was lightened considerably. I also wrote several letters to Europe, and on the morning of 18 April I started on
my way. Mr. Kamelkowski was kind enough to lend me two
of his people to start me on my way. They undertook to take

me from the Kuskokwim in a southeasterly direction over the mountains to the mouth of the Togiak River and so to the coast. We had all together twenty-four dogs, of which fifteen were mine. We started down the Kuskokwim and made a fast trip, arriving at sundown at the deserted village of Jotsitle, where we spent the night. The next day the journey continued downstream and in succession we passed the villages of Ago-laremiut [Arolik], Kaoweangemiut, Semeriangemiut, Illin-tongemiut, and Senneremiute. At the last place we found a warehouse to which a trading vessel came every year to leave its cargo. We spent the night in one of the two unoccupied Eskimo houses there.

The two guides, with whom I could converse either in a general Eskimo dialect or in English, were the best I had had on any part of my journey. Large and well-built, with tremendous body strength and the great flexibility of early manhood, never tiring in packing, skillful and imaginative in overcoming any difficulty, always cheerful and alert, they were just right to face the extra endurance it took each of us to negotiate the climb into the mountains. The next day we still continued downstream, always on the east bank of the Kuskokwim, and passed the village of Oejak, where we saw more grave monuments such as have already been described, and around noon came to Kwinnekaremiut. From here the ice on the river was not passable, and so we decided to go into the mountains, es-pecially since we engaged a native of the region as another guide.

The trail led next across tundra landscape on which there was scarcely any snow. Fortunately, the many little lakes and ponds were still covered with ice, so that we could make rela-tively fast headway. We reached the Agalik River, which was already open, and even on the banks there was no snow. Here the skill of my guides showed itself most clearly when they carried one heavy sled after the other over a terrain full of deep holes. We used fully three hours to cover an English mile. The hardships of the day caused the last guide engaged to leave secretly in the darkness while we were camping the follow-ing night.

The next morning we continued along the river. Fortunately, even though the middle of the stream was clear there was a little strip along the shore on which we could use our sleds. Toward noon we met some Eskimo fishing along the river. The river was full of fish, so it was not astonishing to see the great catch they had made. I identified in this catch at least four kinds of salmon trout and one fish I did not know, which the Eskimo called *sullukbauk*. The young men who belonged to this group were all out hunting; so as I wanted to engage

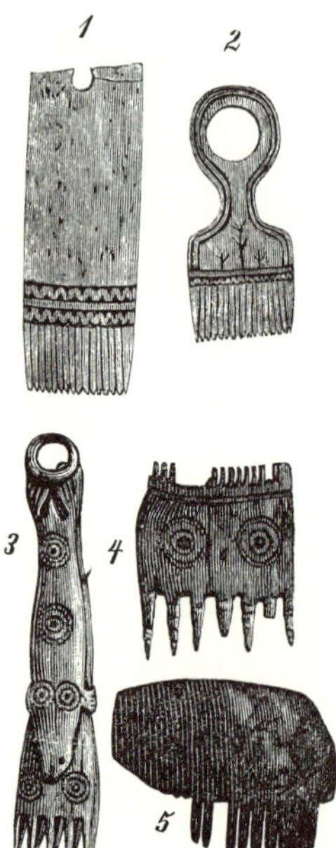

Fig. 58. Combs carved of (1–2) mammoth tusk; (3–4) walrus teeth; and (5) caribou hoof. Kuskokwim River.

one of these people to guide us through the mountains, I stayed
with the fishermen and set up my tent. The fish were so cheap
that not only did we have plentiful meals, but our dogs were
treated to fresh salmon trout. Toward evening the hunters returned and I found a guide.

During the night there was a heavy storm from the southeast and I was afraid my tent would be blown away. The
night's rest was also disturbed by a bloody fight that broke
out among our dogs. In the course of this one of the dogs was
thrown against the tent, and the cotton material, which had
had much wear, gave way, flinging the dog directly onto my
stomach. The next morning we supplied ourselves amply with
fish and broke camp. We had been right at the base of the
mountains and at the entrance of a valley. We went upstream
and started climbing gradually. The ice cover on the river became stronger, and there were only a few places where we
had to drag the sleds over the bare ground. Since even at this
time of year the day is sixteen hours long, we were able to
cover a considerable distance in daylight.

In the course of the afternoon we left the river and climbed
over the first mountain range, where the snow was beautifully
hard and right for the sleds. Our trail led us between two volcanic ranges with jagged points and crater crevasses. In this
region we passed a long lake that had no known name, just
like everything else here.

From this lake there is an outlet southeastward into a valley,
but the ice cover on the river was broken, so we had to change
our course. We started out over a steep 4,000-foot-high peak
on which the snow was very favorable for us. When we started
down again we had to unharness the dogs and let the sleds
run down without any help. It was a mad ride, for the sleds
turned over and ran into each other, but as usual in adventures
of this sort we came through without an accident.

When we were at the highest point the scene was beautiful
and awe-inspiring. Before us lay a great valley with many small
mountain streams and rivers, and farther to the south and
southeast hundreds of jagged peaks were visible.

After we descended into the valley we had much trouble
fording a rapid little stream with steep banks. We followed
farther into the valley and came to a stately river that was fed
by many tributaries and flowed southward, where it emptied
into Kuskokwim Bay near Cape Newenham. I called it Virchow
River, but the Eskimo call it Katzarak.

During the night the frost diminished, and it seemed as if
it might snow with the coming of the south wind. By morning
this actually happened, and it looked as though we should stay
on Virchow River. But the fact that our food was running low

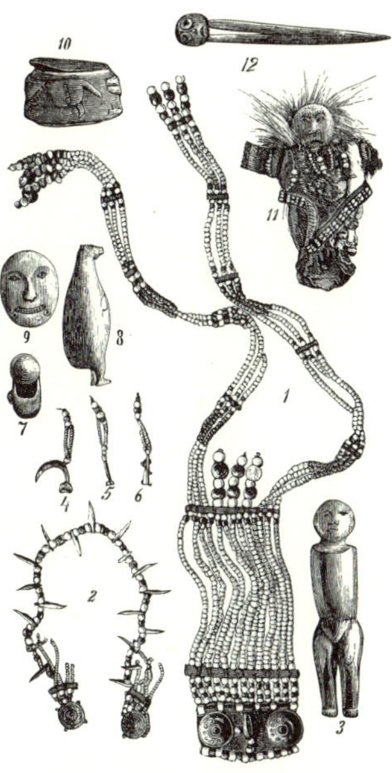

Fig. 59. Objects made of
bone, from the Kusko-
kwim River: (1) girl's hair
decoration; (2) earrings
fastened to a necklace;
(3) doll; (4–6) lip orna-
ments for girls; (7) joint
for a harpoon line; (8)
carving of a polar bear;
(9) plug for opening in
skin of female seal; (10)
snuffbox; (11) doll
representing a female;
(12) bodkin.

and we needed food for our dogs forced us to start out in spite of snow flurries and without knowing whether there was any stopping place in this unknown mountain wilderness. The storm from the south was our only directional guide and we were forced to head constantly into it. The storm also cleared the snow away from our trail, thus forcing us to follow every little brook where there was ice and every patch of snow. So gradually we climbed over a mountain range, beyond which we again found a valley.

After following the waterways a short distance we again came to a large river and followed its course. The river flowed first southeast and then southwest. Everywhere the current had broken the ice cover and we wandered helplessly, looking for a place to cross. At last we found a ford and reached the opposite bank safely. It seemed that this river received much of its water from the east side of the peninsula that ends in Cape Newenham, and that it emptied east of the cape into the Bering Sea. I gave the name William Schönlank to this river. The Eskimo call it Koggaklek.

Searching for a place to cross the river took us off our principal direction, but the storm caught up with us again and brought us back on the right track. We followed a small side stream and climbed into the mountains again. It was the same range we had seen on the horizon the day before. Even though I was accustomed to Arctic storms, not only in Alaska but also in my northern native country, and though my companions were also brought up in storm and wind, the biting wind and drifting snow of that south storm were almost impossible to face. Only our necessity drove us on through unbroken fields of boulders and deep holes.

Fortunately it cleared a little at about two o'clock in the afternoon so that we could see our way. We climbed another ridge and came to a valley of another river that the Eskimo call Matlogak. To the southeast of this river the mountains rose at least to 6,000–7,000 feet. The Eskimo called the range Katlarijok. We followed the river until evening and marched uninterrupted even though in many steep places we had to pull the sleds up the slope. I am certain that without the remarkable help of my guides I could not have gone so far that day. In these untrodden valleys, during our crossing of the mountains, we met swarms of ptarmigan; I have never seen so many of them together. Nor is this region devoid of game. Frequently we met red foxes. Our dogs decided to pursue one of these, but Master Reynard fled up a mountainside that the dogs could not climb. We saw no caribou, although our dogs occasionally showed such excitement that they were hard to control, which the Eskimo attributed to their sensing their presence. With all this abundance of game I had to forego the pleasure of hunting because of our need for haste. We stayed during the next night along this river, and the next morning continued this arduous journey. We pressed on the whole day without stopping because we wanted to reach the station at Togiak on the coast.

I had become so snowblind that I could barely see and suffered severe pain in my eyes. We went over another row of hills and rocks and passed four mountain streams. At eleven o'clock in the morning we crossed the last pass on the south side of the mountains and from its summit had a panoramic view of the coast and the outlying island, Hagemeister. The weather on this day was fine, but much too warm for the time of year. The storm of the last few days seemed to have broken up the ice on the sea and scattered it far beyond sight, showing the clear surface of the water. As it developed we had failed to find the correct passage through the mountains and by chance had taken one that brought us to a point much farther west than we had expected.

Luckily the snow on the south side of the mountains had not yet melted, so our descent was relatively easy, and after a stiff march of six hours we reached the north point of the fjord in which Togiak Bay lies. Here we met a group of Eskimo fishing, whose territory was in the Nushagak River valley. We passed them without stopping, went across the Togiak River, which empties into the fjord, and at seven o'clock in the evening reached the village of Togiak. The trading post of the same name was four to five English miles away, but the snow ended here and we had to leave our things. I could say with luck I had used the Arctic winter in Alaska from the first snowflake to the last for expeditions by sled. For fully six months, from 23 October to 24 April, I was able to use sleds. Now the trip halted for the moment. We stayed at the place for the night because the travel of the last few days had aggravated the condition of my eyes so that the pain was almost unbearable and gave me sleepless nights.

I now had to think about continuing my journey along the coast, leaving the sleds and the dogs here. It was painful to think of leaving the dogs, because most belonged to the same old pack that had been with me throughout the journeys by sled. Over many hundreds of English miles these animals had taken me, often sharing hunger and discomfort with me, and we had become good companions, as is necessary on such trips. Suddenly, through the melting of the snow, we now had to part. As much as I am free from sentimentality, and though on our trips I often had to drive them to greater efforts with the whip, still they felt attached to me. They watched atten-

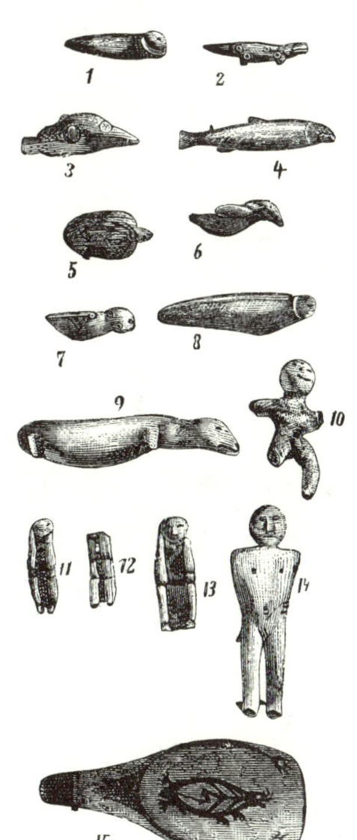

Fig. 60. Small carvings from the Kuskokwim River: (1, 2) figures of mammals; (3, 4) fishes; (5–7) birds; (8) fish; (9) polar bear; (10–14) figures representing people; (15) wooden spoon.

tively while the larger part of my goods was loaded into five kayaks I had rented. They knew each load as well as I did, and they accompanied me to the kayak with each load. When I called them all together and patted them, they jumped up and licked by hands. Then came the worst moment, when we climbed into the kayaks and left them behind; some sat on the shore raising their heads and howling woefully, while others ran along the beach and barked. Truly this was harder than parting from some people.

23

It was toward noon when we arrived with our baggage at the trading post at Togiak; the trader and station manager was not at home, but he came later in the day from his trip and rented me three little craft with four oarsmen. Then after I had paid off my Eskimo and given them something extra for their good service and arranged for the care of my dogs, I continued my journey along the coast toward the east.

The coastline here is sometimes very steep and appears to consist of caverns and palisades like stone walls. The whole region seems to be a favorite playground for the seals and walrus. During the day of my stay the Eskimo from Togiak had caught seven seals and one walrus, an unusually large catch. As we traveled along the coast we noticed summer camps of seal hunters wherever landing was easy.

After we had crossed several large bays, we saw on a projecting height an unusual natural phenomenon created of stone, the figure of a woman about fifteen feet high with a cap on her head. Its realism was so exact that it almost appeared as though human hands had helped form it a little. The woman of stone is widely venerated by the Eskimo, and no one who passes here fails to stop and make an offering. We also landed to climb up to this figure, which the Eskimo called Arningaktak. Some of my men brought dried salmon along, laying a piece at the base of the figure and burying another behind it, while a third one was laid on the top. As remains of former offerings one saw the bones of many sea mammals and birds.

After this we continued on our way and spent the night on the shore of a small bay. The next two days brought high winds and breakers, so that we had trouble rounding Cape Constantine. Close to this point one of my men had an amusing experience with a young seal. He had noticed from the kayak that this young one had crawled up on the shore. He landed at once and tried to grab it by the hind flippers. The frightened animal curled around and tried to bite its attacker. So both parties rolled around in the sand, to our great amusement, and I thought of the folksong about the musician and the crocodile on the Nile. Finally the Eskimo succeeded in holding onto the animal and bringing it alive into the kayak. There, however, it bit him so furiously that he had to kill it.

Spring now forcefully announced its presence. We saw wild geese, ducks, and swans, as well as eider ducks and other birds. It was interesting to observe the courtship antics of some ducks about the size of an eider.

East of Cape Constantine Nushagak Bay cuts deeply into the mainland where the Nushagak empties into the northeast corner. This is the location of Fort Alexander, the headquarters of the Alaska Commercial Company. When I landed here I was heartily welcomed by the station manager, Mr. Clarks [Clarke]. Physically I was really "done in," since my snow-blindness had still not been cured and my feet pained me considerably from sitting for days in the kayak. I could hardly have found a better place in Alaska to recover for a few days than this post. Mr. Clarke took the best care of me, giving me a place to stay in the building of the meteorological station that belongs to Fort Alexander. This station was unfortunately without an occupant because Mr. Mackay, who had been there, was drowned during a hunting expedition. In Fort Alexander there was also a Russian church under the supervision of a priest and a deacon.

My necessary business was quickly transacted. The guides were paid; my dogs, which had been left in Togiak, were made over to Mr. Clarke to pick up later; and my ethnological collections were arranged and packed. It was not possible for me to find anything for the Ethnological Museum in Berlin at this place because before my arrival the deceased Mr. Mackay had bought everything the natives possessed for the Smithsonian Institution.

It was now necessary to make plans for continuing my journey. Fort Alexander is the innermost corner of the penetration of the Bering Sea into southern Alaska, while the large Alaska Peninsula extends to the southwest like a great wall, closing off the Bering Sea and stretching with its long chain of islands almost into the Old World. If I were to continue going eastward, and this was my intention, I would have to cross this peninsula. Since it is covered with high mountains, a crossing must be found at a suitable spot. Such a one is at the base of the peninsula between Bristol Bay and Kamischak Bay. At this point the peninsula is almost cut off from the mainland by Lake Iliamna, about ninety miles long, which has a waterway that can be reached in a few hours from Kamischak Bay and brings one into an entrance to Cook Inlet. I had no choice but to take this way, but in order to do this I had to extend my stay at Fort Alexander for another two weeks because the ice was still on Lake Iliamna. At this place I became acquainted with a young man, Mr. Kasernikoff, whose father had been murdered a few years before at the trading post at Nulato on the Yukon.

A few days after my arrival at the post a fishing schooner that had left San Francisco on 7 April 1883, came in after thirty-two days at sea. The last news from the outside world had reached Fort Alexander on 7 August 1882, so it was not surprising that everyone was overjoyed to get newspapers. On board the schooner were all the facilities for catching and salting fish. The vessel was actually a few days too early, since the Nushagak River had not yet broken up and the first king salmon would not arrive in the river until about 17 May.

Two days after this date I left Fort Alexander in a skin boat I had rented from the Russian deacon there. My crew consisted of three Eskimo and a half-breed with his wife and child, who took the opportunity to make the trip across the peninsula with me. It took us several days to reach the northeast end of Bristol Bay, for the shallow water left us high and dry at low tide. In the region I saw caribou on the shores, which according to the natives, occurred often because they find fertile meadows with plenty of reindeer moss. This area would be a perfect paradise for the Reindeer Laps of my homeland.

On 24 April we reached the mouth of the Iliamna or Quitzak [Kwichak, 1875 map], into which we passed, thus leaving the Bering Sea. Here we met many natives from the village of Mannek, who were engaged in hunting the white whale. In the evening the first mosquitoes announced the coming of the Arctic summer, as did the presence of small meadows with green grass.

We pulled our boat upriver against the current, and along the way we gathered the eggs of seabirds because our food supply was dwindling. The warm weather had broken the ice on Lake Iliamna, and it came toward us in great masses. Fortunately it was so soft and mushy that it floated on the water and did not harm our boat. My crew pulled bravely on the line and when the shore was impassable waded chest deep in the icy water.

On 29 May we reached Lake Iliamna, which was of ocean-like extent and was whipped into great waves in the wake of a storm. I had been warned at Fort Alexander about the waves that often appear suddenly on this seldom-traveled water, caused by the wind against the steep mountains on its shores.

In this lake, which in its western half is about forty to forty-five English miles wide, there are supposed to be many fish, as well as spotted seals, some measuring six or seven feet in length.

The storm forced us to stop even though we were almost without food. During the five days we were obliged to stay here we had little success in hunting and our meals were restricted. At last the storm abated, and on 2 June, at four o'clock in the morning, we started our journey across the lake with a weak northeast wind. After seven hours of the most strenuous work we arrived at an island where we gathered 120 gull eggs that had not yet hatched. I observed that the Eskimo were not at all concerned with whether the embryo was at an advanced stage of development; in fact, they ate the more advanced ones with greater pleasure. We left the island as soon as possible, but we were not more than an English mile away when a storm arose from the northeast, and even though we headed at once for the south shore close to us within seconds of landing our boat was already half full of water.

We paddled along the shore and entered the mouth of a small stream and satisfied our hunger by quickly cooking the eggs. Then we set out again along the shore and found a small Eskimo settlement, where we obtained ample food, including two sides of elk, trout, and eggs, to last us at least eight days. The storm forced us to spend the night on the shore a short distance from the settlement.

As early as two o'clock in the morning we got under way again in quiet, foggy weather, and in the forenoon we passed around a tall rock formation on the south shore that projected far into the lake. I named it "Cape Schleinitz." At this point the lake widened toward the south and formed a great bay covered with hundreds of small and large islands. The largest, where we landed to gather gull eggs, I named "Le Coq's Island."

Not far away on the south shore is the Eskimo village of Kaskanak, which we passed because I was in a great hurry. We continued paddling until late in the evening, when we were completely worn out and came ashore for the night after having covered about fifty English miles that day. It was said that this region should be heavily stocked with elk, caribou, and brown bears.

In the morning there was a strong breeze from the west, mingled with rain. We set sail and headed for the northeast end of the lake, where high rock formations lined the shore. We sailed past a large island that still had no name and arrived at noon at the far end of the lake at the mouth of the

Nusaktolik River, which the Russians called Adematzensky. A short ride of about five English miles brought us at about two o'clock in the afternoon to the village of Iliamna, a trading post of the Alaska Commercial Company. I discovered, much to my sorrow, that the yearly trading vessel that comes to this port early in June had left three days before.

The station at Iliamna consists of five huts and is the boundary between the Eskimo and the Ingalik people. South of here and past the whole length of Lake Iliamna all the coast to Cape Newenham is inhabited by the Nushagak; to the north are the Ingalik.

Now I was separated from the north Pacific Ocean only by a short distance of a few English miles that led in a slow climb to a steep mountain pass on the other side where one descended into the valley of Iliamna Bay. There I was greeted in the friendliest fashion by the trader at a summer post and a few gold miners who had left San Francisco on 9 May.

My possessions, which had been carried over the mountains by six men, were again put into several small boats, and after a short night's rest we started out the next day eastward along the south coast. The Pacific Ocean reaches far inland here and forms Cook Inlet, which extends from southwest to northeast between the mainland and the Kenai Peninsula. This was my goal. The shore here is steep and high and stretches for many miles where there is no place to land, so that one must be very cautious in observing the weather when traveling in small boats in order not to be surprised by a storm.

The country along the shore is enchanting. The mountains have high, sharp peaks and are close to the sea. From here we could see in the distance smoke from the volcano Mount Iliamna. The snow that covered the highest peaks formed several glaciers, while the shoreline was covered with the lushest green. A lovely odor filled the air and seemed to come from the clusters of birch trees. The rocky coast was irregular through the action of erosion and water and fell into ravines, coves, and pillars—a painter's paradise.

As we passed Saunitas Bay we saw smoke pouring forth in three places under the crest of Iliamna and also noticed that the snow below the crater was a dirty gray, as though unclean water had been poured over it. In order to make tea we went as usual into the mouth of one of the many streams that emptied into the sea here, and we noticed the tracks of brown bears everywhere. We had also veered away from the shore several times during the trip because of these animals. The brown bears, however, did not show any fear of us and in one place we saw two large ones rolling on a snowfield near a cliff and playing together like young cats; and at another place a bear stood for a long time and watched our expedition until at last he plunged into the undergrowth and ran away.

This region is a positive El Dorado for hunters and tourists. The landscape, the volcanic outcroppings, glaciers, fantastic rock structures, waterfalls, grottoes, and caves combine with a wealth of animal life such as I have seldom seen. The rivers swarm with salmon and other fish, the sea offers seal hunting, bears and caribou are there in quantity, the rocks are covered with gulls' nests—and on each one we passed sat a female hatching while the male flew about making so much noise that we could hardly hear each other.

The 2,000-foot-high cliff on Assik Island is an example of such a rookery, for near the top the air is constantly dark with flying birds while on the shore is a carpet of blue and red flowers. We were detained here by stormy weather and stayed for a day on the mainland opposite the island.

Some distance farther to the northeast we passed an Ingalik village. The Indian population, which is known by the name Kenaiski, does not differ in physical appearance and language from the Ingalik I saw in the interior on the middle and upper Yukon. I bought here the first king salmon of the 1883 spring, and this was a sign that the salmon fishing season had begun.

The dwellings in this region are very peculiar in their structure. They represent a combination of the standard houses built of wood used by the southern Indians and then they are covered with sod like those of the Eskimo. Such a house consists of a square structure with walls made of horizontal planks. This building constitutes the center of the complex and contains the communal fire and work space for drying salmon in rainy weather. Around this central building and at right angles to its sides are erected from two to six huts about one and a half meters high, that serve as sleeping and living quarters for individual families. These are also covered with earth. Because of its contact with San Francisco, the civilization here has expanded so as to include glass window panes in most of the houses.

In continuing my journey to the northeast I passed long, low Kalgia Island and landed at the village of Kastarnak, where fishing was in full swing. The farther we penetrated into Cook Inlet, the more sea life we saw. A large bay that we crossed north of Kalgia swarmed with seal and white whales, while the fishermen worked hard to get their catch. In one village I found a large supply of smoked king salmon. My destination in Cook Inlet was Tagunak, the trading post of the Alaska Commercial Company where the half-Russian manager, Mr. Dimidoff, received me in a friendly way. Securing ethnographic specimens on the whole southern coast of Alaska was not very successful, since the Nushagakmiut had few original utensils. In Cook Inlet I had somewhat better luck, especially at Tagunak, where I obtained clothing of caribou and elk skin and wooden bows and arrows as well as several other interesting objects; however, the prices demanded for these articles were considerable. Here the trade and barter articles that up to this time had been regarded as satisfactory for my purchases were not accepted, and in their place money was required—and a good deal of it. The local inhabitants were earning much by hunting and fishing, especially for sea otter, and were not willing in this year to part with ethnological pieces.

On the evening of 12 June there was a little feast at Tagunak, in which I participated. The dances were all different from those of the Eskimo, being wilder and more emotional, as were the songs. The Eskimo songs usually have a simple melody and end on the syllables "anga—jangah—jah!" The songs of the Indians in Cook Inlet have the refrain, "Haah haah, heeh heeh, heih heih!" Whereas the Eskimo move their feet very little in their dances, the local Ingalik twist and bend their bodies with great force and liveliness and jump backward and forward. The dancers here had painted their faces black, and instead of the feather ornaments of the Eskimo wore a handkerchief in their hair. The movements of the dancers became so wild and excited that the audience could only imagine that they were about to scalp one another. Every dancer held a feather in each hand. After the dance, in which five men participated together, gifts were distributed and received; in short, it reminded me in many ways of the dances of the Indians to the south in British Columbia.

Since Mr. Dimidoff planned the next day to move to the station at Tagunak for the summer, in order to be at Fort Kenai on the Kenai Peninsula on the other side of the inlet, I accompanied him, even though at first my people refused to go across stormy Cook Inlet. We sat in covered skin boats so that only our heads caught the waves, which could do us no harm since our outer clothing was fastened to the opening through which we entered the boat. After a hard struggle with wind and waves we reached the shore on the peninsula at two o'clock in the afternoon and made a good landing with the tide at a nearby spot. About nine o'clock we started again and reached Fort Kenai at three o'clock in the morning in a stormy sea.

The manager of the trading post of the Alaska Commercial Company at Fort Kenai was Mr. Wilson, a Scotsman by birth, who greeted me kindly. I also became acquainted with Captain Harendin, whose bark *Korea* was waiting to load salmon from the cannery of the California Packing Company, which was close by. Captain Harendin invited me to go with him to visit the cannery, an invitation which several days later was repeated by Mr. Fred Kendall, the superintendent. I accepted this with pleasure and learned that in the short time since this operation started, about three thousand cases of salmon had been packed. Mr. Kendall hoped to bring the total for the season to fifteen to twenty thousand cases.

I experienced the greatest disappointment of my whole journey at Fort Kenai. I had been away from San Francisco more than a year and was in Alaska for the whole winter without any news from home. In several letters I had given orders that all mail, telegrams, and such should be forwarded to Fort Kenai. I had hurried my trip as much as I could and still faithfully carry out my obligations; yet at Fort Kenai I did not find a single piece of mail. It seems that the letters intended for me had been sent to Unalaska.

At Fort Kenai I had to make a decision on how to continue my journey. Since at its base where it separates from the south coast of Alaska the Kenai Peninsula is only a few miles wide and easily passable, it suggested itself to me that I should go again to the northeastern point of Cook Inlet and from there go overland to Prince William Sound. But Mr. Wilson, who best knows the condition of this area, urged me against this, assuring me that I could not get any men on the east side of the peninsula. He had recommended this route to the well-known American traveler Mr. Petrof, who was forced to return. Mr. Wilson suggested as an alternative that I go to Fort Alexander in the southern part of the Kenai Peninsula where I might find a passage to Kodiak Island, opposite the Alaska Peninsula across Shelikoff Strait. At Kodiak he assured me that I would be able to find a small vessel and a crew for a passage to the southern part of Alaska, including Sitka. As little as I liked this plan, since it took me in a roundabout way, I finally had to accept it.

It was necessary for me to reduce my baggage, so I gave Mr. Wilson the trade goods I could no longer use since on the remainder of my voyage I would have to use money.

After hearty farewells I left Fort Kenai on 18 June and followed the coast to the southwest. In a few hours I arrived at the fish cannery on Kasiloff River, where I spent a pleasant evening, after having shared in a birthday celebration on my first visit there when I became acquainted again with champagne and cake. Captain Harendin and Mr. Kendall quickly wrote letters for me to take to Kodiak.

From the Kasiloff to the village of Ninilschik, which we reached in about seven hours, we found the sea very shallow and covered with rocks the size of an European room. We could see one of these rocks protruding above the water at low tide, about five English miles from Ninilschik, a Russian settlement where the vegetables bespoke a settled agricultural community. Mr. Alexius, a handsome inhabitant, served me milk and fresh butter with my snack.

Along the northwest coast of the Kenai Peninsula, the steep shores have occasional veins of coal alternating with pebbles and sand. The largest veins I saw were three to six feet thick. The shore of the lake is covered for quite an area with pieces of coal. Some of the pieces lying around had not completely turned to coal. I found here several petrified pieces of plant foliage, of which I took samples, since they might be important aids in the analysis of the Arctic flora of past geological periods which through the Nordenskjöld Expedition has expanded our knowledge of the circumpolar regions. The occurrence of volcanic eruptions in this area has been determined by layers of ash and the pressure of volcanic rock on the shore.

We continued our journey on the same day and by evening reached Anchor Point, a rocky projection that marks the south end of Cook Inlet. Beyond this point the coastline of the Kenai Peninsula turns at a right angle to the left and extends from west to east. Here the peninsula is indented to the northeast by Kachekmak [Kachemak] Bay, which penetrates far inland.

We spent the night at Anchor Point, or rather Leida, where a large number of sea otter hunters with their boats also spent the few hours until morning. About three o'clock in the morning the hunters left and I woke my crew so that they could make tea and prepare for departure. While I took a little more rest the crew did likewise, and when we woke again we found we had missed the tide for departure and had to wait until the afternoon. The stormy weather forced us to go far into Kachemak Bay before we could cross to the other shore, which we followed to the southwest, reaching Akedaknak in Seldovia Bay for our next night's camp. Here we found the dwellings that the sea otter hunters we met the night before had used. This village had been the location of a trading post of the Western Fur Trading Company that had been abandoned in May. Because of this the price of a good sea otter pelt fell from $112 to $35.

The next morning we set out in favorable tide and wind. We moved swiftly and quietly and observed some halibut that played on the surface of the sea or chased small fish. This aroused a desire to hunt, and in seconds harpoons were seized and a colossal flatfish weighing about forty pounds was struck. These fish are very tough, and it cost considerable effort to bring it aboard and kill it. A second, even larger fish escaped the harpoon by turning and diving into the depth with a great swish of its tail. The captured fish was by no means one of the largest of its kind, for I have seen halibut weighing 250 pounds in my native Norway.

At about nine o'clock in the morning we landed at Fort Alexander, a trading post of the Alaska Commercial Company, managed by Mr. Cohn, who was born in Berlin. This gentleman, who greeted me very kindly, has been with this company for a long time and through his position was able to make observations about the region which he shared with me during my short visit and which proved of good help. This Fort Alexander should not be confused with another of the same name at the mouth of the Nushagak River.

24

At Fort Alexander, on the southern tip of the Kenai Peninsula, I found a schooner from Kodiak under the command of Captain Sand and Mr. Frank. These gentlemen were engaged in salmon fishing and expected to return to Kodiak with their load after a fortnight. The entire population of the place was occupied with sea otter hunting, so that it was difficult if not impossible to hire any of the men. But even if I had found any I would not have trusted myself to ride with them in the skin boats of questionable seaworthiness across the wide strait between Kodiak and the Kenai Peninsula. Only under the most favorable circumstances do these people venture out on this passage; in many instances they would rather wait for weeks for better weather.

Mr. Frank told me on the day of my arrival that in the interior of the region of Kachemak Bay, which I had just crossed, there were ruins of an old, deserted Indian settlement called Soonroodna, and that it might be worth my while to do some excavation at this place, which the Eskimo called Hardak or Hardanak. Since I had to wait for the schooner longer than a week I decided to use this time for such excavation, even though I would have to retrace my journey by about thirty English miles. After I had hired some people at a high price, we left Fort Alexander on 26 June and arrived that same afternoon at Akedaknak in Seldovia Bay, where I engaged as a guide an old Indian whose father had lived in this abandoned village. We continued that same day to a little island, Yukon, where we first collected bird's eggs and shot some birds and then spent the night in a house that belonged to our Indian guide. He sold me several old stone lamps and a pair of dance rattles.

The next morning we circumnavigated Yukon Island, and on the shores we shot ten sea parrots and some auks, as well as a large flecked seal, which booty extended our provisions considerably. After several hours of fast sailing we arrived at last at the ruins of the village of Soonroodna. It is situated at the foot of the third glacier on the south shore of Kachemak Bay.

Soonroodna was a village of considerable size even before 1794 when the Russians came there. Shortly after they had built Fort Kenai the Russians one day went over to Soonroodna in many boats to carry out a second "Rape of the Sabine Women"—they took as many of the young girls and women as they could back to the fort and kept them as wives. In deep sorrow the Indians left their village because they realized that against the Russians they were powerless. They scattered among the Eskimo villages on Kodiak Island.

The ancient inhabitants of Soonroodna before the arrival of the Russians cremated their dead and buried the remains. These were all that were left when the people deserted the village. Objects that remained with the dead, like old dance masks, were collected in a cave and remained there in respect for the ancestors. Everyone that visited the abandoned village made an offering to these masks, which represent the dead. This offering was usually food, but was also small baskets of excellent workmanship that the people made then and still make today. They used baskets for cooking with hot stones. Our old Indian guide said he remembered one place where the dead and these offerings had been put. This was the place we wanted to find. But with the passage of time the rock cover had sunk and all the offerings were crushed, as could be clearly seen. All efforts to move these great blocks of stone were in vain. It was only possible to dig a few fragments out from under the stones.

We then visited a small cave that was used as a burial site after cremation was no longer practiced. There I found a staff similar to those used in ceremonial dancing and also a figure of a woman and a square piece of wood with a hole in the center. Its use could not be determined.

We commenced our excavation on the spot where our old Indian guide told us the house of the most important chief of Soonroodna once stood. Beside the house I assumed that the next structure might have been the chief's cache. This consists in this region of a small house raised on four posts for storing dried fish, meat, and skins out of reach to dogs.

Five persons dug until late in the evening, to a depth of about five feet. The site yielded the following: a layer of firm sand, then a layer of ashes, broken shell, and charcoal, obviously the remains of the first occupation of the site. Here we found as evidence of occupation small pieces of pottery such as they use along the Yukon River. Also we found fragments of bones of bear, fox, porcupine, several kinds of birds, beaver, white whale, seal, and sea otter. These bones were clearly very old and brittle. Above this lowest culture-bearing layer was a layer of clear sand and gravel as though this site had been flooded for a long time. On top of this was another layer that also consisted principally of shells of marine forms and seemed to be better preserved than the same material at the lower level. In this layer we also found several arrow points and harpoon points of bone. Above this there was the customary layer of dark earth mixed with bone and ashes, in which I found lance points, a piece of wooden lance shaft, a small piece of copper that had probably been a knife, a small iron knife, a blue glass bead, two bone harpoon points, and many bones of a variety of animals. My guide explained that formerly the value of a small iron knife was equivalent to two slaves and the same evaluation was also made in terms of one hundred marten skins.

In order to make the excavation less costly, I sent the old guide back the next day and continued with the other men. At one place under the first shell layer I found two short pieces of whale ribs that had been cut with a stone or some other unsuitable instrument.

According to my helpers these bones were prepared to be made into arrow points; at least they were the proper length. In addition we found more potsherds and spear points, a stone lance point, and, a foot beneath the surface, an iron ax, and more animal bones.

On the second day we examined a cave that was known as a shelter for hunters. I had the ground dug up and found many signs of ashes and charcoal as well as a Russian iron ax. We also made another attempt to penetrate the cave I described earlier, but we were not successful.

In the surrounding hills we found many signs of human habitation, especially great shell heaps. This led one to believe that the old settlement of Soonroodna was of considerable size.

On the third day we intensified our efforts at digging. It was the general opinion that the principal part of the village was down near the shore, not ten to twelve feet above the tide line like the chief's house. Here we began our investigations. In the lowest culture stratum I found old potsherds, a harpoon for sea otter and seal, a piece of a well-made stone spear point, a piece of iron ore, a straight iron knife about five inches long, a horseshoe-shaped iron knife with its cutting edge on the outside, which according to my Indian informants was a type used as a fish knife, worked bone which was used for needles and awls, and many animal bones. This ended our excavations at Soonroodna.[33]

The next morning we began our journey back. The wind had

eased and we added to our food supply by hunting marmots and sea birds. When it began to storm we stopped our hunting and went farther into Seldovia Bay, where we spent the night with Captain Sand and Mr. Frank. The former promised me that he would bring me to Kodiak Island within the next eight days if I could get a few people to work on the schooner.

The following afternoon I returned to Fort Alexander and sorted my collection and engaged two natives to work on the schooner. I obtained some very interesting details about the life of the sea otter from Mr. Cohn of the Alaska Commercial Company at Fort Alexander. As we know, sea otter feed mostly on fish, shellfish, and seaweed. The sea otters, whose forepaws are webbed, are skillful in diving, often as deep as thirty to forty fathoms, bringing up shellfish and crustaceans. They break the shells in an extraordinary way. They lie on their backs so that they float on the water and break the shells by beating them against their chests with their forepaws. For this reason the sea otters do not have any hair upon their chests. When the shell is broken, the sea otter turns over in the water so that the shell sinks and the flesh of the creature is held against the breast with the paws. Then, lying on his back again, he bends forward to eat the meat.

A favorite food of the sea otter is fish eggs or spawn, which in stormy weather are deposited on cliffs near the shore. The sea otter that has given himself over to this kind of gourmandizing often does not even notice the approach of a boat. Sea urchins are also delicacies for the sea otter. When a hunter suddenly comes upon a sea otter he will not take to flight, for the sight of human beings is not strange to him, even though the hunter has evil designs on him. He rolls over on his back and waits for the hunter's arrow. An old and experienced sea otter seems to understand how to divert the arrow with his forepaws. This reminds me of the behavior of an old male walrus in the sea near Spitsbergen. The animals, which are hunted during most of their lives, recognize the harpooner and throw their heads backward when he raises his harpoon. As it leaves his hand they are ready to divert the projectile. In this way many a hunter has lost a walrus. I knew a skillful harpooner in the Spitsbergen Sea who threw the weapon with such force and so swiftly that he got his animal without fail.

Often when a sea otter has diverted an arrow his forepaw is struck, so he bites off the arrow and often saves himself by doing this. However if he is harpooned the hunter usually succeeds in getting him since he cannot pull the harpoon out of his flesh. In the Aleutian Islands the sea otters are now usually shot or caught in nets. It is pitiful to watch a female not leaving her young while the male escapes if he can. According to Mr.

Cohn the sea otters mate every year. They live in large herds within which there are bloody conflicts among the males for possession of the females. A grown sea otter is about five feet long. There are now many whites who take part in sea otter hunting in Alaskan waters.

After the schooner belonging to Sand and Frank was floated in the spring thaw, we sailed from Fort Alexander on 7 July, passing Barren Island, and the next day passed Afognak and Marmot Islands, arriving the third day at eight o'clock in the morning in the harbor of Saint Paul on the northeast coast of Kodiak Island.

Here I found Mr. Macinture [MacIntyre?], the local general agent, very busy. He was occupied with outfitting several schooners with food and fishing gear after they had brought in a load of salted salmon. It had been my hope that I would get an opportunity for a quick trip to San Francisco, but I found that there would be no ship sailing before September. So it meant I again had to have patience and put up with the circumstances. I decided therefore to visit the remainder of the south coast of Alaska and especially the region east of the Kenai Peninsula, the archipelago of Prince William Sound, and the Copper River in order to get ethnographic objects. The difficult problem again was securing transportation. The only schooner the Alaska Commercial Company had at this station was on a trip west, so I had to wait for another opportunity. Fortunately I found one the next day in a good, seaworthy craft called *Three Brothers*, belonging to Captain Anderson and the Carlson brothers from Sweden, which had brought a load of salmon to the harbor. I attempted to charter the boat and found that Captain Anderson did not object to a trip to Prince William Sound for several reasons.

In Saint Paul I made several interesting acquaintances. First I met Mr. Fischer, an officer of the Coast Survey who was also collecting for the Smithsonian Institution, Mr. Washburne, the assistant to Mr. MacIntyre, and Mr. Petrof, who is well known for his extensive travels in Alaska and to whom we owe the best large map of Alaska. He acted several years ago as special agent for the tenth census and is now a customs officer on the island. His wife is the only American woman on Kodiak. In addition to these people there were quite a number of Norwegians who were engaged in sea otter hunting.

On the day after my arrival one of these Norwegian sea otter hunters married a Russian woman born in Saint Paul. I was invited with several other Norwegians to the ceremony. I will give a description of the occasion as I have it in my diary. In the Russian church the congregation stands throughout such a ceremony, which is very tiring. Before the marriage ceremony, mass took place. Then a red handkerchief was laid in front of the bride and groom. After the mass the rings were put on their fingers, and the wedding party were led closer to the middle of the church, where a table was set up on which they laid their hands while a cloth was put over it. Two people from the congregation took two brass crowns decorated with glass beads and held them with outstretched arms over the heads of the bride and groom. During this another long mass was recited while the men who held the crowns, as well as those in the congregation, were blessed. Then the priest handed the bride and groom a goblet of port wine from which each drank three times. After another short mass the ceremony was over.

After the wedding ceremony we assembled for a festive dinner, where for the first time in my life I drank *kwas*, a kind of Russian beer. This was followed by dancing, which lasted until one o'clock in the morning. At that time the young couple withdrew but the wedding guests stayed, and it was clear that some secret was being planned. After giving the newlyweds a short rest, each of the guests armed himself with the loudest noisemaker he could devise—a foghorn, tin boxes, empty oil cans—and at a signal began to use them, making the loudest caterwauling possible. It was a long time before the couple showed any sign of life. The part they were supposed to enact was to be aroused from a deep sleep and face the audience with a distressed expression. Our couple was well prepared and invited all those present to drink up a barrel of beer that was ready for them. During the drinking the teasing continued, and before each guest drank he raised his glass and cried "sour." Then the couple had to kiss, whereupon the beer was declared no longer sour.

The next day I transacted some business, bought some ethnographic objects, and wrote letters to San Francisco and Europe which Mr. Vanilius, the captain of a sea otter tender ship, would take with him to the west islands to see whether he would have any chance of sending them south.

I had made a contract with the owners of the schooner *Three Brothers* which included that they should take me to Cross Sound in the southern part of Alaska near Sitka and would also let me visit Prince William Sound and the several native villages on the coast on the way to Cross Sound. This undertaking for which I was preparing myself seems to have been regarded by everyone as hazardous, and I was warned against it, because the population in the area I wished to visit is regarded as the most dangerous on the whole Alaskan coast. The northern Tlingit equal the Indians of West Vancouver Island in their thieving habits. It was necessary that we arm ourselves heavily for this journey.

We left on 13 July. On board were Captain Anderson, the Carlson brothers, my interpreter, a Tlingit Indian, and our cook. I had also taken on a good supply of trade goods for barter. With a fresh breeze we reached Marmot Island on the same day and the next afternoon we got to Seal Bay, which is on the east coast of Afognak Island. Here we found the third owner of the vessel, whom we had to notify that the vessel would be away from Kodiak for the next five weeks.

Close to Seal Bay there is supposed to be the site of a formerly occupied village, which I attempted to excavate for any ancient remains; but in the stony ground our shovels and other tools broke and we had to give up the project. In the evening we started to hunt a brown bear, but that also brought no results. Disregarding a "counter" breeze we sailed away in the morning and spent all day trying to get out of the bay. The younger of the Carlson brothers shot a young seal from the deck of the ship and gave us a fine supper. Since it was now a whole year since I had had a saltwater bath, and that was in the Bering Sea at about the same latitude, I initiated the season that day in Seal Bay. The water was not very cold.

We spent the night in a small bay and sailed the next day in a good breeze. We passed Barren Island and a few hours later passed Cape Elizabeth on Kenai Peninsula. We noticed many fur seals here, playing in the sea. The Kenai Peninsula has many glaciers that reach to the sea. The wind brought us quickly along the coast so that the next day we came to Seal Rocks, where we saw many sea lions and albatross.

Soon the wind changed and we faced a strong east wind. We were in sight of Montague Island and we cruised back and forth looking for a good anchorage before dusk. In this we were not successful, for the glacier-cut shore is very steep and there was no place to drop an anchor. So we had, for better or for worse, to stay under sail the whole night, which in the pouring rain and the complete darkness was very unpleasant.

As soon as dawn broke we started north and arrived at Knight Island about nine o'clock in the morning. According to Petrof the village of Chenega is here, and we searched for it for several hours without success. Finally a skin boat arrived with some natives from whom we learned that the village was two to three English miles away on a neighboring island of the same name. We went there and landed about four o'clock in the afternoon, and with this I had arrived at the next goal of my expedition, Prince William Sound.

<h1 style="text-align:right">25</h1>

In Prince William Sound I had the opportunity to learn about the former culture of the area. After we landed at Chenega, a local inhabitant told me that a few English miles away there was an old burial site. So I rented a small skin boat, took my interpreter and a native with me, and went to this place. It was at once obvious that someone had collected the pieces before me. I found only two broken masks, which I took. In the evening I returned to the village, where I bought all the ethnographic articles available. The inhabitants of this village are Eskimo and speak a dialect similar to one heard along the Nushagak River. The pieces I bought here were stone axes, wooden plates inlaid with beads, large stone lamps, beadwork, and jackets of eagle skin.

After tending to all our business in Chenega we sailed away and in a few hours were becalmed in an unfavorable tide so that we were forced to anchor. We were only a short distance from the burial ground I had visited, so I went there again with Captain Anderson and my interpreter. After a long search we found mummies—an adult and a child. They were in poor condition, but with great care I managed to get them aboard. As far as could be determined the bodies were in a squatting position, covered with skins tied together with thongs and a second cover of sealskin. The mummies had been in a cavelike depression. The remains of the child were so poor that they could not be transported. In spite of their condition, I could not assume that these mummies were of a great age, for I found near them a piece of wood that had been cut with a saw.

In our boat we cruised along the steep overhanging cliffs with many caves and found a second burial site where there were more mummies, also in such advanced stages of decay that we could find just one small example. This was also wrapped in skins and was lying on a wooden hoop that reminded me of a Labrador snowshoe and was possibly a child's cradle. Fortunately, at this place we found a well-preserved skull. Perhaps the cave had been flooded by a high tide from the sea and the other remains had been washed away. As grave offerings I found a few pieces of wooden masks but no weapons or hunting gear, as is customary. I had made an agreement with Captain Anderson that half of all finds would go to Mr. Fischer in Saint Paul. Without such an agreement I probably would not have had the opportunity of being there at all.

Captain Anderson personally helped in the search for caves and worked with the fervor of a born anthropologist and ethnologist. We went a few miles farther in the boat and discovered another burial site. Here the roof of the cave had broken and fallen on the human remains, so we first had to clean all this away before we could excavate the graves. After much effort we succeeded in finding a well-preserved skull. This appeared to be the oldest of the sites we found, not because of the state of preservation but because the bodies were covered with pieces of wood and planks that had not been touched with modern tools, but were cut with axes. Some of the bodies were also covered with cedar bark. It struck me that these old graves bore a likeness to the ones of the old population of Labrador; but the difference was that the latter had many offerings and did not have any wooden planks. There should be more and larger burial sites in this vicinity on Chenega Island with mummies in caves, but we could not get any information from the local inhabitants.

The next day I went with Captain Anderson and an Eskimo over to Knight Island, where, as I expected, we found an old burial place under an overhanging rock. Like the last one of the previous day, the body was in a box made of rough planks. All the burials were almost completely decayed, so that from all the graves we had only four mummies. We also found six skulls. In one grave there was a woman and a child. Hard as I tried to preserve them I did not succeed, and I came away with only the woman's skull and the child's cradle. It was a great problem to transport the skeletons to the water's edge. We were not the first visitors here, for the collector from the Smithsonian Institution had preceded us.

On the same day we continued with our schooner on a course around Knight Island and along the east side of the island to Green Island. From the deck of the vessel we saw a large fish swimming near the surface of the water, which we took to be a whale. We put a boat in the water at once and I asked my people to go with me and follow the fish. As we came closer we discovered that the black monster was a shark about thirty to thirty-five feet long. We shot a few bullets into his abdomen and he quickly died and, with mighty blows of his tail, vanished.

We sailed northward around Montague Island and landed on the north coast of Nuchek Island, at a trading post of the Alaska Commercial Company, where I made the acquaintance of Mr. Lohr, the agent. The information he could give me about my plan was not encouraging, as we later found out. He told me that in the stretch of nearly 10° latitude between the mouth of the Copper River and Cross Sound, there were only three native settlements, and that I could not expect to make any large collections. He also declared that the weather in Prince William Sound and along this coast was either stormy or without wind.[34]

Captain Anderson had undertaken to pick up a number of seal hunters on Middleton Island. I arranged with him that at the same time I would go from the northeast of Prince William Sound to the mouth of the Copper River and would wait for him at Cape Martin.

We separated and I rented a small boat after going to a distant place on the island, where we made a small excavation that resulted in getting fifteen broken axes.

We departed from Nuchek Island on 27 July 1883, with the interpreter and a young Tlingit on board. I had trade goods and provisions for four to five days. From the northwest coast of Nuchek we went to Hawkins Island, where we spent a sleepless night because of the mosquitoes.

Hawkins Island is separated from the mainland by a narrow strait that we crossed in the early hours of the day. The next part of the coast consists of a steep projecting peninsula that is part of the delta of the Copper River. The natives take a portage overland. The peninsula has an inland lake with a west shore that is very close to the west shore of the peninsula, and its end is connected with the delta of the Copper River. This lake and river are called Konno.

As we approached the peninsula we saw fire on the west shore. We landed and met some men from two wooden canoes. These people, with whom we started a conversation, were from Iggiak on the Konno River. We followed their advice and went a little farther up the west shore of the peninsula and found a small bay with a flat beach. Here we landed and pulled up our boat, for this is where the portage begins. At first we pulled the empty boat across the new flat land until we were about half an English mile from the shore, and we carried our load at the same time. After the canoe was loaded again we crossed the lake and came at noon to Iggiak, a village of about ten houses that belongs to the Tlingit Indians. The inhabitants here are supposed to have formerly belonged to another tribe that was once very powerful. This tribe had been almost eliminated by the Eskimo and the Tlingit in warfare, and it was only through intermarriage with their conquerors that anything was left of them.

Actually these people are another type, different from the Eskimo and the Tlingit, and their language also differed to such a degree that my interpreter could not understand a word of it. I also realized that I had never heard a language so completely unintelligible. We could make ourselves understood because a few of them knew a little Eskimo.[35]

I obtained a few ethnographic articles from them, but the stone amulets they wore around their necks were not for sale. In trading these people used all the well-known Indian stratagems, so I am inclined to think they may have had their origin somewhere in the interior of North America. It appears that polygamous marriages are not rare with them.

We spent the night in Iggiak, and early the next morning we paddled in two hours to the mouth of the Konno River. This river flows with the principal arm of the Copper River and therefore the tide of the North Pacific Ocean reaches far up these rivers. The mouths of these rivers are so wide that it is difficult to see the opposite shore, but the delta is so shallow that at low tide one can scarcely pass with any kind of boat.

We went upstream from the mouth of the river for about three to five miles, against the tide, and arrived at the village of Allaganak[Alaganikis],where to my surprise I found three American prospectors who had come from Sitka to test the Copper River for metals. They had come from Cape Martin up the eastern mainstream of the delta, and because of the numerous waterways and canals they became confused and passed the principal arm of the river and arrived at Alaganik, without, however, being able to communicate with the inhabitants. They were surprised and very pleased at my arrival, for not only could I direct them, but also through the advice of Mr. Lohr, the station manager, I could tell them where on the Copper River the greatest bed of copper lies. With the help of my interpreter I could also arrange for the engagement of a local native who would guide them to the place. The inhabitants had been surprised when three white men came from the east who could not understand them, and right after them one white man came from the west who greeted them joyfully. The last comer, myself, was also distinguished from the others because he carried a hunting knife and a revolver in his belt. Such a man, the natives decided, could only be an officer of the United States of America, who had come to determine the opinion of the local population in regard to the shooting of one of their tribesmen who had murdered two white men and was captured by a gunboat that took him to Portland.[36] My appearance also caused a delegation of the natives to come to us in the evening and state that the whole village was very much frightened by my presence.

One might have thought in the circumstances that the inhabitants might have been more willing to sell the few articles I wanted for a lower price, but on the contrary I had to pay exorbitant amounts for them.

The competition of the two principal trading companies had spoiled these people also. I found a number of carved wooden utensils that resembled those of British Columbia. By the way, I must mention that the night after I bought my pieces, the best one disappeared. I went the next morning and complained in no uncertain terms to the chief of the village, who made a great effort to recover it for me, but without success.

The next noon we left and went upstream on the right arm of the river, then downstream on the left, or western, side, and had such difficulty going against the wind and tide that we camped on one of the islands. When we had set up camp I went hunting in thick brush and had the misfortune to lose my way, getting my gun wet and not being able to shoot anything. I found my way back after several hours.

Now our real difficulties began, for our food supply began to dwindle and the area had no game, no fish, and no birds. It rained constantly and our tent, which was old and worn, began to leak. On the third day the situation improved and we got back to the coast and with a little paddling arrived at Cape Martin, where three families lived. The population of the Copper River Delta, including the village of Tschilkat to the east of Cape Martin, are a related group and move to various parts of the area according to the season.

For this reason when I arranged for the schooner *Three Brothers* to come for me I asked that all the people in the region who wanted to trade should come to Cape Martin, and shortly after my arrival they came. I bought a number of pieces, principally masks and carved bone objects. I was happy to find a good supply of food here so that we could remedy our starved condition.

Storms from the east and a terrible plague of mosquitoes drove us almost out of our minds, for it was a whole week before the schooner came from Middleton Island. In this time I had an opportunity to study the customs and habits of the people of the Copper River Delta. The medicine men make their magic equipment or consecrate amulets in the following way: the shaman first puts on ceremonial clothes, which consist of an apron decorated with birds' beaks and the feet of the mountain goat. He paints his face, puts on a proper hat for the kind of medicine he expects to make, puts on a mask, and carries a rattle. In the middle of the room a large fire is built, around which the audience watches him dance. The shaman impresses the audience with the idea that the fire will not harm him. He picks up glowing embers on his hand and shows them around and throws them through the opening in the roof without burning his fingers. The men sit around the fire, against the walls of the house. Each one has a stick in his hand to beat on a plank. An old man undertakes the beating of the large drum. All take part in the singing, including the women, who sing as loudly as possible. It is a strange custom of the women to hold some favorite article in front of their mouths as though to prevent the entry of a demon.

The shaman goes on making all kinds of tricks to astonish his audience. One of his most enjoyable bravado pieces consists of asking two pairs of men to stand opposite each other across the fire and hold heavy tow cords down close to the fire. The shaman lies or hangs on these and the men swing him to and fro. Often the cords catch on fire, and then the men let him out. Another trick is that the shaman eats a long bone in the sight of the public, and to their astonishment pulls it out of his throat again in one piece. The magician also takes a red-hot knife in his hands and licks the blade without any sign of pain. Some shamans also practice ventriloquism. In the middle of a song there is often a pause and the shaman bends over toward the ground and seems to answer an evil spirit that lives deep below the surface.

The time I was there was not the season for dances and other ceremonies, so I can describe those events only from the information I obtained from Captain Anderson, who some time ago spent a whole year in the area.

As soon as a song is finished and another ready to start the medicine man changes his clothing or his mask or headgear and sprinkles eagle-down on his head. The shaman can cure illness by taking a handful of down or a live mouse from the patient, and so that the sickness cannot enter another person, he eats them in front of the spectators. Throughout this the patient plays a passive role; he must be completely quiet and seem lifeless; he may lie, according to the wishes of the sha-man, in the sight of the audience or behind a screen. The sha-man then approaches his subject while the drummers and singers maintain complete silence, listening for the shaman's spirit to speak. When the spirit has spoken a few words, the singers exclaim "A–h! A–h!"

The shamans are highly respected by the people. Cap-tain Anderson told me that once when he was waiting for a schooner, a shaman offered to tell him whether it would come soon. So a group of people gathered and he performed his usual tricks. While he was being swung on the cords over the fire, the cords broke and he fell into the glowing embers. Quick as lightning he jumped out of the fire, and this fast flight on the part of a man who was supposed to be nonflammable made some of the audience laugh. The shaman directed his anger against the unlucky ship and cried out that it would have an accident. By chance the ship ran aground in the same year, near Saint Paul on Kodiak Island. This made the prestige of the shaman rise so that even today he is still considered one of the most important practitioners in the region. The clothing, masks, and other gear of shamans is not kept in the house but is hidden in the bushes. The natives know these objects, but would not touch them. When a shaman cures an illness he is given blankets. The shaman also prepares amulets and love potions made of a particular herb and finds a grateful and believing public especially in young people. Every village has a shaman.

I also had the opportunity to observe some of the domestic and family activities of the Copper River Delta Indians. Like all other Northwest Coast Indians they are married young. When a daughter is born she often is betrothed on the first day of life, but she is not married until she is from twelve to fourteen years old. If her father should die before she is this age, her future husband must take his future mother-in-law as his wife. As with many native peoples, the girl's puberty is celebrated with special ceremonies and a feast. During this period the young girl is separated from the rest of the family and stays in a small closed-off space in her parent's house. She must stay there for thirty days, and during this time is given very frugal meals by a woman attendant. When she lies down her head must face south. After her confinement she lives in the house again and is given a new dress and some festive gifts from her father and close relatives. If she marries very soon, as is customary, the parents also receive gifts.

It is the custom to prevent the birth of deformed people, so when such births happen, the infants are not allowed to live and are immediately cremated; the same always happens to the afterbirth. These practices are carefully watched, and disobedience may be punished with death. As soon as a child is born its septum is pierced and a ring inserted.

If a murder has been committed, the relatives of the victim immediately arm themselves and go to the home of the murderer. They demand wergild, and if it is refused a bloody revenge is bound to follow. Both sides call a family council and determine the number of blankets that must be paid to absolve the crime. If the amount demanded is considered too large by the murderer's family, who either cannot or will not pay it, several young people in the murderer's family will be given into slavery and through their services wipe out the crime. There are many slaves among the Tlingit, where they seem to have as much freedom as their masters.

On 8 August a small canoe came from Nuchek Island with the news that the schooner *Three Brothers*, for which I had impatiently waited, had tried four times to come to Cape Martin but was forced back by wind and tides. In the last three days there was no storm, but a calm in which it could not travel. This information confirmed my fears that it would be impossible for me to go to Cross Sound in this seasonal change. I had also heard that in the long coastal stretch there were few opportunities for collecting ethnographic artifacts. This was substantiated by Captain Anderson and Mr. Carlson when they arrived. They were very certain of the approach of severe storms, but they offered me a refund because they could not carry out our original agreement and said they would take me back to Saint Paul. They also realized that they could not prepare properly for the coming fishing season and that their future income might be light.

I asked for a few days for readjustment, and during this time I bought many pieces that I had expected to get on the proposed trip south, because many people from that area were here.

In 11 August the east wind brought heavy rain, so I concluded with the owners of the *Three Brothers* to go no farther to the east and southeast but to return to Kodiak Island, where I would try to find transportation to San Francisco. Among other favorable actions before I started my journey back, Captain Anderson gave me his half of the excavations and mummies we had gotten together.

We sailed [from Cape Martin] at ten o'clock in the morning and arrived in the harbor at Nuchek Island the next afternoon. To show how much I had learned of the customs of the coast inhabitants, Captain Anderson, Mr. Carlson, and myself decided that I should dress in a shaman's costume I had bought, paint my face black, and appear at Nuchek in this costume.

After I had completed my metamorphosis the station manager, Mr. Lohr, came aboard. His first question was, "Why are you returning so soon? Weren't you going to Cross Sound? Where is Captain Jacobsen?" They replied that they were bringing the medicine man who had killed Jacobsen. He looked scowlingly at me as I sat fastening the sails, when he became more disturbed. Anderson and Carlson started to laugh and explained the joke. At first he would not believe this until I spoke to him. He took a deep breath and said it was lucky for him and for me that he did not have a revolver with him, because in his excitement he could have shot me without mercy. I told him I had thought of that and was ready to prevent any accident.

Then Mr. Lohr suggested that I go ashore in this costume to see what impression it would make on the Eskimo population on Nuchek Island. This was done, and when the people heard that I had murdered Jacobsen they became very frightened and fled from me wherever I was seen. Later the situation was cleared up to the common amusement when they saw me again as a white man.

After transacting some necessary business we started on our six-day trip to Kodiak, anchoring in Saint Paul harbor on the evening of 18 August.

26

[Jacobsen was ready to take the first ship out of Kodiak that would take him to San Francisco so he could start for home. He found a little steamer, the *Korea,* which he boarded 28 August. When he arrived in San Francisco there was mail for him, all very welcome except one letter from the museum asking him to make a quick trip to Arizona and visit the Yuma, Pima, Maricopa, and other tribes. Since the account of this trip is likely to hold little interest for those who enjoyed the rest of the book, it is not translated here.

After several very disappointing weeks visiting the groups mentioned above Jacobsen returned to Tucson and took the train to Deming, El Paso, Saint Louis, Washington, and New York. He arrived in Berlin 23 November 1883.

As his collections were being unpacked, an exhibition of many of the artifacts was made at once, to the great satisfaction of the people who had been following his journey through his letters, printed as news items in the local papers.]

I was born on 9 October 1853 on the small island of Risø (70°
north latitude, 16° east longitude) in the neighborhood of the
Norwegian city of Tromsø. Even in my early childhood I became acquainted with the sea, because almost daily we went
between our little islands in our boats to hunt and fish. Every
spring about the end of April the sea gulls and eider ducks
came by the thousands from the southern regions to build
their nests. At the beginning of May the owners of the islands
began collecting the eggs of the sea birds, as many as three
thousand a day, which they sold in Tromsø and the surrounding area.

In the late 1830s my father moved from the city of Tromsø
to Risø, an island he had bought, and engaged several young
people to join him in fishing. The principal fish we obtained
were haddock in winter and, in summer, a similar fish called
"sei," which came by the thousands and were caught in large
nets about one to three miles from the island. Another good
source of income was the down of the eider duck, which was
cleaned and sold to Russia. We and our neighbors, however,
lived mainly on the income from fishing. In addition to the
fishing carried on by the men, it was the practice to keep three
to ten cows and ten to fifteen sheep, goats, and pigs. During
the nine months of winter the cows had to be fed in their
stalls, and since there was little hay, they were fed cooked fish.

For a city dweller in a southern country this type of life
must seem terrible, but the people who live here not only find
it tolerable but would not live anywhere else. The one difficulty is that we island people do not have schools, whereas
the city people have schools patterned after the German edu-
cation. The reason for being so backward is that for nine
months the communication between the islands and the mainland is very difficult. In the three summer months children as
young as seven years old go fishing with their parents. An

attempt was made to have a seven-week school period in the spring and fall, but even then the weather was too uncertain to carry this on. What one learned in the schools in those days was principally "religion," reading, and a little writing and arithmetic. If one went until about thirteen or fourteen years of age one had the opportunity to learn a little geography and church history. I don't want to give the impression that the northern islanders were behind the southern islanders. When there were better schools, in fact, I found that most of my young friends were just as intelligent and knowledgeable as any people who fish. This probably is due to the experience they get traveling south as far as the coast of Russia and meeting different people. Most of the fishing people travel at least half the year. They also like to read newspapers, and nearly every fisherman subscribes to at least three even if it takes several months to get them. Now, at least, every fishing station has mail and telegraphic connection with the outer world.

As far back as my memory goes I can remember struggles with the watery elements that my father and his crew had to pass through on their fishing expeditions. Again and again the lives of all aboard depended on their coming through the winter storms. Sometimes notices of death would reach the neighbors when a boat capsized and someone found his grave in the waves. I think I can be certain that about a third of the male population met a watery end.

When my oldest brother was fifteen years old he went to sea and visited many parts of the world and wrote letters from the United States, Peru, Australia, Java, and China, which aroused in me a desire to see strange countries and their people as my brother was doing. My father had secured an atlas, and we could find the places from which my brother wrote. By quiet industry and savings my parents had accumulated a little money, and at the beginning of the 1860s the "America" fever broke out and our neighbors whose island was on the Icy Sea wanted to exchange their land for a home in the United States. So my father bought the island, and together with ours it made a good piece of land.

One day in the spring of 1865 a number of boys, including myself, went to the highest point of our island, and we saw two large ships through the fog. And at the moment we saw them one ran onto a reef of rocks covered with water, and the other one steered out to sea. Naturally we ran home as fast as we could, and immediately my father put out a boat with his son-in-law and two other men and sailed to the wreck. From our outlook high on the island we saw many fishing boats going to the wreck. Toward evening my father came home with two pilots and two sailors who wanted to go to Tromsø and get a tow ship to help get the ship loose from the rocks. The wrecked ship was a bark from Dundee, Scotland, which was new and well equipped, making its first voyage to Archangel. Later that evening my father and one of their younger boys went to Tromsø, while the other eleven men on the ship refused to leave it. The next morning a bad storm began, and early we saw the emergency signals from the ship. Several fishermen tried to approach the wreck but it was not possible in the rough sea. It began to look as though the whole company on board would sink with the ship. The waves had demolished the ship's boats. The masts fell overboard, and we expected that in the next few hours the ship would be battered to pieces. My mother and sisters, who had only been observers, with tears in their eyes had our young brother-in-law, who was an excellent seaman, make another attempt to bring the poor people off the ship. My brother-in-law and another young man took the largest boat and approached the ship. The waves made a circle about a half mile wide around the ship. They succeeded in bringing the eleven off the ship and safe to land. The captain had swallowed so much water that he fainted, and many others were also sick from the water. Half an hour later, when there were no more people on the ship, it sank without a trace. My mother and brother-in-law, who rescued the crew, each received from the British government through the British consul in Tromsø a silver spoon engraved "For your deed."

In the summer of 1866 my older brother came home from his long journey. It was a joyous greeting, for he had been away eight years. My brother went up to the highest spot on the island with a telescope and saw out at sea some "bundles" swimming. I ran home and told my father, who started out with a boat and crew and found that what he had seen was a dead whale. It looked like a little island itself. At home I got my sisters and three maids to help. None of them were seamen, and every wave that broke on the boat was greeted with screaming. After several hours of hard sailing we arrived at neighbors. I piloted my boat and was very proud of my achievement.

In autumn of the same year my father bought a small ship that my older brother used. The ship was new, a good sailer, and was called *Elida* after Frithjof's famous ship. The ship was prepared to carry fish that were purchased. I received permission from my parents to go with it. My first occupation aboard was as cabin boy. In March 1867 we left our home and traveled to the fishing stations where we sold fish as well as caught them. There were not many, so we did very little business. At the end of May we returned home and the ship was prepared to go to Spitsbergen, but I did not get permission to go along. My brother had success in Spitsbergen and came back home in September. At the end of September the ship was prepared to go to the Lofoten Islands to buy herring, and I went along. We had little luck because very few herring were caught that year, so we returned home after Christmas.

In February 1868 our ship went again with eight men and two fishing boats to Finnmarken to buy fish and to fish ourselves. A few days after we left home we were overcome by a bad storm that filled our fishing boats with water and sank them. Then two of our crew became ill, and we tried hard to save them. One was a special friend of mine, and the event affected me very much. I had to return home to engage a new man to come with us. This year had been remarkable for storms. Fishing was very good on the Russo-Murman coast, and many Norwegian boats went there. Murman Coast on the Norwegian coast east from North Cape has few harbors, and what ones there are are usually used even in bad storms.

We found ourselves in a hurricane on the Norwegian side and were lucky to hang onto our boat. Some ships that were disabled by the storm were then looted by the Russians living there. In June we returned home. My older brother had accepted a position in Hamburg, but the ship he was supposed to take over was lost in the storm, so he was given our ship. In mid-July we sailed to Spitsbergen. After a few days we met polar ice in the neighborhood of Bear Island. Here we were almost lost because fog covered the land so we could not see it, but we got through without injury.

We crossed on the west side of Spitsbergen that whole summer and landed often at a fjord where there was reindeer hunting. This hunting is exciting and interesting, even though it is associated with many hardships like carrying an animal that had been shot two to four German miles from the mountains to the shore. Even though I was very young I took part in the hunt with great enthusiasm and excitement. And in the evening when the tales of the day's success were told I sat by the fire munching good pieces of meat and thinking I was luckier than any other person. For the night we turned the boat over so it served as a tent. At Spitsbergen there were seals, walrus, white whales, polar bears, and many sharks and eider ducks. The land had little vegetation—so little that one wondered what the reindeer lived on. There is much coal on Spitsbergen, but it is not of good quality.

Hunting on Spitsbergen is now carried on principally by Norwegians, whereas in the past Hollanders, Englishmen, and even Russians set up stations there. Some remains from these people still show, principally leg bones of men who died of scurvy. The following years until the autumn of 1869 I spent the summers at Spitsbergen and every fall wandered back to Norway. I developed myself into a seaman and did the same work as older seamen. In the winter of 1869 many people of Tromsø and the surrounding area migrated to Queensland in Australia, among them our recent captain. There was a shortage of captains and my father was very anxious to keep a captain who was interested in our business. One time when this was discussed, I told my father that I would like this posision. He thought I was too young to handle a ship and oversee the crew, but he responded to my wish by sending me to Tromsø to the navigation school. At the same time, Hans and Søren Johansen and some other young people who later gained fame in polar voyages were there. Hans Johansen was the captain of the *Lena* that went with Nordenskjöld on his journey to Siberia. In April 1870 I finally gathered a crew because the insurance company would not take a sixteen-year-old captain. On 19 April we sailed away and stayed close to the banks between Spitsbergen and Norway, and I must admit I had unusually good luck, for I returned with a very good catch. We unloaded quickly and sailed to Spitsbergen at the end of July. In the middle of September I came in with so much that I used the bladders of seals to pack fat and skins. Before we reached the shores of Norway we heard of the war between Germany and France and of the important battle of Sedan and the capture of Napoleon. That autumn my oldest brother came from Hamburg to visit us, and when he was ready to leave again after a month I had a great desire to accompany him, but my program did not allow it. The spring of 1871 I again spent at Spitsbergen, and in 1872 Nordenskjöld stayed in Spitsbergen for the winter. In this period an unusual number of ships had misfortunes in the neighborhood. Then six of our small boats with about sixty men on board were frozen into the ice. At the end of November the ship could be reached and forty men were brought back, almost starved. Twenty men in another area died of scurvy. There was little ice in 1873–74, and I spent my time on the banks between Spitsbergen and Norway where one catches sharks, which were very plentiful. My brother-in-law bought a ship and did very well with it. In autumn of 1874 when I returned from Spitsbergen I decided to visit my brother in Hamburg; I left Norway in the beginning of October and arrived in Hamburg on 26 October. My brother urged me to go into business and I did so. Then I wrote my father that I was not returning and that our ship should be sold. I stayed in Hamburg through the winter and learned to speak German. In the summer of 1875 I realized that salesmanship was not my line and longed for the sea, so

I planned to travel to another part of the world. A Norwegian captain whose ship was lying in the harbor was going to South America and invited me to go with him. We left on 13 January 1876 and arrived in Valparaiso. Here I left him and was accepted as a pilot. I must say that this was the most disagreeable position I had ever had, since the Chilean sailors were simply useless for European ships. I gave up my position and found a Swedish baker whose main business was in Peru and who had a branch in Valparaiso, of which I became the manager. I had seen as soon as I arrived in Chile that the surrounding waters were rich with fish, so I decided to buy a fishing boat and found a Swede and a Dane as partners. It did not go easily for us because since we were foreigners the government did not allow us to leave the harbor from sundown to dawn. The daytime fishing is very poor, and my companions lost interest and each bought himself a mule and headed for the Cordillera Mountains. While I sold the boat and gear, I looked for employment. I worked as a sailor and workman repairing all the ships that got into trouble rounding Cape Horn. At this I earned five or six dollars a day. In November 1876 a Norwegian ship came into the harbor and I knew the captain and pilots, so I decided to go back to Europe with them.

We sailed in November and reached Hamburg in the middle of February. My eldest brother had married for the second time during my absence and so invited me to meet his new wife and be their guest. One day I heard of a countryman who had sold six polar bears to Mr. Carl Hagenbeck in Hamburg. Hagenbeck had given orders to make ethnographic collections of artifacts used by the Eskimo and to bring an Eskimo family from Greenland. But the captain was going to Novaya Zemlya, where he could not get Eskimos; so I went to Hagenbeck and introduced myself and told him that I knew where the Eskimos were and could get them for him. He gave me the commission and I left the same evening for Copenhagen, since I knew it was the only way to reach Greenland. I took an old Danish brig, the *Whale,* which was making her eighty-fourth trip to Greenland. We had much contrary weather, so we did not arrive on the west coast of Greenland until the middle of June, and on 6 July we reached the trading post at Omenak. I immediately started making my ethnographic collection among the Eskimo who lived there, but to engage a family seemed impossible. On 12 July I met the governor, the "inspector," and asked him for his help with my problem, but he seemed to be very uncertain about taking people to Germany. On 17 July I went to Diskobay in the bark *Thorwaldsen,* but it seemed impossible to get any people here. On 22 July we reached Jacobshavn, where the inspector landed after accompanying us this far. I became acquainted with Dr. Von Haven, as well as with the missionary Rasmussen and the local trader, Fleischer; these three gentlemen were very friendly and promised me their help. During the first eight days I saw little possibility of achieving anything, but as I became familiar with the Eskimo, my prospects became brighter. As I became more certain that I would get some Eskimo to go to Europe I bought many ethnographic objects like large and small skin boats, tents, dogs, sleds, fishing and hunting gear, jewelry, clothing, and tools. On 15 August the *Whale* arrived at Jacobshavn and I at once reserved space for myself and six Eskimo I had engaged. The inspector arrived on the *Whale* and arranged the agreements with the Eskimo. On 21 August I had all my goods aboard, and since I was accompanied by several hundred Eskimo, each anxious to see a relative in his last moments before sailing, there was great danger that some would lose their courage. We sailed between two great icebergs that rose about three hundred feet above the level of the water. On 26 September we arrived at Copenhagen and three days later at Hamburg. We stayed in Hamburg from 29 September to 23 October and had great success, with thousands of Hamburg residents taking the opportunity of seeing Eskimo for the first time in Europe. On 26 October we arrived in Paris, where we had an engagement at the Jardin d'Acclimatation.[37] Here the Eskimo driving their dog sleds and small skin boats [probably kayaks] was new and wonderful. Never before had there been such a display of an ethnic culture in Paris. We stayed in Paris until 17 January, then went to Brussels, Cologne on the Rhine, Berlin, Dresden, Hamburg, and Copenhagen. The Eskimo had an extra six hundred kroner in addition to the money guaranteed them. On 14 May of the next year they went to Copenhagen and arrived home well and happy in the middle of July.

On 14 June I started to go to Lapland in the service of Mr. Hagenbeck to gather an ethnographic collection and bring reindeer and Lapps to Germany. On 26 June I arrived at my dear home, Tromsø, where I stayed two days, and then I went to those places where the Laplanders and their reindeer gathered to make contracts with them, including an order for forty reindeer that were to be collected later when I returned to the north. I visited my old home Risø on 2 July and spent two days there. My brother-in-law accompanied me to Hammerfest. I waited there until 15 July for a passing ship that made the short trip through Porsanger Fjord to two Lapp villages, Karassjok and Kautokeino. On 16 July we arrived at the fjord, and I went at once to a telegraph station. From now on I went in all directions collecting my Laplanders and buying objects and clothing until the end of July. I came upon a large Lapland camp in the mountains, from which I engaged nine persons—three women, four men, and two boys. On 16 August we had the people and the ethnographic objects together, and we went aboard a coast steamer.

On 26 August we arrived in Bergen. There was a circus (Leonhardt), and I decided to take my Laplanders to the evening performance. The Lapps, looking around, saw so many people that they thought they were in church, so they took off their caps. When a horse came jumping into the ring they became frightened and ran up to the gallery, where they turned to see if the horse was following them. Seeing they were not being followed, they calmed down and enjoyed the show, especially the clowns, who were stimulated to do their best work. On 31 August I arrived in Hamburg and visited the Laplanders, and later went with them to Hannover, Paris, Lille, Brussels, Düsseldorf, Berlin, and Dresden. In Dresden I received a note from Mr. Hagenbeck asking me to come to Hamburg in order to go to Le Havre, where he was expecting three Patagonians on a German steamer. With them I visited Hamburg, where I met my Laplanders, just getting ready to embark to go home. By this meeting a funny incident occurred. The Patagonians insisted that they knew the Laplanders and had seen them in the Cordillera Mountains, and they wanted to be taken to the chief of the group in order to greet him. I did this, and immediately our good Patagonians began their customary greeting ceremonies, which took more than ten minutes with bows and body movements. The Laplanders watched with amazement at the idea of greeting an unknown person with their ceremony. The eldest and most intelligent of the Laplanders undertook to reply to this greeting. He mimicked some of the facial movements, and the Patagonians took it as their best. After the ceremonies were over they shook hands and that ended what neither had understood.

For some years Mr. Hagenbeck and I had had a plan to own a little boat that could be used for journeys to all parts of the world to collect ethnographic artifacts, so I went to Norway, where in December 1879 I bought a ship. Our first voyage was to Greenland and the Northwest Coast of America, so I had the ship equipped for a polar voyage. On 27 April we sailed from Hamburg, but the trip was slow because of contrary winds. We had seal and whale hunters on board, for we hoped to take part in the seal hunting near Greenland. For some time on this trip I began to feel sick, and finally I became very ill with cold and fever. On 29 May we saw the northwest coast of Greenland, and a few days later we met some of the Norwegian Seal Clubbing Company, which consisted of about twenty or thirty steam and sailing vessels. I was so ill I did not know what was happening. A strong storm and fog gathered, and we had little luck with the seal hunting. On 21 June we were on the east coast of Greenland and mistook the place by four German miles, so we came suddenly on thick fog and heavy ice to stop us. From the mast I could see some small islands and a fjord going inland. At the end of June we sailed to northwest Greenland and at last arrived on 6 July in Jacobshavn, the place from which I had brought an Eskimo family to Europe. They greeted me with joy and some wanted to go again.

Even though the local inspector prohibited my bringing my ethnographic collection with me and charged duty, I was forced to sail again on 20 July and set my course to the side of Greenland opposite Cumberland. But the condition of the ice would not allow us to land, and we wallowed in ice and storm until 8 August. Then I gave up trying to reach the northeast coast of Cumberland and tried to go to Labrador, where on 11 August we arrived at the harbor of Hebron, a mission station of the Moravian brotherhood. Here I gathered some ethnographic artifacts from the native Eskimo. I found some especially rich graves. To engage a family to go to Europe was impossible because the German missionaries there, who were otherwise friendly toward me, urged the Eskimo not to go to Europe. However, I succeeded in getting an intelligent young Eskimo as pilot and interpreter and sailed on 11 August skirting the coast northward. After much effort I succeeded in getting a heathen Eskimo family from the north, and now when my pilot promised to go to Europe with his family I turned around and returned to Hebron. The pilot got his wife, two children, and a relative, so now we could start homeward again. We had favorable winds and reached Hamburg on 24 September. We made our first exhibition in Hamburg and stayed there until 27 October, when we went to Berlin. Here we performed until 15 November, when we went to Prague, where we stayed until 29 November, after playing to packed houses. On 30 November we went to Frankfurt am Main and on 13 December to Darmstadt and Crefeld, and we proceeded to Paris in January 1881. The accidents and illnesses our expedition suffered are well known. I was so ill that I stayed in France until 10 March, when I returned to Hamburg and made a few business trips for Mr. Hagenbeck.

I offered my services for the collecting expedition that the Berlin Museum was preparing, and for which the "Aid" committee was raising the funds, in the summer of 1881. I was selected and started out to visit the Northwest Coast of North America and Alaska.

1. Stewart's was a department store in New York City.

2. This reference to the Meares expedition as the origin of the Chinook Jargon is not correct. The jargon antedated the coming of Europeans as an Indian trade language, and words from such European languages as English, French, and Spanish joined the potpourri. As trade spread and the Hudson's Bay Company participated, many Europeans came to speak Chinook Jargon; in fact, they often used it in conversation among themselves.

3. This term was applied to those tribes that deformed their infants' heads by applying pressure to their foreheads while they were on the cradle board; it is also the tribal name of the Salish-speaking group in Montana, who do not deform heads. It is no longer applied to any coastal Indians.

4. The Bella Bella are the northernmost Kwakiutl and are seldom grouped with the other three northern tribes.

5. Cattails or split cedar bark.

6. Jacobsen identifies this fish with the northern European "lodde," or smelt, which is a food fish for cod. The species *Mallotus arcticus* he suggests is the same as *Mallotus villosus* (Muller 1772). This fish is six inches long (Fisheries Research Board of Canada 1961).

7. Perhaps these were argillite, made by the Haida, though they are very tall for argillite.

8. This is undoubtedly a Chilkat blanket.

9. There is no "Vancouver Sound"; the crossing is in Hecate Strait (*Gazetteer of Canada, British Columbia* 1966, p. 291).

10. This refers to a prominent Kwakiutl family named Hunt, still well represented in this area. The son George who is mentioned later became Franz Boas's famous informant and co-worker in linguistics.

11. "Kwag.ul" is one of the more modern ways of spelling a word that for many years has been rendered as "Kwakiutl." It may be more correct phonetically, but since the latter spelling is used in most reference literature, "Kwakiutl" will be continued here.

12. It is interesting to compare this account with the more extensive report by Boas (1895).

13. This seems to be a frontlet headdress that sat on the forehead, not a face mask. It was usually inlaid with abalone shell and the opercula of the sea snail. The Tsimshian were famous for making these.

14. This term is misused for the Coast Salish, some of whom had slightly deformed heads. Becher Bay was occupied by Clallam from the north coast of the Olympic Peninsula.

15. These bone "swords" or clubs were carried only by chiefs and other people of rank. The chiefs often had special ritual names for their bone clubs, but if they did not wish to use those names they made up a euphemism like "orphan maker" (Drucker 1951, p. 335).

16. See Sproat (1868), pp. 188–90.

17. A record of this transaction is in the documents of the Alaska Commercial Company at the Jackson Graduate Library of Business at Stanford University, Palo Alto, California.

18. The description of the trip continues in this vein on pages 147 and 148 of the original, which are not translated here.

19. Much of this geological discussion (pp. 170–72 of the original) has been omitted here; it may now be completely out of date.

20. The rest of the paragraph is omitted here.

21. None of the place names could be identified.

22. Jacobsen wrote "kju" to be pronounced "chu."

23. Alternate spelling for Isaak (Ray 1971, p. 27).

24. Jacobsen's spelling of this name varies between "Ki" and "Ku."

25. Named for James Gordon Bennett, publisher of the *New York Herald*; Mr. Woolfe was employed by this paper.

26. "Mr. Hartz" is Jacobsen's rendition of the name of A. B. Hard, one of the original stockholders in the Golovnin Bay area (Ray 1971, p. 25)

27. This is the "Feast for the Dead" described by Nelson (1899, pp. 363 ff.).

28. Nelson (1899).

29. This may be wild parsnip, according to Nelson (1899).

30. After Jacobsen's employer.

31. Jacobsen confused this with Romanof Point.

32. Mumtreklik is the version of the name given in Orth (1967, p. 128).

33. Personal communication from Dr. Frederica DeLaguna (8 October 1975): "Jacobsen dug at an abandoned Indian site on Kachemak Bay, which he called Soonroodna, and which represented the Eskimoized culture of the Tanaina just prior to [?] and just after the coming of the Russians. Although I have not been able to identify the site with certainty, I think it is probably the one I visited in China Poot Bay, although I did not find any pottery there. In both the upper and lower layers Jacobsen found 'a number of small pieces of earthenware cooking pots, of the same kind as are now used on the Yukon.' Unfortunately this description is not more specific."

34. Compare DeLaguna (1956).

35. These people are probably Eyak; see Birket-Smith and DeLaguna (1938).

36. Though the Eyak were disturbed by the incident, it is not certain whether Eyak or Tlingit were involved (Birket-Smith and DeLaguna 1938, p. 340).

37. The Jardin d'Acclimatation is the Zoological Garden in the Bois de Boulogne.

Adematzensky (191). *See* Nusaktolik River.
Adnek (148). *See* Atnuk; mentioned under this name in Ray
(1964, p.69).
Afognak Island (201). NE of Kodiak Island (Orth 1964, p.48).
Agalik River (182). The Agaligamiut have a village, Arolik
(q.v.) on the east bank of Kuskokwim Bay (Orth 1967, p.49).
Possible variant: Agolegma (Zagoskin 1967, p.348).
Ahauset (48). Ahouset, a Nootkan village (BCG, p.5; Walbran
1972, p.4).
Ahts (Indians) (45). The Ahts are the Nootkan tribes occupying the west coast of Vancouver Island from Cape Cook
south to Port Renfrew; first so named by Sproat (Walbran
1972).
Akedaknak (195). Formerly a trading post of the Western Fur
Company in Seldovia Bay; it was abandoned in May 1883
when the firm merged with the Alaska Commercial Com-
pany, which reduced the price of sea otter skins from $112
to $35 apiece.
Akun (82). The strait separating Akun and Akutan Islands.
Named by Krenitzen (1768) from a native name. Name also
used by Veniaminof and Lutka in 1830 (Baker 1966, p.87;
Orth 1967, p.58).
Alberni (44). Modern town on canal at upper end of Barclay
Sound; a division of the Nootka (BCG, p.7).
Alexander. *See* Fort Alexander; there are two forts by this
name.
Allaganak (207). Alaganikis in the Copper River Delta. There
are many variations in spelling. The village has both Eskimo
and Athapaskans and formerly some Ahtena. The village
was visited by Serebrenikof in 1848 and by Lieutenant Allen,
USA, in 1885 (Orth 1967, p.59).
Allert Bay (8). Alert Bay. Modern town and Kwakiutl village
on Cormorant Island (BCG, p.9).
Amelirok (145). On the shore opposite Port Clarence.
Ameoraremiut (178). On the Kuskokwim expedition Jacobsen
passed three villages: Sintuleremiut, Sewartlaremiut, and
Ameoraremiut, in this order. None were occupied.

This glossary includes
the names of natural
features and of places
where Jacobsen traveled,
stayed, or traded as well
as the names of some
Indian and Eskimo
groups. The name as
written by Jacobsen is
followed by the page
number where it first
appears. Next is the
modern spelling found
in Orth, *Dictionary of
Alaska Place Names*,
the *Gazetteer of Canada,
British Columbia* (BCG),
or Walbran, *British
Columbia Place Names,
1592–1906*. Complete
references and other
sources are listed in the
Bibliography. The
references to Petrof,
Nelson, and Zagoskin
are given as consistently
as possible when dealing
with such a variety of
languages. The ending
"miut" on Eskimo
names refers to the
people occupying a
village or area.

Anchor Point (195). A promontory forming the southern point of Cook Inlet, named by Cook because he lost an anchor here. Formerly called Leida, it was a gathering place for sea otter hunters of the Kenai Peninsula (Orth 1967, p.75).

Andrejewski (93). Old Andreafsky on the right bank of the Yukon River was a fort established by the Russians in 1853; a "redoubt" was built, and it was the site of a massacre in 1855 (Orth 1967, p.76). Variants: Andreafsky, now called Saint Mary's; Andreivsky (Nelson 1899, p.19).

Ankasagemiut (95). Alternate Eskimo name Kinegnagamiut (Orth 1967, p.795); Russian name Razboinski (q.v.).

Anvik (98). An Ingalik village on the right side of the Yukon River (Orth 1967, p.82); in 1834 Glazanow found this village of several hundred people; in 1869 Raymond called it Anvic (Baker 1966, p.102); in 1887 an Episcopal mission was established at Kaiayutkhotana, a village at the junction of the Anvik and Yukon Rivers (Orth 1967, p.82); Zagoskin gives Anvig (1967, p.348).

Apoon. *See* Upun.

Arawingenak River (158). A river flowing into Eschscholtz Bay, Kotzebue Sound, and a small village by the same name.

Arolik (182). An abandoned small village on the Agalik River; name means "moon" (Orth 1967, p.87). Also known as Agolaremiut.

Assik Island (192). An island in Lake Iliamna, two thousand feet high; a bird refuge in great use.

Atna. *See* Copper River.

Atnuk (148). On NW shore of Norton Sound (Orth 1967, p.92). Variant: Atnikmion (Zazoskin, map XXI, 1850; Nelson map; Petrof 1880, p.11; Ray 1964, p.60; 1971, p.21).

Azachagyak. *See* Romanof Point.

Aziak (120). Village of Aziagmiut on Sledge Island near Cape Nome; subdivision of Kavaigmiut; named Sledge Island by Captain James Cook, 1778. Variants: Aziyak (Zagoskin 1967, p.348); Ayak (Ray 1971, p.7; Petrof 1880, p.11).

Bajo (50). A promontory on Nootka Island occupied by a few Indian families from Nootka Sound (BCG, p.29).

Barclay Sound (43). A large inlet in Nootka territory (Walbran 1971, p.33).

Barnassella (108). Russian name for Makkiem (Makak, q.v.); modern name Bonasila (Osgood 1940, p.30, map p.40).

Barren Island (201). Between Afognak and Marmot Islands.

Beecher Bay (43). Becher Bay on Becher Inlet, a Clallam village near the entrance of the Strait of Juan de Fuca on the Canadian side (BCG, p.45).

Belase-karat (104). An Athapaskan village on the Yukon River near Norraden and Nusaron; visited on downstream transit of the Yukon River.

Bella Bella (9). NW Coast of Denny Island in Milbank Sound. The Indians speak Heiltsuk, a dialect of Kwakiutl (BCG, p.47); Adaptation of Indian name, which they pronounce "Pil-palla" (Walbran 1972, p.45).

Bethel. *See* Mumtreklik.

Bonilla Island (15). SW of north end of Banks Island; shelter on trip to Queen Charlotte Islands (BCG, p.67).

Bristol Bay (188). North of base of Alaska Peninsula, between Cape Newenham and Alaska Peninsula; named by Captain James Cook, 1778 (Orth 1967, p.160).

Bute Inlet (87). Site of an Indian village, deserted during the fishing season.

Cape Beale (43). Lighthouse at the entrance of Barclay Sound. The Spanish explorer Eliza called it Punta de Alegria; later named for purser on the *Imperial Eagle* (Walbran 1972, p.39).

Cape Constantine (187). At the tip of Nushagak Peninsula, named by a Russian surveyor (Orth 1967, p.234).

Cape Cook (45). Northern boundary of Nootka territory.

Cape (Point) Esteven (50). Named by Captain James Cook (Walbran 1972, p.106).

Cape Jungfrau. *See* Newiarsualok.

Cape Martin (206). South of Alaganik at mouth of Martin River; considered the dividing line between the purer Eyak of the Cordova Copper River delta and the more Tlingitized Eyak of Comptroller Bay and the Gulf Coast (Orth 1967, p.626; Ray 1971).

Cape Newenham (53). On Bering Sea between Kuskokwim and Bristol Bays; named by Captain James Cook and claimed for his country (Orth 1972, p.160).

Cape Prince of Wales (115). On Seward Peninsula, nearest to Siberia. Named by Captain James Cook, 1778; Bering in 1728 named it Mys Gvozdeva (Orth 1967, p.777).

Cape Raget (51). At the entrance to the Nootkan village of Kyuquot.

Cape Romanzoff (93). Point of land at west of Asikmok Mountains between Kokechik and Scammon Bays (Orth 1967, p.814).

Cape "Schleinitz" (190). Jacobsen's name for part of Romanof Point.

Cape Scott (74). North end of Vancouver Island.

Cape Vancouver (93). Promontory on tip of Nelson Island, 125 miles south of Bethel. Discovered in 1821 by A. K. Etolin and named by him for Vancouver (Orth 1967, p.1017).

Chakwaktolik. *See* Kjokkaktolik.

Chawispa (51). Ca'wispa, village in Kyuquot Sound (Drucker 1951, p.222).

Chenega Island (203). Chugach Eskimo village on an island (Orth 1967, p.203. Variants: Chanega, Chenija, Ingamatsha) (Petroff, 1890 census).

Chichinak. *See* Kjikjingemiut.

Chickliset. *See* Tschuklesaht.

Chimenes (79). Chemainus, modern spelling of a town and Indian village on the east side of Vancouver Island, NW of Kuper Island (BCG, p.116).

Chinaman's Hat (11). China Hat, a Kwakiutl village speaking Heiltsuk dialect, on Tolmie Channel and Mussel Inlet (BCG, p.458).

Clahus (80). Klahoose, an Indian village near Clayamen (mainland Salish belonging to Bute Inlet villages).

Clayamen (80). Salish village on the mainland opposite Comox.

Comox (79). Northernmost Salish village on the east side of Vancouver Island; also called the southern outpost of the Kwakiutl, but their language is Salish (BCG, p.136).

Constantine. *See* Cape Constantine.

Copper River (201). Also called Atna; extreme northern limit of Tlingit influence; flows through mountains to the gulf of Alaska (Orth 1967, p.238).

Cowichan (6). Name used for a bay, a Salish village, and also a subdivision of the Salish-speaking people.

Cracroft Island (35). Home of a division of the Kwakiutl.

Cumshewa (20). Haida village on the north shore of Cumshewa Inlet.

Dakketjeremiut (111). Eskimo village on the Yukon River in an area where Jacobsen found many articles to buy.

Deep Inlet (51). On the east side of Kyuquot Sound and east side of Union Island. From this point Jacobsen visited the villages of Queka and Oales. Variant: Amai Inlet (BCG, p.13).

Delsanorvit (103). Village on the Yukon River where a shaman danced, trying to bewitch the boat in which Jacobsen was traveling upstream.

Dininek Lake (141). Lake on the trail to Cape Prince of Wales.

Eckult (44). "Bushes or hill people"; now joined with Seshart at Nootkan summer village; not mentioned by Drucker; listed by Sproat (1868, p.333) as Ekole; Warren Trading Post.

Egavik (165). Igawik, an Eskimo village on Norton Sound. Reported in 1857 by Western Union Telegraph Expedition as Igawik Creek (Orth 1967, p.303).

Ehattesaht (53). Ehatisaht, Nootkan village north side of Esperanza Inlet (BCG, p.198). Important dentalium center. Variant: Ehetisaht (Drucker 1951, p.5).

Eparsluit (109). Russian name given this village by Gregori Schapka, in reference to a sugarloaf-shaped rock six to eight miles away; above Mission.

Eratlerowik (171). At south end of Yukon delta.

Eratlewik (138). Village on Fish River. Variants: Ikalikhoik, meaning "fish place" (Kashervirow 1838); Irathlink (Zagoskin 1967; Ray 1964, p.69). Fish River is also known as the Nerkluk River.

Eritak River (154). River at the divide in the mountains south of Kotzebue Sound. Variant: Errakwik.

Errakwik (146). Village on Maknek River on the journey to Cape Prince of Wales.

Eschscholt Bay (158). In Kotzebue Sound (Zagoskin 1967, p.350; Orth 1967, p.317).

Eyak. *See* Iggiak.

Fish River (138). Also known as Nerkluk with Eskimo village of Eratlewik at the mouth. Variant: Niulak (Orth 1967, p.338).

Fort Alexander (188). Russian American Company established a trading post in Nushagak Bay, probably named for Alexander Baranof (Orth 1967, p.712). There is another Fort Alexander; see next entry.

Fort Alexander (188). On the shore of the Kenai Peninsula on Cook Inlet is a trading post of the Alaska Commercial Company; on maps of Holmberg 1854, and Jacobsen 1869.

Fort Kenai (193). On the Kenai Peninsula diagonally across Cook Inlet from North Foreland, which is approximately at the location of Tyonek; it even may be Tagunak (q.v.) (Orth 1967, p.509). Variants: Fort Nicholas, Kenai Redoubt, Saint Nicholas.

Fort Saint Michael (81). Jacobsen's headquarters for organizing his major journeys; the main port for Norton Sound. Eskimo name Tachek (Orth 1967, p.827). Established 1833, visited by Whymper, 1836; attacked by the Malemiut (Schwatka 1885, p.110).

Fort Rupert (28). On east side of Vancouver Island, south side of Beaver Harbor; a Kwakiutl village (BCG, p. 230).

Friendly Cove (53). Famous location during period of exploration and Spanish settlement in Nootka Sound; name of Indian village is Yuquot (BCG, p.237; Walbran 1972, p.194).

Galownin. *See* Golovnin Bay.

Gold Harbor. *See* Kaisun.

Golovin Bay (85). A lagoon extending south 12 miles to Norton Sound, 45 miles east of Solomon (Orth 1967, p.377).

Golovnin Bay (118). In Norton Sound; Eskimo village reported there in 1824. Also called Chenik Mission. Named by Kromshenko for his brig *Golovnin* in 1821. Omilak silver mine 37 miles away (Ray 1971; Orth 1967, p.377).

Golzowa (168). At Norton Sound at mouth of Golsovia River; 23 miles from Unalakleet; Eskimo name Nygvilnuk (Orth 1967, p.377; Zagoskin 1967, p.350).

Hagemeister Island (185). In Togiak Bay; named for Baranof's successor.

Haida (9). The Indians living on the Queen Charlotte Islands.

Hametze (30). Hāma'tsa, the highest secret society of the Kwakiutl.

Hardak, Hardanak (197). Eskimo name for the village now standing near Soonroodna, an archaeological site in Kachamak Bay.

Hesquiaht (49). Hesquiat, a Nootkan village with a Catholic mission (BCG, p.295).

Holy Cross. *See* Koserowsky.

Hotham Inlet (158). In the area of several rivers that flow into Kotzebue Sound.

Hotlotulei (144). Hotlina mountains, 21 miles SE of Rampart (Orth 1967, p.440).

Igawik (125). Egavik, on Norton Sound, north of Fort Saint Michael; reported by the Union Telegraph Expedition (Orth 1967, p.303).

Iggiak (206). On Konno River, a Tlingit village of about ten houses. This was once a powerful tribe, but warfare with Eskimo and other Tlingit eliminated most of them; intermarriage with Tlingit produced the few remaining members; they are probably Eyak (Orth 1967, p.323).

Iglotalik (124). Iglutalik, an Eskimo village and a river by the same name. Variant: Iglutalik River, Jacobsen 1869.

Igniktok (134). Village on the west shore of Golovnin Bay found by Zagoskin and Petrof.

Ikogmiut. *See* Mission.

Iliamna or Quitzak (189). Kwichak River at head of Bristol Bay; rises in Lake Iliamna; Dall, 1870, called it Kwichag and saw an Aglemiut Eskimo village there (Orth 1967, p.449).

Iliamna, Lake (188). Site of an Alaska Commercial Company trading post. It is the dividing line between Eskimo and Ingalik; south of here and along the lake Eskimo are found and the coast to Cape Newenham belongs to the Nushagak-speaking villages (Orth 1967, p.449).

Illintongemiut (182). Eskimo village on the trail on the east bank of lower Kuskokwim River; last village on the trail.

Ilquigamiut (179). Summer fishing village on the Kuskokwim River.

Imarsok (143). Imuruk Lake and Basin; roughly means "water." On Seward Peninsula. Variants: Emaruk, Imourouk Lake (Ray 1971; Orth 1967, p.452).

Ingalik (91). Eskimo name for Athapaskan people in the Yukon valley, especially the Eskimo Paimiut near Anvik; Ingeletes (Raymond 1967, p.36).

Ingerkarremiut. (111). Eskimo village on the Yukon River near Dakkettjeremiut where Jacobsen camped for the night. Not mentioned by name in text.

Inuktok (157). Eskimo village at the mouth of the Buckland River at the head of Eschscholtz Bay; Eskimo camp 1898

(Orth 1967, p.458; Baker 1966, p.328; reported by Zagoskin in 1844).

Itlauniwik (154). On the way to Kotzebue Sound where the Eritak River flows into the Koyuk; on map, "Kotzebue Sound to Norton Bay."

Joktjitleramiut (179). Summer fishing village on the east bank of the Kuskokwim River. The first village of a group. It may be Bethel.

Jotsitle (182). Deserted village on the Kuskokwim River.

Jucklulaht (47). Ucluelet, Nootkan village near Barclay Sound (Drucker 1951, p.7).

Jukkak (174). Eskimo village at the mouth of the Jukkak River, which empties into Vancouver Bay at the tip of Cape Vancouver.

Juklutok (79). Cowichan summer village near Nanaimo.

Kachemak Bay (195). Archaeological site on Kenai Peninsula.

Kaggan (173). Village at SE corner of Kaggan Lake.

Kaisun (17). Also known as New Gold Harbor; west side of Queen Charlotte Islands.

Kajak (154). Village on the Kiwalik River (Orth 1967, p.528).

Kajaluigemiut (174). On the journey to Bristol Jacobsen found this village with six houses.

Kajuktulik (159). Village where the Selawik River empties into Selawik Lake.

Ka-krome (110). A village on the Yukon River below Mission; nearest to the mythical bird area.

Kaksertobage (140). Summer fishing camp in Eratlewik territory; "Kukesuktopaga" means "a place where there are white hills." White miners changed the name to "Casedepaga" (Ray 1971, p.23).

Kalgia Island (192). On Cook Inlet west of Kenai in Tanaina area.

Kamischak Bay (188). At the entrance of Cook Inlet (Orth 1967, p.491; Kalgin, in Orth 1967, p.488).

Kamschua. *See* Cumshewa.

Kangek River (154). Probably the Kiwalik River as on the Alaska map and in Orth (1968, p.528); Eskimo name established by the British Admiralty about 1880. Variant: Keewal-ik. The Unalitschok River flows into the Kangek.

Kangerenaremiut (179). Large village on the Kuskokwim River.

Kaoweanagemiut (182). Eskimo village on the east bank of the Kuskokwim River together with Agolaremiut, Semerian villages.

Kasiloff River (194). On the Kenai Peninsula.

Kaskanak (190). Eskimo village of the Kiatagmiut division of the Aglemiut who live on the banks of the Kvichivak River and Lake Iliamna (Orth 1967, p.499).

Kastarnak (192). Fishing village on Cook Inlet.

Katlarijok (184). Mountain range in the valley of the Kusko-
    kwim River.
Katzarak (183). Eskimo name for a river that Jacobsen named
    "Virchow" for a well-known German anthropologist.
Kauwerak (138). Largest Eskimo settlement on Seward Penin-
    sula.
Kaviaremiut (155). Name for Eskimo living on Prince of Wales
    Peninsula.
Kawiarak (138). Kauwerak, meaning "gravel bar" (Ray 1971,
    p.22); a historical village east of Port Clarence. Variants:
    Chueweren (Kobelev 1729); Kow-ee-rok (Beechey 1827;
    Ray 1964, pp.4–13).
Kayokaht (48). Kyuquot, Nootkan village on sound by same
    name (BCG, p.366; Drucker 1951, p.4).
Kelsomat. Division of the Ahauset made by the Indian agent
    (Drucker 1951, p.238).
Kelungiarak (140). Keluniak, summer fishing village owned by
    the Eratlewik (Ray 1964, p.70). Variant: Kigluniarpak
    (Bourchier 1851).
Kenaiski (192). Indians on Cook Inlet.
Ketkatle (13). Kitkatla, Tsimshian village on north coast of
    Dolphin Island, south of Porcher Island (BCG, p.79).
Kikertagmiut (90). Eskimo living on Kodiak Island; name may
    be derived from Kikhtowik (Orth 1967, p.535).
Kikertaok (151). Kikertarok, a small Eskimo village about 10
    miles east of Fort Saint Michael. Variants: Kiktaguk (United
    States Survey 1909).
Kikertaurok (177). Large village near Cape Vancouver; ar-
    chaeological site (Ray 1971, p.14). Variant: Klilitauk (Ray
    1971, p.14).
Kinegnagamiut. *See* Ankasagemiut.
Kingegan (138). Village at Cape Prince of Wales; may be re-
    ferred to by Lvov (1711) when he came from Chukchee
    Peninsula (Ray 1971, p.3); named by Beechey (Orth 1967,
    p.1026). Kingegmiut were middlemen between Cape Prince
    of Wales and Siberia (Petrof 1884, p.126).
Kingerumiut (109). First large Eskimo village on the Yukon
    River when going downstream.
King Island (88). Offshore island facing Cape Nome. A group
    of Eskimo came to Fort Saint Michael with many good arti-
    facts that Jacobsen bought.
Kjikjingemiut (177). Chichinak, an Eskimo village in the Kus-
    kokwim mountains where the party stopped for tea. Jacob-
    sen mentions that there were no artifacts for purchase be-
    cause of Nelson's visit (Orth 1967, p.207).
Kjokkaktolik (173). Chakwaktolik, village on the downstream
    transit of the Yukon River near Marshall (Orth 1967, p.
    197); spelling used reported by Jarvis in 1897.
Kjukkarremiut (110). Village on the border of Athapaskan and
    Eskimo locations on the Yukon River.

Kjuwaggenak (131). Eskimo village 2 miles from the mouth of the Kwiniuk (Quinekak) River on left bank; new village at Moses Point, named for a Unalit man who was called Moses in the gold rush (Ray 1964, p.68).

Klaun-lokolte (105). One of a series of four villages passed in quick succession on the downstream trip on the Yukon. They did not yield any good purchases.

Klawitsches (35). Klawitches, Kwakiutl village on Cracroft Island (Boas 1895; Boas 1966, map, p.2).

Klayoquaht (48). Clayoquot, a Nootkan village; trading post of Warren Company; harbor used by fur traders in eighteenth century (Walbran 1972, p.92; BCG, p.126).

Kleitvit, Klaun-lokolte, Kohara (105). Villages in the region of the mammoth bones; Kohara may be Kokara.

Klekusiremiut (179). On the Kuskokwim, left bank.

Klokare (103). Athapaskan village on the right bank of the Yukon River above Nulato.

Klu (19). Klue, Haida village on Tanu Island, named for a chief (BCG, p.358).

Knight Inlet (32). On coast of mainland facing the east side of Vancouver Island.

Knight Island (203). Off Kenai Peninsula; Jacobsen tried to excavate an archaeological site there (Orth 1967, p.533).

Koggaklek River (184). Named for William Schönlank by Jacobsen.

Kokara. *See* Kleitvit.

Kommensita (104). Athapaskan village on the Yukon River near Nusaron. Formerly one of the sites of Old Lowden (Orth 1967, p.598).

Konno Lake and River (206). Eyak Lake and River.

Koserowsky (108). Also Holy Cross, on the west bank of Walker Slough off the Yukon River, 34 miles from Anvik. Variant: Anilukhtakpak (Zagoskin 1967, p.137).

Koskimo (37). Subdivision of the Kwakiutl on the south side of Quatsino Sound (BCG, p.533).

Kotzebue Sound (118). Large bay in Bering Strait in territory of the Malemiut Eskimo.

Kuikak (124). Eskimo village near Eisak's village on Norton Sound.

Kujikuk (104). Koyukuk, river flowing into the Yukon River near Nulato. Variant: Yunnaka (Zagoskin 1967, p.144); whole length explored by Lieutenant Allen in 1885.

Kujuk (153). The Koyuk River.

Kulewarewialeremiut (179). Place on Kuskokwim River where Jacobsen changed guides.

Kumsche. *See* Cumshewa.

Kupfer Island (78). Kuper Island was named for an early settler, not for the metal copper, as the German word implies (BCG, p.363). See also Pinalekaht.

Kusilwak (90). Chnagmiut village on Kusilwak Island at the mouth of the Yukon River; a Roman Catholic mission was built there; name also applied to a mountain visible from 50 miles away (Orth 1967, p.554).

Kuskokwimiut (90). Eskimo living along the Kuskokwim river.

Kuskoqwim (86). Kuskokwim, the second largest river in Alaska.

Kutlik (91). Kotlik, village of the Chnagmiut on Kotlik River about 30 miles from the Apoon mouth of the Yukon River (Orth 1967, p.542); 1878 trading post called Kwutlek, meaning "trousers" (Father Barnum, Baker 1966, p.380); breeches names fork of river at Koatlik, the home of an old Russian who had trade goods (Schwatka 1885, p.110).

Kwag.ul (29). Division of Kwakiutl at Fort Rupert; one of the recent attempts to get a more accurate phonetic spelling.

Kwikluk (178). Kwethluk, Kwik, Kwikak River. Kwik River; former Eskimo village. First reported by the Western Union Telegraph as Kwikmute (Orth 1967, p.558); reported by Cook (1784, date of publication of his Third Voyage, not date when he was at this place). He called it Bald Head; reported by Giddings (1964, p.179) as Kwik. In Unalit Bald Head is known as Uluksak (Giddings 1964, p.179) for slate found there. Kwik River is an ancient site at the mouth of the river with berry-picking camps (Ray 1964, p.68).

Kwik Pak (90). Kwikpak, "the great river." The Eskimo living near the mouth are called Kwikpakmiut and those above Andreafsky, Ikogmiut, and speak a Yupik dialect (Orth 1967, p.559). Variant: Kvishpak (Zagoskin 1967, p.353).

Kwiniuk or Quinekak (131). "New River" (Ray 1964, p.68); Kjuwaggenak village is on this river (q.v.).

Kwinnekaremiut (182). On the Kuskokwim River after passing the Agolaremiut group.

Kyuquot. *See* Kayokaht.

LeCoq's Island (190). In Lake Iliamna there are many nesting places for sea birds, where Jacobsen and others went to collect eggs.

Leida. *See* Anchor Point.

Makah (4). Nootka-speaking tribe at Cape Flattery and Neah Bay (Drucker 1951, p.4). Not named in text.

Makakkerak (157). Village in the Kotzebue area on the Kiwalik or Buckland River.

Makkatmekettan (104). Abandoned village of the Athapaskans between Moose point and Old Melozi.

Makkiem (108). Makak, village on the right bank of the Yukon River below Anvik; former Eskimo settlement reported in 1881 by Tikhmenof (Orth 1967, p.616); Malegimiut at division of Eskimo and Ingalik (Schwatka 1885, p.104). Variant: Makki (Zagoskin 1967, p.353). Russian name Barnassella.

Maknek River (141). This river is reached after crossing Dininek Lake.

Malaspina (80). Indian village near Bute Inlet.

Malemiut (90). Eskimo living between Norton Sound and Kotzebue Sound are known by this name. Variant: Mahlemute (Petrof 1880, p.125).

Mamelellika (33). Kwakiutl village on Village Island at the south end of Gilford Island. Variant: Mamleleqala (Boas 1895, p.330).

Mamtratlagemiut (180). This may be modern Bethel.

Mannek (189). Village famous for hunters of the Beluga whale.

Markaht (51). Nootkan village in Kyuquot Sound.

Marmot Island (201). Near Afognak Island (Orth 1967, p.623). Known to many explorers.

Masset (19). Haida village at entrance to Masset Sound (BCG, p.4).

Matlogak (184). Matlogak River flows 28 miles SW to Hagemeister Strait and 10 miles N of the same; in Kilbuck Kuskokwim Mountains (Orth 1967, p.629). Variant: Matuwalk on Jacobsen's 1869 map.

Metlakatla (14). Village that Father Duncan moved from the mainland to Annette Island. The people are Tsimshian.

Milbank Sound (9). Between Price Island and Nardswell (BCG, p.436). Locale of Bella Coola Indians.

Mission (96). In 1843 the Russian Orthdox church established a mission here; Ikogmiut Eskimo village means "Point People" (Baker 1966, p.34); store kept by Aleut priest's brother, employed by Alaska Commercial Company (Schwatka 1885, p.109); portage from Mission across the Yukon River to redoubt on the Kuskokwim; Ikogmiut now named "Mission" and speak Yupik.

Moaht (53). Moachat, Nootkan village (Drucker 1951, p.5).

Montague Island (203). Large island in Prince William Sound occupied by Chugach.

Moses Point. *See* Kjuwaggenak.

Mumtreklik (180). "Smokehouse" Kuskokwim village on west bank of river; modern Bethel; Moravian mission founded 1886 (Orth 1967, p.128).

Muschlaht (54). Muchalat, Nootkan village (Drucker 1951, p. 5; BCG, p.454).

Nakortok (71). Subdivision of the Kwakiutl living on the east side of Vancouver Island.

Nanaimo (79). Modern town in the area where there had been a Salish village.

Nanowarogemiut (112). Very old village on the lower Yukon River below Andreafsky.

Nanuwarok River (170). Passes a village of the same name where Jacobsen found care for his injured foot and his snowblind eyes.

Napariaseluk (141). Eskimo hut on the way to Kauwerak.

Nemkis (8). Nimpkish, Kwakiutl village on the east side of Vancouver Island on Seymor Inlet (BCG, p.373).

Nerkluk River. *See* Fish River.

New Gold Harbor. *See* Kaisun.

Newiarsualok (132). Temporary quarters used in March, April, and May by seal hunters at Cape Jungfrau.

Ninilschik (194). Village on Kenai Peninsula occupied by Russians; a very "settled" community with agriculture.

Noatak River (157). River near Kotzebue Sound.

Nogemiut (177). Village near the Kjikjingemiut where Nelson bought all the artifacts that were for sale.

Noksiaremiut (178). Rest stop on the Kuskokwim River.

Nooette (32). Newette, Kwakiutl village on Hope Island.

Norraden (104). Athapaskan village downstream from Makkatmekettan and close to Belase-karat at the mouth of Melozi River.

Nuchek (206). Town on Hinchinbrook Island, also listed as Nuchek Island, where there is a deserted Eskimo village. The Russians built a stockade post there about 1793 and called it Fort Constantine for the younger brother of the czar (Orth 1967, p.706).

Nukakiet (103). Athapaskan village at the mouth of the Nowitna River, opposite Moose Point; seen by Jacobsen on his passage down the Yukon River.

Nuklukayet (98). Village near the junction of the Tanana and Yukon Rivers; former trading camp and settlement on the right bank of the Yukon River. Trading post established by Arthur Harper (Orth 1967, p.708).

Nulato (99). On the right bank of the Yukon River, 25 miles west of Galena; a Kaiyuhkho village, founded by Russian Creole Malakov in 1838; burned by Indians in 1839; Derabin rebuilt it in 1841 and all the inhabitants were killed in 1851; new village built in 1853 (Orth 1967, p.709).

Nulleslugemiut (175). Village between Jukkak and Cape Vancouver; Jacobsen met an Alaska Commercial Company trader there.

Nunalinak (110). The nest of a giant bird allegedly is near here; articles about it appeared in *Daily Entertainment* magazine in Germany during Jacobsen's journey and in *Lubecker General Anzeiger* 3 May 1891; Jacobsen bought some artifacts here.

Nunapiklogak (170). Village with three houses near the Nanuwerok River in the delta of the Yukon River.

Nusaktolik River (191). The river flows into the southeast side of Lake Iliamna. The Russians call it Adematzensky (q.v.).

Nusaron (104). Athapaskan village on the Yukon River near Belase-karat and Norraden.

Nuschagak (86). Nushagak Eskimo live in the region from the north shores of Lake Iliamna to the coast at Cape Newenham. The Nushagak River and Nushagak Lake empty into

Bristol Bay at Fort Alexander. Variant: Bristol River named
by Captain Cook 1778 (Orth 1967, 712).
Nutschatlitz (52). Nuchatlitz, Nootkan village at the entrance
of the inlet by the same name; trading post of Spring and
Frank (BCG, p.482).

Oales. *See* Queka and Oales.
Oejak (182). Village on the banks of the Kuskokwim River.
Oheiaht (44). Ohiat, Nootkan village with a Catholic mission
under Father Justus (Drucker 1951, p.7).
Ojaralik (134). Ojeralik was passed on the way from Singek
to Igniktok (Ray 1964, p.70).
Ommekomsiut (176). On the peninsula formed by Cape Vancouver. There are three villages as one approaches the cape
from the north.
Opettisaht (46). Hopachisat, a Nootkan village (on Drucker's
map [1951, p.59]).
Orowignarak (118). Ogowinagak, an important Eskimo village
at the mouth of the Mukluktolik River on the north shore
of Norton Sound (Orth 1967, p.716). Variants: Orowignarak, Ogowinana (Petrof 1880); phonetically, Ukvignaguk
Ray 1971, p.271).
Orrutoremiut (178). Place where women had many necklaces
of beads but no ethnological pieces. On southern trip in the
Kuskokwim Valley, near Sintuleremiut.

Pastoliak (89). Eskimo village on the right bank of the river
of the same name; 1849 name used by Tebenkof (Orth 1967,
p.742). Variants: Dall wrote it Partoliak (Baker 1966, p.
490); Pastolyak (Zagoskin 1967, p.354).
Pastolik (170). River and Kwikpakmiut village in the delta of
the Yukon (Orth 1967, p. 742). From Paimut to Pastolik the
people are Okogmiut (Nelson 1899).
Peimilliagaremiut (176). Village near Cape Vancouver, one of
the three as one approaches the cape from the north.
Pikmiktalik (89). River and Eskimo village about 25 miles SW
of Fort Saint Michael; a native name (Baker 1966, p. 497,
Orth 1967, p.754); village mentioned by Zagoskin (1967, p.
355).
Pinalekaht (78). Penelakut, Salish-speaking village on Kuper
Island and Galiano Island (Walbran 1972, p. 379); Penelakut
is in the Cowicham Indian Agency (Boas 1966).
Pinjakpagemiut (177). Paingakmiut, a small village in the se-
quence of settlements on the way to Cape Vancouver; on
left bank of Johnson River, north of mouth of Pikmiktalik
River (Orth 1967, p.754).
Port Clarence (141). On Seward Peninsula.
Port Essington (7). Modern cannery town and Indian settle-
ment; in Tsimshian territory (BCG, p.522).

Port Simpson (27). South shore of Port Simpson harbor (BCG, p.522); Tsimshian town.

Potogroak (160). On south shore of Selawik Inlet, Kotzebue Sound.

Pujulik Creek (155). Principal route from east fork of Koyuk River to Buckland River was down the Pujulik River—the "river with smoke"—a tributary of the west fork of the Buckland River; well-traveled route before the caribou disappeared.

Quakult (29). Kwakiutl name for the tribe in some ethnographies, though phonetically not correct; *see also* Kwag.ul (Boas 1966, p.3[a]).

Quamichan (78). Division of the Cowichan; a Salish village on Cowichan Bay, east side of Vancouver Island.

Quatsino (37). Neighboring village of Koskimo; north side of Quatsino Sound (BCG, p.523).

Queka (35). Kwexa, Kwakiutl village on Cracroft Island; also known as Q!o'moyae (Boas 1895, p.331). War name was Kue'xa, meaning "beheaders."

Queka and Oales (51). Two Nootkan villages in Deep Inlet (Amai), east side of Kyuquot Sound (BCG, p.13).

Quigiorremiut (178). Across the Kuskokwim River from the group of three villages.

Quinekak (131). Kwiniuk River was followed on the trip to Bering Strait.

Quitzak River. *See* Lake Iliamna.

Razbolniksky (95). Razboinski, Russian name for Eskimo village of Ankasegemiut (q.v.), on lower Yukon River near the delta. Russian name means "robbers"; Nelson saw the Feast for the Dead there.

Romanof Point (154). East entrance to Pastol Bay on Norton Sound. Variants: Eskimo name Asiatchak recorded by Lutke, and Aziachek recorded by Tebenkov in 1852 (Orth 1967, p. 813). Also called Azachagyak by Zagoskin (1967, p.349).

Saanich (5). Indian reserve north of Victoria, Vancouver Island (BCG, p.565).

Saint George's Canal (12). Strait of Georgia.

Saint Mary's. *See* Andrejewski.

Saint Michael. *See* Fort Saint Michael.

Saint Paul (86). Town on Kodiak Island.

Sakara (105). Village near mouth of Innoko River where a famous shaman had died just before Jacobsen arrived. He described the burial. Probably former Grayling (DJR).

Schaktolik. *See* Shaktolik.

Seeschaht (45). Seshart, Nootkan village at end of Alberni Canal. Drucker called it Tsisaaht (Drucker 1951, map).

Selawik River (155). Important river in Kotzebue area.

Seshelt. *See* Sechelt.

Semeriangemiut (182) and Senneremiut (182). Eskimo villages on east bank of lower Kuskokwim River where there is a warehouse visited by trading schooners every year. Jacobsen passed them on his trip down the river.

Seshelt (80). Indian village on Sechelt Peninsula (BCG, p.581).

Sewartlaremiut (178). Another village like Semeriangemiut.

Shaktolik (123). Malemiut village on the east shore of Norton Sound. Inhabited by descendants of native Malemiut invaders from Kotzebue Sound (Orth 1967, p.859).

Shelikoff Strait (194). Between Kodiak Island and the Alaska Peninsula.

Sinaogak (146). Sinar, village of three houses on the Seward Peninsula. Variant: Sinarmete (Orth 1967, p.876).

Singakloget, Singek, Sinuk or Singuk (134). These places are very confused and cannot be placed in Orth. Sinuk or Singuk is the name of a river near Cape Rodney (Ray 1964, map #2).

Skedans (21). Haida village on the east coast of Louise Island (BCG, p.602).

Skidegate (17). Haida village on Skidegate Inlet (BCG, p.602).

Sledge Island (120). Aziak, named Sledge Island by Captain Cook because they found a sled where they landed (1785, 2:441). Variants: Jacobsen's spelling Sleads; Sauer Auak; Beechey (1831, p.831) noted Cook's statement (Orth 1967, p.888).

Soonroodna (197). Ruins of village at Kachamak Bay where Jacobsen excavated.

Tachek (81). Eskimo name of the village at Fort Saint Michael.

Tagunak (192). Alaska Commercial Company post at the head of Cook Inlet, diagonally opposite Fort Kenai.

Takkjelt-Pileramiut (109). Eskimo village on the Yukon River below Anvik and above Mission.

Tananah River (108). Tanana River, which flows into the Yukon near Rampart.

Tanoo (21). Tanu, a small island between Logan and Richardson Inlets, Queen Charlotte Islands (BCG, p.650).

Tlingit (9). Indians living in the SE archipelago of southeastern Alaska.

Togiak (185). Name of a river and villages. Variants: Tugistak (Sarichev 1806–7, map 7); Tunjiyak River and Bay (Holmberg 1854); now two villages, Togiagegamiut and Togiak Station (Orth 1967, p.972).

Tschilkat (208). Village at the Copper River Delta, to the east of Cape Martin; in former Eyak territory.

Tschuklesaht (93). Chickliset, a Nootkan village on Clayoquot Sound; called "rhubarb people" (Drucker 1951, p.5).

Tschuktschen (82). Chukchee Peninsula, Siberia.

Tsimshian (9). Indians along the Skeena River, village Hazelton.

Tsisaaht. *See* Seeschaht.

Tuenirok (93). Side canal of the Yukon River; also a vessel by that name.

Tukkerrovik (143). Village of three houses near Lake Imuruk.

Tuklomare (158). Lake four miles wide SW of Selawik (Orth, p.989).

Tununak (175). Village on west coast of Nelson Island. Variant: Tunniakhpuk (Petrof 1884, p.12); near Cape Vancouver.

Ucluelet. *See* Jucklulaht.

Unaktolik (124). Eskimo village on river of same name. Variant: Ungalik (Orth 1967, p.101; Ray 1964, p.69).

Unalaklik (120). Unalakleet, terminus of winter route from Anvik on the Yukon River; last of the Kwikpakmiut villages on the river upstream; mixed population of Eskimo and Ingalik (Orth 1967, p.1008; Baker 1966, p.651).

Unalitschok River (156). River Jacobsen called Hagenbeck in honor of his sponsor; near the mouth of the Kiwalik River.

Upun (91). Apoon, on the northern delta of the Yukon; a Chnagmiut village at the north mouth of the Yukon. Variants: Abkun (Tebenkof 1852); Apkun, later, by Russians; Aphoon (Zagoskin 1967, p.348). Jacobsen entered the northeast mouth of the Yukon (Kwikpak) on 4 August 1882 (Orth 1967, p.84). "The natives compared the delta of the Yukon with its mouths to a human hand and have named it 'Apoon,' the thumb" (Baker 1966, p.103).

Walinsel (118). Whale Island, close to Fort Saint Michael. Jacobsen went there to find an archaeological site.

Wetkelt-tokara. *See* Kleitvit.

Bailey, G. W. 1880. *Report on Alaska and its people*. United States Senate, 46th Congress, 2d session, doc. 132. Washington, D.C.: Government Printing Office.

Baker, Marcus. 1966. *Geographic dictionary of Alaska*. Bulletin no. 299, U.S. Geological Survey. Washington, D.C.: Government Printing Office.

Beechey, Frederick W. 1831. *Narrative of a voyage to the Pacific and Beering's Strait*. 2 vols. London: Henry Colburn and Richard Bentley.

Birket-Smith, Kaj, and DeLaguna, Frederica. 1938. *The Eyak Indians of the Copper River Delta*. Copenhagen.

Boas, Franz. 1895. *Social organization and secret societies of the Kwakiutl Indians*. U.S. National Museum Report. Washington, D.C.: Government Printing Office.

————. 1966. *Kwakiutl ethnography*. Ed. Helen Codere. Chicago: University of Chicago Press.

Bourchier, Thomas. 1851. Reports of the "Plover."

Dall, William H. 1870. *Alaska and its resources*. Boston: Lee and Shepard.

DeLaguna, Frederica. 1956. *Chugach history: Archaeology of Prince William Sound*. Publications in Anthropology, vol. 13. Seattle: University of Washington Press.

Disselhoff, H. N. 1935. Bemerkungen zu einigen Eskimomasken der sammlung Jacobsen des Berliner Museum für Völkerkunde. *Baessler Archiv* 18:130–37.

————. 1936. Bemerkungen zu Fingermasken der Beringmeer Eskimo. *Baessler Archiv* 19:181–87.

Drucker, Philip. 1951. *The Northern and Central Nootka*. Bureau of American Ethnology, Bulletin no. 144. Washington, D.C.: Government Printing Office.

Elliott, Henry. 1897. *Our Arctic province*. New York: Scribner's.

Fisheries Research Board of Canada. 1961. Bulletin no. 68.

Gazetteer of Canada, British Columbia. 1966. Geographical Branch, Department of Energy, Mines, and Resources. Ottawa.

This bibliography lists books about the Northwest Coast and Alaska based on travels in these regions at approximately the time Jacobsen was there, as well as other works cited in the notes and the glossary. Comparing Jacobsen's remarks with later studies or much earlier accounts does not give a clear picture, because the nineteenth century was perhaps the greatest period of change this population had experienced; but the more recent studies of the people of this area will provide further information obtained by anthropologists doing fieldwork and by travelers.

Giddings, James Louis. 1964. *The archaeology of Cape Den-bigh.* Providence, R.I.: Brown University Press.

Guernsey, H. H. 1896. An artist in Alaska. *Harper's* 30:589–602.

Healey, M. A. 1887. *Cruise of the revenue steamer "Corwin" in the Arctic Ocean in 1885.* Washington, D.C.: Government Printing Office.

Hoffman, Walter J. 1883. Comparison of Eskimo petrography with those of other American aborigines. *Transactions of the Washington Society of Anthropology,* vol. 11.

————. 1897. The graphic art of the Eskimo. *United States National Museum Report.* Washington, D.C.: Government Printing Office.

Holmberg, Henrik. 1855. *Ethnographische Skizzen über die Volker des Russischen Amerika.* Part 1, vol. 4. Helsingfors.

Howard, W. L. 1886. Sledging expedition to the "NO-TALK" River, 1 December 1885 to 5 April 1886. Unpublished. Houghton Library, Harvard University.

Jacobsen. 1869 (map). *See* United States Coast Survey. 1869.

Moravian Church. 1886–99. *Proceedings of the 110th General Meeting and 99th Anniversary of the Society of the United Brethren for Propagating the Gospel among the Heathen.* Bethlehem, Pa.

Nelson, Edward W. 1899. The Eskimo about Bering Strait. *Report of the Bureau of American Ethnology,* vol. 18, part 1.

Orth, Donald J. 1967. *Dictionary of Alaska place names.* Geological Survey, Professional Paper no. 567. Washington, D.C.: Government Printing Office.

Petrof, Ivan. 1880. Population and resources of Alaska. 46C: 3s, H.R. Ex. Doc. 40 (serial 1968).

————. 1884. Report on the population, industries, and resources of Alaska. In *United States Tenth Census.* Washington, D.C.: Department of the Interior, Census Office.

Ray, Dorothy Jean. 1964. Nineteenth century settlement and subsistence patterns. *Arctic Anthropology* 2 (2):61–94.

————. 1971. Eskimo place names in Bering Strait and vicinity. *Names* 1:1–33.

Sarichev, Gavril. 1806–7. *Account of a voyage of discovery to the northeast of Siberia, the frozen ocean and the Northeast Sea.* 2 vols. London.

Schanz, A. B. An Alaska expedition. 1881, 1882. *Frank Leslie's Newspaper,* vol. 72.

Schwatka, Frederick. 1885. *Along Alaska's great river.* New York.

Sproat, Gilbert M. 1868. *Scenes and studies of savage life.* London: Smith, Elder.

Tebenef, M. D. 1852. *Atlas of the Northwest Coast of America.*

United States Coast Survey. 1869. Map of Alaska and adjoining territory.

United States Survey. 1909. Map of Alaska.

Walbran, John T. 1972. *British Columbia coast names, 1592–*

1906. Reprint edition. Seattle: University of Washington Press.

Zagoskin, Lavrentii. 1967. *Travels in Russian America, 1842–1844.* Ed. Henry N. Michael. Published for the Arctic Institute of North America. Anthropology of the North: Translations from Russian Sources, no. 7. Toronto: University of Toronto Press.

Note: Under Jacobsen's spelling of a place name, only the first reference and the glossary reference are indexed. For further occurrences, see the modern spelling given in brackets after Jacobsen's spelling. Page numbers of illustrations are given in italics.